DATE			

The Quest
for Quality

Lewis B. Mayhew
Patrick J. Ford
Dean L. Hubbard

The Quest for Quality

The Challenge for Undergraduate Education in the 1990s

Jossey-Bass Publishers

San Francisco • Oxford • 1990

THE QUEST FOR QUALITY
The Challenge for Undergraduate Education in the 1990s
 by Lewis B. Mayhew, Patrick J. Ford, and Dean L. Hubbard

Copyright © 1990 by: Jossey-Bass Inc., Publishers
350 Sansome Street
San Francisco, California 94104
&
Jossey-Bass Limited
Headington Hill Hall
Oxford OX3 0BW

Library of Congress Cataloging-in-Publication Data

Mayhew, Lewis B.
  The quest for quality: the challenge for undergraduate education
in the 1990s / Lewis B. Mayhew, Patrick J. Ford, Dean L. Hubbard. —
1st ed.
      p.   cm. — (Jossey-Bass higher education series)
   Includes bibliographical references.
   ISBN 1-55542-254-3
   1. Education, Higher—United States—Curricula.   2. College
credit—United States.   3. Higher education and state—United
States.   4. Education, Higher—United States—Finance.   I. Ford,
Patrick Joseph, date.   II. Hubbard, Dean Leon.   III. Title.
IV. Series.
LB2361.5.M386   1990
378.1'99'0973—dc20   90-34307
                                                                  CIP

Manufactured in the United States of America

The paper in this book meets the guidelines for
permanence and durability of the Committee on
Production Guidelines for Book Longevity of
the Council on Library Resources.

JACKET DESIGN BY WILLI BAUM

FIRST EDITION

Code 9062

The Jossey-Bass
Higher Education Series

Contents

Foreword

The Quest for Quality: The Challenge for Undergraduate Education in the 1990s is about more than surviving the 1990s. It is about the academic quality of undergraduate education in any decade. A similar comment could be made about Mayhew's earlier book, *Surviving the Eighties: Strategies and Procedures for Solving Fiscal and Enrollment Problems,* which was actually about effective administrative leadership, a topic important in any decade. I view these two books as falling not in a chronological sequence but in a content sequence — the earlier one being on leadership and the second on the objects of leadership. Both books will be as applicable to the first decade of the next century and to succeeding decades as they are to the 1980s and the 1990s.

    Surviving the Eighties, in my judgment, was actually not about the eighties as they turned out. It was published in 1979, when the following decade was expected to entail a struggle to survive, in which some institutions would find their very existence jeopardized because of the anticipated demographic depression in enrollments. This depression never took place; although it was the almost universal expectation, there was no struggle for survival. Yet that in no way detracts from the value of the book, because its principles are valid for any time.

    This book on the nineties is also placed in the context of a single decade, a decade of increased global competitiveness

for the United States, as the authors say. True, but I do not
believe that restoring quality to undergraduate education has
much to do with global competitiveness in the nineties. It has
much more to do with the quality of individual lives and of
citizenship over the next half century.

Thus, I recommend this book not for its importance for
this decade in particular, but as an excellent review of the current status of the nearly eternal problems with the quality of
undergraduate education and the means for its improvement
in this and any foreseeable decade. In the same way, I can also
recommend the previous book on the basis of its timeless discussion of effective administrative leadership.

Lewis Mayhew, along with his two coauthors, is as well
qualified to review undergraduate education as he was to discuss
administrative leadership. I know of no one who has read more
widely in the higher education literature or who has evaluated
that literature more carefully. I went back over the reference
list of this book because I knew that it would provide a select
listing of the best of the literature. Mayhew also has been on
more campuses — and consulted on more campuses — than anyone else I know. Consequently, he has a comprehensive, direct
contact with reality to supplement his grounding in the literature.
He is also a devotee of the golden mean, as I am. Thus, whenever I have wanted to discover the "current wisdom" about higher
education, I have asked myself, "What is Lew Mayhew thinking and saying?" When I do not agree with him (and I do not
totally agree with everything in this book), I know that my views
are at odds with the current accepted wisdom.

This leads me to several qualifications about *The Quest for
Quality*.

First, how bad is the situation? The authors detail some
aspects of contemporary undergraduate higher education that
point to a deterioration: fewer well-qualified entering students,
more part-time faculty members, spectacular grade inflation,
a drastic decline in the attention given to liberal education, and
a parallel decline in the emphasis on basic skills. I agree. But
such evidence as we have — and it is not very complete — indicates
that test scores of college graduates have on the average fallen

less than test scores of high school graduates, a fact that implies (even if it does not prove) that higher education has increased its "value added." I agree that we can and should do better for many reasons—but not because we have been doing so much worse than before. The war has not, in my opinion, clearly been lost as far as quality is concerned.

Second, I agree that higher education must improve to meet the challenge of global competitiveness facing our nation. Yet we draw more talent from more areas of society than most of our competitors do, and we have clearly the best training at the highest levels of intellectual attainment, and the best basic research, in the world. We should improve our performance, but more for the sake of the quality of our total society than to face global competitiveness.

Third, I agree that the attempted reforms of the 1960s almost universally failed to catch on and usually disappeared without a trace. But it was important at that time in history to give the spirit of reform a chance, and there was one triumph: greater access to education. The sacrifice of academic quality in the interest of egalitarian gains was, in my judgment, really not very great.

Fourth, I agree that equal share and outstanding performance are, to a degree, in competition with each other, but more in theory than in practice. One of the great advantages of the American system of differentiation of functions is that some institutions concentrate on equal share and others concentrate on outstanding performance; and we should keep it that way. Thus, I believe that we can excel with both the equal share and outstanding performance standards at one and the same time—but it will not be easy.

Fifth, the authors have a point that because of their rhetoric, the reader may suppose that they worship the status quo. They do show reverence for "parsimony," for tradition, and for realistic expectations. The reader who looks at the detail, though, will see what excellent suggestions they make for improvements. Mayhew, Ford, and Hubbard appear to me to be more ameliorators or even outright reformers than all-out supporters of the status quo ante; they actually seem to be heirs of the reformers of the 1960s who have learned that it is better to be sound than just experimental. I recommend universal consideration of the many possible reforms that the authors suggest, which constitute a real program for substantial improvements in the 1990s.

Sixth, I agree that the emphasis is now on basic skills, basic courses, basic student services, and all the other basics; and that emphasis on the basics will require some contraction elsewhere. But let us not close the door entirely to expanded possibilities. The American system was founded on the expansionist philosophy of any person, any study. Many mistakes have been made in pursuit of this philosophy, but it has also served American society well.

The gist of what I am saying is that Mayhew, Ford, and Hubbard are expressing the current wisdom and that the burden of proof lies with those who challenge it. All policymakers should fully familiarize themselves with the insights in *The Quest for Quality* and should heed them. A few may wish to step cautiously beyond them — but it will be at their peril. In summary, reading this new book and rereading the earlier one should make it easier to survive any decade, and indeed several decades into the future.

Berkeley, California   Clark Kerr
July 1990   President Emeritus
                                          University of California

Preface

This book is intended as a sequel to *Surviving the Eighties: Strategies and Procedures for Solving Fiscal and Enrollment Problems* (Mayhew, 1979). *The Quest for Quality* stresses achieving, maintaining, and restoring academic and intellectual quality, whereas the earlier book stressed sheer survival without explicit concern for matters of quality. The current effort was stimulated, in part, by a reviewer of *Surviving the Eighties* who praised it but wished that the author had examined something more than just institutional survival.

In this book, we argue that, especially since 1970, there has been a serious decline in academic and intellectual quality throughout American higher education, although it has been more precipitate in some kinds of institutions than in others. We adduce several lines of evidence to support this contention; for example, we see a deterioration in the meaning of academic credit granted toward degrees. At the same time, inflation of academic grades has become so widespread that grades no longer define different levels of academic performance.

During the 1960s and 1970s, the previous rather well-thought-out, generally prescribed education for college students was discarded; as a result, the undergraduate curriculum lost rational form and structure, except for the order imposed through the interest, desire, and choice of individual students. At the same time, requirements were lowered for English, mathematics, and foreign language. This erosion of requirements resulted in a generally recognized decline in college graduates' verbal and quantitative literacy.

Although the academic qualifications of full-time faculty members in four-year institutions that granted bachelor's degrees remained relatively stable, overall the academic preparation of those teaching college and university courses deteriorated seriously through widespread use of part-time faculty who were not fully qualified or whose preparation was simply some particular kind of work experience. Accompanying this decline in faculty qualifications was a decrease in the amount of faculty-student contact, as institutions embraced independent study, which is financially more affordable than regular, sustained faculty-student interaction in the classroom.

Overall, there has been a serious dilution of guiding purposes for higher education as institutions have sought new activities and markets and expected faculty members to demonstrate new abilities for which they were unprepared. Thus, some institutions attempted to become brokers for whatever kind of service a particular constituency wanted, and these schools expected faculty members to deal with such disparate matters as counseling the aged or instructing the illiterate and unmotivated and to tailor their programs to all conceivable needs or conditions of individual students.

Although the decline in quality resulted from many factors (including institutions' need to survive financially), it was in large measure an unanticipated effect of colleges and universities' attempt to satisfy the nation's demand for greater participation in higher education by all segments of the society. In pursuing this goal, some egalitarian reformers argued that colleges and universities should meet whatever needs any individual or groups of individuals had, whenever and wherever they arose. These reformers spoke of universal postsecondary education; "educare," comparable to Medicare, to provide any desired educational service; nontraditional pedagogy for nontraditional students; interruption of the academic lockstep by awarding credit for whatever experience seemed to produce improved skills, behavior, or attitudes; and curricular attention to whatever individual talents, traits, and abilities seemed to need cultivation. In our judgment, these efforts, though well-intentioned, led to a blurring of educational purpose and a decline in quality.

Throughout this book, two interrelated themes are developed. The first is the meaning of academic and intellectual quality and judgments concerning its components. Academic quality, an abstraction, is determined through informed judgment, as is esthetic quality. Traditionally, though, academic quality has essentially meant intellectual quality. The medieval university emphasized the life of the mind, nourished through sustained intellectual interaction between students and faculty; among students; and among members of the faculty.

Employing a more contemporary rhetoric, we argue that the essential mission of the undergraduate institution is to prepare learners through the use of words, numbers, and abstract concepts to understand, cope with, and positively influence the world in which they find themselves. This position does not insist that other human traits and needs are unimportant or that they should not receive institutional attention. The human needs for religion, physical and emotional health, companionship, jobs, and political expression are all important, but it is not necessarily the duty of colleges and universities to fulfill them. If collegiate institutions are expected to assume primary responsibility in these areas, less attention is paid to proper educational responsibilities in the attempt to offer services that many collegiate institutions are ill equipped by either tradition or experience to provide.

The second pervasive theme of *The Quest for Quality* is public policy concerning the proper expenditure of public funds for education. While we recognize that there are many worthwhile human needs, the policy issue is whether the public has a responsibility to provide funds to meet all these needs. The point of view we espouse here is that public responsibility for the support of higher education should be limited to those activities leading either to academic degrees or to vocational preparation and competence on a reasonably sophisticated level. The justification for public support should be society's need for an educated citizenry, well-qualified leaders, and competent professionals to provide essential services. Rather than support rapidly escalating additional services, we suggest, even affluent societies must establish priorities for the use of finite resources.

Throughout this book, we urge a narrower definition of academic credit than that currently in acceptance and recommend that institutions find alternate ways of recognizing participation in many admittedly desirable activities. Before the 1970s, except in publicly supported two-year community colleges, academic credit was usually reserved for academic courses presenting a certain content and level of complexity (except that some institutions awarded token credit for courses in physical education). Generally, degree credit was not awarded for remedial work, subcollegiate courses, skills courses, fieldwork, work experience, internships, or foreign travel.

Since 1970, however, virtually any sort of human experience has been judged by at least some institutions to warrant academic credit toward a degree. Although the primary focus of this book is on undergraduate higher education, addressing this issue has necessitated some discussion of community colleges, which frequently award credit and then insist that it be accepted as applying toward the baccalaureate degree. We argue that awarding academic credit for noncollegiate activities results in diminished educational quality and recommend that community colleges, like more traditional institutions, adopt a more realistic view of the institutional mission and jettison services and activities that schools are not designed to provide.

This probably means that there should be a primary, and in some cases singular, focus on technical or vocational training programs. Where college-level work is offered, academic courses should be clearly identified, and traditional methods and expectations should be adopted. Also, people who teach such courses should meet traditional standards of preparation and performance. This solution is the only politically plausible and educationally defensible one, and it has been applied already in many regions. However, this solution will be weakened as long as public subsidies — especially state subsidies — are inextricably linked to the awarding of academic credit. If state funds are provided only for courses granting academic credit, then institutions will resort to any relabeling or redescription of programs necessary to justify awarding academic credit.

We argue throughout for parsimony; that is, we advocate an important but limited set of functions for collegiate institutions. Similarly, we suggest that faculty members can accomplish a limited number of things well, but that faculty members are not omnipotent and should not be expected to be all things to all people. We further consider departments, separate schools, and single campuses more effective and conducive to quality than suprainstitutional organizations and agencies and ad hoc academic organizations such as interdisciplinary centers.

In arriving at such recommendations, we examine the principal innovations of the 1960s and 1970s and judge most of them to have made only a modest impact on orthodox academic degree programs in American higher education. For example, the net result of the experimentation with the academic calendar seems to have been that the first semester now generally ends before Christmas. Competency-based education has been adopted by only a few institutions. Cluster colleges, with a few exceptions, have not proved to be particularly popular.

The principal lesson for American higher education is that those institutions that have remained reasonably faithful to their traditions are generally the ones in the most stable financial condition and are also the ones most likely to have preserved academic and intellectual quality.

Audience

We believe that *The Quest for Quality* will help a variety of individuals, especially professors and students of higher education. It also should be used by college and university presi-

dents, deans, and other administrative officers such as department heads, directors of institutional research and of long-range
planning, and directors of counseling centers. It can also be used
with profit by people on governing or coordinating boards and
their staffs, as well as others who work in the higher education
infrastructure.

Overview of the Contents

In Part One we take a look at past and present forces that
have an impact on quality in undergraduate education in this
country. Chapter One reviews the recent history (the last five
decades) of higher education. We discuss how collegiate institutions have met significant challenges and how some of these
challenges have led certain institutions to embark on overam-
bitious new missions. In Chapter Two, we seek to define and
illustrate different kinds of quality and to pinpoint the aspects
of undergraduate education that appear to be declining in quality. Chapter Three traces the changes the undergraduate curriculum has undergone from the 1930s to the present. We
describe the rise and fall of the general education movement
of the 1930s, 1940s, and 1950s and the concurrent rise and fall
of institutional selectivity; we attempt to evaluate the curriculum
reform of the 1960s and 1970s and consider a current trend—
the search for ways to restore the earlier form of general education.

In Part Two we examine how faculty and administrators
can take the lead in strengthening academic quality. Chapter
Four outlines historical concepts of academic quality and changes
in standards over the last several decades. Chapter Five focuses
on the contributions of campus life outside the classroom to
overall academic excellence. In Chapter Six we discuss the role
of the faculty and explain how it has contributed to academic
quality—but also to its deterioration. Chapter Seven presents
an overview of college teaching. We argue that teaching, though
an important element in college education, is not necessarily
the most significant one. Chapter Eight traces the emergence

of the college presidency, the forces that have shaped it, and developments that have contributed to a decline in its historic role. We suggest means for restoring leadership, especially at the presidential level. In Chapter Nine, we argue that the highly centralized system of administration that has long characterized higher education has proved inappropriate for changing conditions. It appears that a new administrative structure is called for that would balance centralization with decentralization.

Part Three covers monitoring and coordinating agencies and their role in maintaining academic quality. Chapter Ten reviews the evolution of voluntary accreditation, evaluates its successes and failures, and offers suggestions on how to retain the effective aspects of accreditation and eliminate the dysfunctional elements. Chapter Eleven discusses an array of suprainstitutional organizations, their success or lack of success in carrying out their missions, and their probable future course and configuration. In Chapter Twelve, we present our concept of academic quality, stressing the importance of traditional education and the necessity of recognizing institutional limitations. The book concludes with a comprehensive application of the principle of parsimony to the educational enterprise.

Acknowledgments

Particular mention should be made of the contributions of John R. Thelin, Chancellor Professor of Higher Education at the College of William and Mary in Virginia. Thelin has reviewed the manuscript several times, each time making significant and critical comments and recommending specific ways in which the manuscript could be strengthened. His thoughtful suggestions were a timely and extremely useful contribution to the final form of the book, which we hope will achieve the stature that Thelin felt it should attain. We also must acknowledge with gratitude the critiques and suggestions of Neal Buckaloo, Ellen Chaffee, and Melody Lowe. Their impact on the final product was substantial. However, we of course accept responsibility for the views presented. Mary Ann Grimes Carey, Cynthia Garvin, and Forbes Rogers each made important contributions to an early draft of the manuscript. And finally, we gratefully admit that the project would never have been completed without the bibliographic and word processing skills of Allen Henry, Susan Mattson, Laura Prusch, Marcia Renouard, Donald Sharp, and Lora Wilson.

This book is reverently and lovingly dedicated to the memory of an extraordinary woman, who profoundly influenced the lives of the authors: Dorothy C. Mayhew, wife of one, friend of the others, and an inspiration to all who knew her.

July 1990   Lewis B. Mayhew
                                                   Stanford, California

                                                   Patrick J. Ford
                                                   Spokane, Washington

                                                   Dean L. Hubbard
                                                   Maryville, Missouri

The Authors

Lewis B. Mayhew is professor emeritus of education, Stanford University, where he taught full time for twenty-five years. Before that, he taught at Michigan State University and at the University of South Florida. From 1957 to 1974 he served as part-time director of research at Stephens College in Columbia, Missouri. Mayhew received his B.A. and M.A. degrees (in 1938 and 1947, respectively) in history from the University of Illinois and his Ph.D. degree (1951) in history from Michigan State University.

He has written more than 45 books and 200 articles about higher education in the United States, consulted widely (for more than 500 institutions), and served on many different regional and national committees, such as the Educational Testing Service Board Committee on Test Development and the Senior Commission of the Western College Association. He was consultant to the White House Conference on Education during Lyndon B. Johnson's administration and president of the American Association for Higher Education, and he was rated one of the forty-four most influential leaders in higher education in the *Change* magazine survey of 1974.

Patrick J. Ford is a Roman Catholic priest and a member of the Society of Jesus. He is currently the academic vice-president and professor of higher education at Gonzaga University,

Spokane, Washington. Previously he served as dean of the graduate school and dean of the College of Arts and Sciences at the same institution. He received both his B.A. degree (1966) in philosophy and classical languages and his M.A. degree (1967) in sociology from Gonzaga University, his Ph.D. degree (1972) in administration and policy analysis in higher education from Stanford University, and his M.Div. degree (1974) in pastoral theology from the Jesuit School of Theology, Berkeley.

Ford's research interests have been in the areas of curriculum improvement, graduate and professional education, institutional evaluation, and organizational theory and practice. He served on the editorial advisory board of the *Educational Record* and is currently a trustee of two private universities and a member of the Commission on Colleges of the Northwest Association of Schools and Colleges. Together with Mayhew, Ford coauthored *Changing the Curriculum* (1971) and *Reform in Graduate and Professional Education* (1974). He has made accreditation visits for three regional and two specialized accrediting bodies.

Dean L. Hubbard has been president of Northwest Missouri State University since 1984. His administrative career in higher education began at Loma Linda University in southern California, where he served as assistant to the president and director of institutional research (1974–1976). Subsequently, he was academic dean (1976–1980) and then president (1980–1984) of Union College. He served as a commissioner of the Commission on Higher Education of the North Central Association of Colleges and Schools (1980–1984) and, as a consultant-evaluator for the commission, evaluated twenty institutions.

After receiving a B.A. degree (1961) in speech and theology and an M.A. degree (1962) in systematic theology, both from Andrews University in Berrien Springs, Michigan, he served as a pastor in northern Wisconsin from 1962 to 1966. Hubbard spent the next five years in Korea, where, after graduating from the Korean Language Institute at Yonsei University (1968), he founded an English language school that trained 2,000 students. After his return to the United States, he earned a Ph.D. degree (1979) in administration and policy analysis in higher education from Stanford University.

Since 1980 Hubbard has concentrated in his research on the definition and management of quality, primarily in education and the health care industry. He has acted as consultant in the areas of strategic planning and managing quality to eleven colleges and universities, eighteen insurance companies, twenty-nine hospitals, and two religious denominations.

The Quest
for Quality

Part One

Forces Affecting
Quality in
Undergraduate Education

ONE

The Challenges to Educational Quality Since World War II

Since 1980, there has been a rising tide of interest in school reform. At least thirty national reports have suggested changes for elementary and secondary schools. The fifty states have appointed some 300 task forces and sent them out in search of quality. At the postsecondary level, eleven major reform reports were released within a recent four-year period. In our opinion, the most notable of these was the National Institute of Education report, *Involvement in Learning* (Study Group on the Conditions of Excellence in American Higher Education, 1984).

The nation's newly aroused interest in quality education is a continuation—indeed, an outgrowth—of concerns regarding quality that started with cameras and stereos in the 1960s, continued with televisions and automobiles in the 1970s, and moved on to electronics and the full range of consumer goods in the 1980s.

There is good reason for the outcry. America seems to be losing its preeminence as the industrial leader of the world. Trends and events in the 1980s showed that high labor cost was not the primary reason for the nation's competitive slide; rather, the reason was the poor quality of American goods. When blatant industrial shortcomings are juxtaposed with more than a decade of declining scores on tests such as the Scholastic Aptitude Test (SAT), American College Test (ACT), and Graduate Record Examination (GRE), certain questions seem inescapable.

Are such phenomena short-term historical aberrations or are they characteristic of modern American society?

Are the good old days gone forever — the days when "Made in USA" set the standard of quality for the world?

Are there cultural differences that make it impossible for America to compete? In other words, does America's stress on equal opportunity preclude achieving the heights of excellence obtainable in other more homogeneous and/or selectively structured societies?

Or, on the other hand, has this nation experienced cultural changes that have resulted in poor quality and doomed the society to mediocrity? Is that the reason today's generation seems less well-educated in an absolute sense than their forefathers?

Educators must be attentive to these issues. Self-interest, if nothing else, demands it. The applicant pool of traditional students is declining and will continue to decrease until 1995. Competition for scarce resources between state agencies has intensified in the wake of the withdrawal of federal dollars, and some states have started to consider whether some colleges or universities should be closed. As the nation struggles to reduce its deficits, such debates will doubtless continue. Educators must be prepared to demonstrate the quality of their institutions to legislators and, increasingly, to the general public.

Current interest in improving the quality of undergraduate education comes after a twenty-year period of general neglect for the academic integrity of the enterprise. The purpose of this chapter is to review the forces that have shaped higher education in America since World War II and that have led up to the current debate.

Challenge and Response of Higher Education

A major component of the history of American higher education since 1940 is a chronicle of responding effectively to a series of serious, but quite different, challenges rooted in demographics, economics, changing societal values and priorities, and now quality. The first of these challenges was coping with the almost 40 percent drop in enrollment during the most intense period of World War II. With the aid of various military and other federal training programs, and helped by the departure of many professors for military or government duty, institutions were able to stay in operation and were not forced to make serious cutbacks in faculty. In addition to concentrating on survival, many institutions took advantage of the pause in enrollment to engage underutilized faculty in serious curricular planning.

The second challenge was to cope with the unexpectedly large number of veterans who entered college after the war under the GI Bill of Rights. Responsible educational leaders had estimated that, of 11,000,000 people in the service, probably no more than 700,000 would enroll in college. In fact, over 2,000,000 veterans attended college under the GI Bill (Henry, 1975). Institutions responded creatively by entering vigorously into temporary and permanent housing programs; by creating counseling, testing, and guidance centers; by developing books of readings as substitutes for inadequate library holdings and lack of available textbooks; and by putting into effect programs of general education designed to preserve, albeit in an attenuated form, the virtues of previous general education programs grounded in the liberal arts and sciences.

The next great challenge came during the 1960s in the form of what Ronald Thompson called an "impending tidal wave" of students (Thompson, 1954). Birthrates began to increase enormously in 1945, producing large groups of potential students who would begin to apply for college in the early 1960s. The 1940 aggregated enrollment of 1.5 million students jumped to 3.6 million in 1960, 8.5 million in 1970, and just over 12 million students in 1980.

In response to this challenge, throughout much of the late 1950s and early 1960s, normal schools were upgraded to state colleges or regional universities, campuses were expanded, residence halls were constructed, and new campuses were created on the average of one every other week. In the same way that the military created new divisions during World War II around

cadres of commissioned and noncommissioned officers drawn
from existing divisions, educational leaders in the 1950s and
1960s frequently moved junior faculty members and administrators from the senior institution within a state to form the nucleus
around which a new institution would be built. In some cases,
within a scant three years from the time of the decision to expand, a new multicollege university would emerge with a reasonably full complement of undergraduate, professional, and
graduate programs. Across the country, graduate programs were
increased substantially to produce the needed faculties, and in-
genious schemes were developed to make use of retired faculty
and to attract qualified people working in other industries.

Although no major curricular synthesis appeared during
this period, the response to numbers represented a real flowering of the American system of higher education. Strong regional
state universities and private institutions became national research centers, a powerful new system of junior colleges came
into being, and the proportion of faculties holding terminal
degrees increased.

This expansion occurred during a tumultuous period, a
part of which saw campuses torn by perhaps the worst period
of unrest in the history of higher education in the United States.
Nonetheless, during even the worst excesses of campus protest,
institutions accepted increasing enrollments and produced increasing numbers of graduates needed to staff the steadily increasing national economy, and these achievements were made without seriously reducing traditional standards of academic quality.

The next challenge (in about 1970) was nationally more
symbolic than real, although some institutions and even categories of institutions faced genuine threats. This challenge was
the sudden onset of what was to be called the new depression
in higher education, or, to use economic terms, the end of the
bull market. Institutions saw a steadily widening gap between
increases in income and increases in expenditures. Perhaps one-
third of all institutions found themselves in financial difficulties,
as defined by the inability to offer programs judged essential
for the institution. Another third found themselves heading for
financial difficulty, while the remaining third were in reasonably

good financial health (Cheit, 1971). Some institutions began to experience stabilizing or declining enrollments, and a larger number began to expect declines before the end of the decade. Leaders of individual institutions and systems of institutions responded by reducing expenditures and by improving budget development and management procedures. By the middle of the 1970s, many institutions had achieved a precarious financial equilibrium. Nonetheless, throughout the decade quite a few institutions had to cope with annual operating deficits, and the number of institutions closing or merging began to increase.

By the end of the 1970s, the effective responses of most institutions to real or anticipated problems had turned an expected time of disorder into a reasonably healthy decade for higher education. Most institutions, including private institutions, gained full-time equivalent enrollment despite the widening gap between tuitions of private institutions and those of public institutions. (The resilience of private institutions in such circumstances may be attributable to the fact that privately paid tuition did not rise as fast as disposable family income.) Overall, the notion that institutions had been starved for money proved to be a myth; actual expenditures on instructional costs per student in constant dollars remained steady, and the states, even in the face of the unfavorable publicity resulting from the student protest movement, increased steadily the funds available for educational and general purposes.

With respect to curricular changes, the major educational efforts between 1940 and 1980 (apart from a short burst of focus on science and math in the late 1950s after the launching of Sputnik) consisted of the integration of interdisciplinary programs in general education and the refinement of counseling, testing, and guidance programs. Both derived directly from planning during the war years.

The 1980s: A Changing Agenda

Despite three decades of success, leaders in higher education faced the 1980s feeling increasingly threatened. Several scenarios for the future were advanced. The pessimists projected enrollment declines of 40 or even 50 percent. They suggested that such declines in enrollment, coupled with inflation and the redirection of public monies to other social purposes, would produce a serious crisis in the financing of higher education. Colleges and universities would enter a period of bitter competition for students and resources that would adversely affect educational quality. Faculty members would react defensively to preserve their positions, thus blocking new intellectual blood from entering the professoriate. Students, using their competitive advantage, would force institutions into catering to their desires for less demanding work and for accelerating their receipt of diplomas.

On the other hand, optimists expected enrollments to increase as much as 25 to 40 percent, with older persons and foreign students taking the place of the missing eighteen- to twenty-five-year-old students. While resources might diminish in response to a variety of factors, they suggested that declines could be accommodated and that the trend of three decades of expansion would allow institutions to turn their energies to curricular matters, with more time and thought being given to educating new and diverse student bodies in new and creative ways.

Neither extreme view matched reality. In fact, enrollments remained rather stable. Although some oil-producing states were forced to reduce funding for higher education as oil prices fell, other states were able steadily, if not dramatically, to increase their support for higher learning.

With the appointment of Terrel Bell as the Secretary of Education, quality rapidly emerged as the theme of the decade for all levels of education in America. In 1981, Bell appointed an eighteen-member National Commission on Excellence in Education, chaired by David Gardner, then president of the University of Utah. The commission's report, *A Nation at Risk: The Imperative for Educational Reform* (1983), received broad attention throughout society. In rhetoric uncommon for such documents, the authors branded what had happened at the elementary and secondary level as "unilateral educational disarmament." They referred to "a rising tide of mediocrity," pro-

ducing masses who are "scientifically and technologically illiterate." True, these ominous assessments were slightly attenuated by a few buried kudos for American education, such as
the conclusions "that the average citizen is better educated and
more knowledgeable than the average citizen of a generation
ago" or that there are "a number of notable schools and programs" in the country (pp. 5–12).

However, even such compliments were shaded by observations that "the average graduate of our schools and colleges
today is not as well educated as the average graduate of 25 or
35 years ago," and that the outstanding programs that do exist
"stand out against a vast mass shaped by tensions and pressures
that inhibit systematic academic and vocational achievements
for the majority of students." The report concluded that America's "once unchallenged preeminence in commerce, industry,
science and technological innovation is being overtaken by competitors throughout the world" (pp. 5–12), a judgment since but-
tressed by a strong wall of facts.

Even though the focus of *A Nation at Risk* was on elementary and secondary education, attention quickly was drawn to
higher education as well. Within a short time, studies began
to appear that examined the various components of higher learning, particularly the undergraduate experience. As in the case
of elementary and secondary education, all investigators seemed
to agree that this segment, too, had experienced a serious decline
in quality over the last fifteen or twenty years. Three common
complaints consistently emerged: the baccalaureate degree as
currently structured lacks common focus and definition; the
typical education received at the baccalaureate level is only
marginally relevant for tomorrow's world; and today's baccalaureate degree lacks integrity.

Some observers, such as James March (1974, p. 133), suggested that society's expectations had simply outrun education's
capabilities. It was expecting too much to think that education
could produce quality and at the same time single-handedly
eliminate racism, the lingering effects of ghetto upbringing,
and the recalcitrance of social systems deeply rooted in class
and sex distinctions. Furthermore, higher education's unclear

goals rendered impossible a consensus regarding what essential knowledge, skills, and experience every college-educated person should share. In such an environment, it was inevitable that quality in an absolute sense would begin to wane. Indeed, during the 1960s and 1970s, grades were inflated, requirements were generalized and diffused, validating tests were abandoned, and semesters were shortened while educational leaders concentrated their energies on maintaining whatever portion of society's resources they had grown accustomed to receiving.

One result was a steady decline since 1964 in student performance on eleven of fifteen sections of the GRE, with the sharpest declines occurring in subjects requiring high verbal skills. Another result was the explosion of industrially based, postsecondary education programs along with the rapid growth of community colleges, vocational/technical schools, and other alternatives to what mainstream higher education had traditionally provided.

Higher education's conspicuous failures, in combination with its strident denials of responsibility, would almost certainly have led to continued ennui on the part of society in general were it not for one fortuitous (from higher education's perspective) change in events: the emergence of the global economy. As long as attention was focused on declining enrollments, excess capacity, and entry-level vocational skills, most traditional institutions were in trouble. Like it or not, community colleges, technical schools, apprenticeships, and industrial training programs had all demonstrated their ability to outdistance liberal arts–based programs when it came to providing entry-level skills. However, when concern shifted to America's long-term competitiveness, a new agenda began to emerge. The debate began to center on creativity, flexibility, and global awareness. Derek Bok, the president of Harvard University, reflected this change of emphasis in his book, *Higher Learning* (1986, p. 5): "More and more, therefore, the United States will have to live by its wits, prospering or declining according to the capacity of its people to develop new ideas, to work with sophisticated technology, to create new products and imaginative new ways of solving problems. Of all our national assets, a trained intelligence and a capacity for innovation and discovery seem destined to be the most important."

The National Governors' Association Task Force on College Quality, chaired by Missouri Governor John Ashcroft (1986, p. 154), reflected a growing public impatience: "The public has the right to know what it is getting for its expenditure of tax resources; the public has a right to know and understand the quality of undergraduate education that young people receive from publicly funded colleges and universities. They have a right to know that their resources are being wisely invested and committed."

Under the heading: "Where Do We Want to Be in 1991?" the report charged institutions to assess and publicly report student achievement (p. 159): "Public policymakers, taxpayers, students, and parents should expect colleges and universities to fulfill their promises. To assure accountability, post-secondary institutions must assess student learning and ability, program effectiveness, and institutional accomplishment of mission."

The report concluded with six recommendations (pp. 160–163). The first exhorted institutions clearly to define their role and mission. The second stressed "the fundamental importance of undergraduate education." The third recommended the use of multiple measures to assess undergraduate student learning. The fourth recommendation urged "Governors, state legislators, and state-wide coordinating boards [to] adjust funding formulas for public colleges and universities to provide incentives for improving undergraduate student learning, based upon the results of comprehensive assessment programs." The fifth recommendation reaffirmed a commitment to access to public higher education for students from all socioeconomic backgrounds, and the sixth urged accrediting bodies to focus on the measurement of outcomes.

The Egalitarian Reformers

The decrease in the quality of higher education described above was not deliberate; in fact, it was seldom perceived. Understanding why attention was not paid to quality during the late 1960s and 1970s requires a closer look at America's social agenda during that time. During that period, enormous energy was directed toward attracting to higher education segments of the society who had previously been underrepresented. This focus was articulated in 1968 by The Carnegie Commission for Higher Education as reflected in the title of their book, *Quality and Equality: New Levels of Federal Responsibility for Higher Education* (1968). Indeed, the federal government did invest millions of dollars through Title III in remedial programs designed to shore up deficiencies frequently found in newly recruited students and caused by substandard elementary and secondary education. In some important ways, such efforts seemed to achieve (at least partially) the equality portion of the equation as the number of women, blacks, and other minorities entering college increased steadily.

Nurtured and propelled by those gains, however, was a profound change in the way that higher education was viewed. The earlier, generally accepted synthesis of higher learning as essentially an intellectual undertaking gave way, at least in part, to the notion that colleges and universities were essentially institutions that provided social service and were obligated to provide whatever kinds of service anyone wanted. That shift in perception may very well be a major cause for the observed decline in academic quality.

Before the late 1960s, statements about higher education, reflected substantial agreement about its mission and characteristics that stands in sharp contrast to concepts developed and expressed later, especially during the 1970s. The earlier, sharply defined purpose of higher education was well stated by Millett (1952, p. 11):

> If higher education is to have meaning as a distinct function in our society, it must have some core of purpose which is unique and different from the activities of any other institution, and if higher education is to assert some such purpose, then it must, from time to time, reassess all of its activities in the light of that central purpose. The common denom-

inator in the work of higher education lies in the concept of intellectual content. Above all other characteristics, higher education requires two qualities in its staff and students. These are individual aptitude and commitment to exercise imaginative intelligence. It is not easy to define imaginative intelligence, except to say that it implies the exercise of the highest reaches of the mind. There is at least one other close corollary. This is the open mind, fortified by a basic moral or spiritual conviction in the worth of man.

Given such a concept of the essential nature of higher education, general agreement followed as to what were the requisite traits of college teachers. Harold Taylor (1958, p. 151) caught the essence of that belief when he wrote, "The attitude of a teacher should be primarily that of an intellectual leader who . . . should stand before his pupils and before the community at large as the intellectual leader of his time. If the teacher thinks of himself as the intellectual leader of his students, he then finds ways in which the students can respect his opinions, and learn from his range of intellectual experience and from the knowledge which is his personal possession."

Those same general principles were stated by the senior author of this book: "Education was judged to be a rational, intellectual and professional enterprise serving quite specific needs of clients." Further: "College education was judged to be intellectual and conceptual; hence, college teaching should deal with intellect and concepts. Comprehension of intellectual and conceptual matters required specific intellectual abilities; hence, quality in teaching relied, in considerable measure, on quality of students" (Mayhew, 1977, pp. 19–20, 39).

The validity of the preceding ideas regarding higher education came under serious attack beginning in the late 1960s because of the increased heterogeneity of college students, the criticism of higher education implied by the student protest movement, and the realization that adherence to the older conception of higher education could very well produce significant drops in enrollment by the end of the 1970s. The number of institutions, the size of institutions, and the number of faculty and administration personnel all had increased steadily throughout the 1960s, but when those increases appeared threatened by declining birthrates and the resulting prospect of declining enrollment, a different ideology about higher education started to emerge.

This new gospel was promulgated by a relatively new breed of professional critics of higher education, who, although academically prepared in one of the traditional disciplinary or professional fields, gained recognition and achievement not in that field but in the emerging fields of educational commentary and criticism.

Two generalizations about this group of critics seem valid. First, they created new roles for themselves in new kinds of activities. They had left — for one reason or another — the established reference group of their chosen academic disciplines or professions to establish new reference groups and reputations. Second, the titles of the new positions frequently implied a bias toward certain new kinds of activities. For example, in a list of college occupations, the 1974 *Current Issues in Higher Education* included a mentor in a learning center, a coordinator of a student lobby, a director for educational research and innovation, a director of courses taught through the newspaper, a specialist in media programs, a director of an open university, and a director of planning studies.

The main elements of the critics and commentators' goals were revealed in the writings of several individuals who held different points of view, but who, in aggregate, represented a significant drive to change rather completely the historic profile of American higher education. In one way or another, all adopted the social meliorist position; how each would attain ameliorist goals differed somewhat from individual to individual, however. They urged and foresaw a universal higher education that would seek to enhance whatever traits any individual wished to develop. Joseph Katz (1968, p. 4), highly visible among such critics, argued as follows:

Higher education seldom gives the student sufficient opportunity to develop the non-intellective parts of his character. The development of more autonomous identity, of the capacity for intimate communication with other people, and of taking responsibility for others is not brought to the fruition that most students implicitly desire but cannot realize without further educational help.

The college years bring many difficult psychological tasks and problems. Separation from home and parents, confrontation with a wide variety of peers, and high standards of academic performance create insecurities and a questioning of one's power and identity. Older problems and feelings, often dating back to childhood, are revived once more, and many students find themselves more or less consciously struggling with derivatives of earlier feelings of narcissism, omnipotence, or passive dependency. . . . The tasks are so staggering that many individuals let some or most of them go by default; and institutions rarely address themselves in sufficient detail to the problems of helping their students cope with these many-faceted problems.

Another theme that appeared often was that formal higher education must reflect the profound changes in society and the equally profound changes in the life patterns of individuals. These changes include the increased longevity of Americans, the earlier physical maturation of youth, the decreasing amount of time spent at work, and the changes in family structure. Ernest Boyer (1974, p. 7) was one of those who argued that education must adapt to these developments:

For years we have just assumed that life for all of us was neatly programmed. There were the early days of freedom; then came formal education, after

that, work; then abrupt decline. And we quite properly built colleges and universities to fit this rigid
cycle, serving principally the young and unattached.
Now with the birthrate falling off, we are inclined
to panic; we fear a new depression as we lose our
natural clientele.

But it seems clear that the old life-patterns
are beginning to break up and that is another way
to view the present scene . . . Even though the
baby-boom has slackened, there are still more people to be served. Mid-career people have more
leisure time, and they face the crisis of early ob-
solescence. Older people retire earlier, live longer,
have more free time, and are often socially unattached. Now we have blocks of freedom throughout
all of life, and for the first time in our history higher
education may be viewed not only as a pre-work
tradition, but as a process to be pursued from eighteen to eighty-five.

Another pervasive theme of the 1970s was to choose some
presumed social order of a particularly visible and dramatic
nature and then to suggest, frequently with dramatic prose, how
education could solve that particular problem. In urging such
solutions, reformers claimed a role of universal service for collegiate institutions. Gollattscheck suggested that a college must
no longer be just an agency to provide service to the community;
it must be a vital participant in the total renewal process of the
community (Gollattscheck and others, 1976, p. 12). Gollattscheck's ideal college would be committed not just to degrees
and credentials, not just to job training, and not just to service
for the community. It would, rather, be committed to the continued improvement of all aspects of the community's life and
dedicated to the continued growth and development of all citizens
and all social institutions. Political action, social work, and even
evangelism are seen as legitimate educational activities.

Such reform doctrines of the 1970s provided the base for
what has come to be called the nontraditional movement. Thus

the Commission on Nontraditional Study (1973) argued that the first set of patterns should be woven around the philosophy of full educational opportunity. The goal should be to ensure that each individual (regardless of age, previous formal education, or circumstances of life) receives the amount and type of education that would add to and develop his or her potential. Achieving this goal would require different elements of structure, method, content, and procedures that would combine to create a new, flexible education. Implementation would require calling seriously into question the historic educational virtues of intensity and continuity of study, traditional subjects and modes of study, and the use of trained professional faculty. The commission seemed almost to urge that instead of using professional faculty, instruction be assumed by business, industry, labor unions, cultural, governmental and social agencies, military commands, proprietary schools, correspondence institutes, and others (Commission on Nontraditional Study, 1973). Also, it assigned considerable prescience to individuals by suggesting that each student search for the kind of education suitable and necessary for himself or herself. Furthermore, it urged individualized responsibility whereby each student, having decided on his or her educational goals and course of action, would document motivation by satisfactory progress toward that goal. In what manner individuals are expected to develop such insights was not indicated.

Another tenet of this Commission seemed to reject any validity for specialized, organized, and focused study by proclaiming that all knowledge, regardless of where acquired, and all behavior, regardless of how modified, are worthy of academic credit. Such a point of view would support granting academic credit for such activities as experiencing an annual physical examination, enduring an audit by the Internal Revenue Service, taking traffic school to avoid paying a fine for a traffic citation, or witnessing and being moved by televised scenes of earthquake destruction. The widespread adoption of this tenet has allowed granting of college academic credit to displaced Vietnamese for learning basic English and to Seattle residents for taking a class in order to appreciate better a display of Egyptian art. Without doubt, all these experiences can produce useful knowledge and presumably change behavior in reasonably sophisticated ways, but useful knowledge and changed behavior are not sufficient for the awarding of academic credit.

Such themes have received substantial attention within higher education for at least a fifteen-year period. Indeed, they still influence the behavior of some institutions, primarily publicly supported, two-year community colleges; private, invisible liberal arts colleges in financial difficulty; the new, tuition-driven institutions created during the 1970s; and, in certain limited ways, state colleges and universities. However, the names of established private colleges and universities and flagship state universities almost never appear on the lists of institutions that are seriously and comprehensively participating in radical reform.

The Ameliorists Challenged

These themes of the 1970s and early 1980s were based on a set of beliefs that can be questioned seriously on both theoretical and empirical grounds. The first of these beliefs is the great importance of education as compared with other social institutions. Throughout the egalitarian-reform literature is the implicit or explicit acceptance of the beliefs that (1) higher education is the pivotal institution in society and (2) if only the problems of education can be solved, the quality and tone of all American life would be improved. Actually, a case can be made that higher education historically has been important in American society but never preeminently significant. The eight colonial colleges did add something to colonial society, but the major institutional contributions were made by churches, marketplaces, families, and small towns — and especially by the existence of a frontier.

In the late nineteenth century, colleges, land-grant colleges, and newly created private universities were beginning to have some influence on America as a civilization, but this influence was still modest compared to the influence of churches, eighty-acre family farms, village life, growing cities, burgeoning marketplaces, railroads, and the military. Even in the last half of the twentieth century, as higher education has been gaining its greatest level of visibility, financial support, and attention, a case can be made for the even greater formative impact of other competing social institutions (for example, corporations, the military, labor unions, factories, television, and even nonacademic intellectual communities).

Related to the error of overstating the importance of higher education is a second error: grossly expanding the activities deemed appropriate for higher education. If any activity that changes behavior in people over eighteen years of age is judged to reside within the domain of higher education and therefore to be worthy of academic credit, then establishing priorities, allocating resources, and making decisions become essentially capricious or political processes.

A third associated error is the assumption that an infinite amount of financing will be available to enable collegiate institutions to provide virtually any service. Generally, advocates have assumed that American financing capacity is infinite. Given the size of the national debt and the cost implications of an increasingly aging population, higher education during the last years of the twentieth century more likely will receive a decreasing percentage of the gross national product, forcing educational leaders to establish priorities and make decisions on the basis of financial limitations.

The generally expansionist educational philosophy led inexorably to a third error, which involved the question of who would deliver the needed services. On the one hand, expansionism led its interpreters to argue that professors, trained to do one thing, should willingly submit to training to do many other things and should be willing to do them. In Chapter Six we note that people who become professors early in their careers develop an interest in a certain topic and that, over time, involvement with that subject becomes one of the essential elements of their lives. Expecting such an individual not only to forsake that interest but also to be happy about it is most likely expecting the impossible. Of course, the other possible solution would be to reject professionally prepared professors and to replace them with people from many different walks of life, expecting these new teachers to cultivate new skills, interests, and motivations in return for love, satisfaction, or money. For example, either the professor would become a therapist, or the therapist would become a professor; such a profound change for either type of person implies many complex consequences.

A last error was different: a tendency for the reformers to resort to hyperbole as they criticized the grievous shortcomings of education and proclaimed the possibilities of the paradise that could come through an embracing of their ideas. Thus, according to these critics, education was judged to have failed miserably in a number of ways: it had not prepared people adequately for change; it had failed to renew cities; and it had inculcated rigid ways of thinking in those who passed through its system. Given such failures, "revolutionary" changes were prescribed, and the particular revolutionary change was any special preoccupation of the commentator (for example, community education, community renewal, lifelong learning, or competency-based education).

The dangers of such beliefs are multiple. Elaborate claims as to the primacy of higher education and its potency to positively influence all aspects of American life can and likely will lead to frustration, disillusionment, and a weakening of public regard for education. Indeed, the elaborate claims that the public school system would lead to a better life for all contributed to the disrepute into which public education had fallen by the 1970s. When attempts at omnipotence failed and the public schools turned out millions of functional illiterates, public disregard inevitably followed. Similarly, the judgment that every kind of life activity is worthy of academic credit undermines the entire national system of imposing standards for the preparation of those who will perform critical tasks for this society.

For example, educational reformers might decide that college courses in mathematics, chemistry, biology, physiology, and physics — typical requirements in the premedical curriculum — are irrelevant to eventual successful performance as a physician. Logically, however, a connection exists between organic and inorganic chemistry, pharmacology, and the prescription of appropriate medication in the treatment of disease. This logic is absent from the clearly implied beliefs of many reformers that the undergraduate credits awarded for such things as military service and successful avocational experiences should be counted as important parts of an undergraduate degree — a degree on which students can base an application for medical school. Also, the contentions that anyone who can do a task well can teach college students to perform that task well and that individuals who can teach effectively should perform a wide variety of other helping services lead to considerable confusion as to what the public can rightfully expect from collegiate programs.

In many respects, the best reaction of institutions to these cries for reform (especially the demand for unlimited service) is benign neglect. Certainly, any individual (or majority of voting citizens) has the right in a free society to demand and provide monies for higher education or postsecondary education institutions in which a wide range of activities are performed by instructors with varying training and experience. On the other hand, quality-conscious colleges and universities will very likely continue to perform as they have in the past and pay little attention to the rhetoric of the reformers. These institutions might even serve as sanctuaries for some recommended instrumentalities of reform (such as the improvement of instruction), which could be useful for many but which probably will not dramatically change established and traditional practices.

However, some consequences of this proposed neglect ought at least to be explored. The most serious consequence is that people who participate in some kind of educational activity may be misled into believing that they are in fact receiving a full college education (or at least the elements of one). It is dishonest to offer academic credit for remedial reading courses, and to tell students that this kind of work can be applied as electives to an associate's or a bachelor's degree. It is also deceitful and misleading to award bachelor's degrees largely on the basis of life experiences and to imply to recipients that, should they desire it, they are fully prepared and qualified to enter graduate or professional programs in traditional universities. Furthermore, it is misleading to imply to participants in an external doctoral degree program that a course in statistics and research design taught once a month for three months by a competent individual will prepare that student to do graduate-level, sophisticated research. Here, the matter of nomenclature is important. It would not be misrepresentation to create new names for newer nontraditional graduate programs if those names clearly describe the programs.

A second consequence (particularly important for publicly supported institutions but also relevant to privately supported institutions whose students receive tax-provided financial support) is the matter of fundamental public-finance policy. Of course, American citizens tax themselves to support virtually every kind of activity not precluded by the federal constitution or the applicable state constitution. However, the government has generally restricted its involvement in education to community-wide, statewide, or nationwide concerns and objectives. For example, this restriction is reflected in categorical federal grants to produce physicians, basic researchers, and agriculturalists.

States similarly have created colleges to prepare teachers and universities to prepare doctors, lawyers, social workers, engineers, and businesspeople. The real worth of some of these programs might be questioned; however, in the face of clearly limited resources, other programs can be challenged even more seriously when public money is used to teach car repair, language-refresher courses, or current events — and these types of courses are labeled higher education. Our diverse population has many real, important human needs, but there is a limit to the needs the public should be expected to support through the collegiate education, which was originally intended for quite definite and limited purposes.

In summary, higher education in America has been remarkably responsive to changing demographics and to society's shifting social agendas. However, the nature of the educational enterprise precludes successfully addressing every perceived need if it is still to fulfill its historic mission. The emergence of an information-based, technologically driven economy requires citizens who are facile with the higher-order cognitive skills of analysis, synthesis, and evaluation and who can express themselves clearly in verbal, written, or numerical form. Providing educational experiences that produce such outcomes requires a severe sharpening of the focus of those institutions that wish to provide what honestly can be called "higher" education.

TWO

Current Perspectives
on Academic Quality

The purpose of this chapter is to set forth a definition of quality undergraduate education that will (1) provide an adequate context within which to evaluate the current status of American undergraduate education and (2) suggest directions for improving this most vital component of the nation's educational system.

Defining Quality

A major item for clarification before quality can be addressed directly is nomenclature. Every educational institution insists that its primary commitment is to "quality" or "excellence," terms that are used interchangeably. Indeed, in spite of considerable deviation from ideals, for over 300 years a general consensus had existed regarding the characteristics of quality higher education. The designations "higher education" or "higher learning" implied some generally accepted qualitative norm. These phrases suggested which activities were appropriate for colleges and universities.

However, during the 1970s, at the urging of various reformers and reform groups and later through direct federal action, the term "postsecondary education" came into vogue as an umbrella for an enormous range of activities ranging from counseling programs in death and dying to doctoral programs in theoretical physics and to postdoctoral programs in esoteric medical specialties. The very term then allowed many institutions to undertake almost any conceivable kind of activity and to call it postsecondary education.

To some extent, this was probably a necessary accommodation to reality. The American system (or more precisely, the nonsystem) of higher education consists of many different types of institutions to serve a wide variety of students desiring some form of structured learning. There are technical institutes, junior colleges, community colleges, liberal arts colleges, church-related colleges, regional universities, and comprehensive universities polarized around science and technology. These institutions properly offer a variety of programs and activities that include many different preparations for vocations; preservation of the culture through libraries, museums, and galleries; and service as a community-learning resource. In this sense, all these institutions share important purposes and values in common; therefore, although important differences exist between a technical institute in Appalachia and a research-oriented university in California, both share the basic goal of meeting the educational and cultural needs of the citizenry and of inducting and socializing youth into American civilization and society. Furthermore, these new programs provide expanded learning opportunities for segments of the population previously excluded from higher education.

However, collegiate institutions are important but limited institutions that cannot and should not attempt to perform too many functions. Colleges and universities, for example, can have little effect on fundamental character traits such as honesty, optimism, or sense of humor. Those traits are formed much earlier and by different processes. Colleges and universities are at their best when they develop skills and abilities resting on the uses of words, numbers, and abstract concepts. Institutions organized to emphasize other goals (such as narrow vocational training, disseminating the joys of gardening, the cultivation of spiritual serenity, or therapeutic self-expression) are not institutions of higher education, even though they may be quite laudable in their ability to improve the human condition. We doubt that many Americans would wish to return to an era when only the privileged had access to any education after high school. However, a more practical educational policy would establish (as many other industrialized nations have) higher education as one entity and a variety of postsecondary educational services as another; in this type of policy, the two entities are in no way equivalent and do not use the same criteria for defining quality.

Quality is always an elusive concept. In *Quality Is Free* (1979, p. 13), Philip Crosby suggests that quality is like sex: everyone is for it; everyone claims to understand it; few are willing to attempt to explain it to anyone else; execution is simply a matter of following natural inclinations; and, when problems occur, they are always someone else's fault! Similar complexities arise in discussions regarding quality (or the lack thereof) in undergraduate education.

While quality as a concept shares certain abstract dimensions whenever it is discussed, it lends itself to so many different perspectives that meaningful dialogue is impossible unless the participants agree on a common approach. In *Managing Quality* (1988, pp. 39–46), David Garvin quotes from various authors to illustrate at least five different approaches to defining quality that are used frequently in industrial settings. All these approaches have, at one time or another, been applied to education. For example, the "product-based" approach suggests: "Differences in quality amount to differences in the quantity of some desired ingredient or attribute" (Abbott, 1955, pp. 126–127). Those who insist that the relative quality of an institution may be judged by its students' performance on nationally standardized tests seem to be working from such an approach.

On the other hand, egalitarian reformers work from a completely different approach, which assumes a "user-based" definition. From this perspective, quality can be equated with consumer preferences; in the words of the well-known industrial quality expert J. W. Juran (1974, p. 22), "Quality is fitness for use." Of course, such an approach has appeal for those undergraduate students who judge their education only in terms of how well it facilitates securing their first job and those adult part-time learners who only select courses which appear to be immediately applicable to their current job.

A third definition was popularized by Crosby (1979, p. 15) when he defined quality as "conformance to requirements." He illustrates the utility of his approach by noting that it allows for both high-quality or poor-quality Rolls-Royces and Ford Escorts. Once set requirements are met, the product has quality. Competency-based and criterion-referenced approaches to education reflect this approach.

A fourth definition, termed "value-based," implicitly acknowledges that standards must at times be compromised because of lack of resources. "Quality is the degree of excellence at an acceptable price and the control of variability at an acceptable cost" (Broh, 1982, p. 3). Legislators who must grapple with distributing scarce resources often fall back on this definition.

Of all the approaches outlined by Garvin, the "transcendent" approach mirrors most closely the historic view of quality education. Barbara Tuchman (1980, p. 38) stated it thus: "Quality is achieving or reaching for the highest standard as against being satisfied with the sloppy or fraudulent." While this definition clearly focuses on rigor, is challenging, and historically has enjoyed the widest currency among Americans, it provides little specific help for those charged with the task of improving undergraduate education.

No review of approaches to defining quality would be complete without W. Edwards Deming's definition (1986): quality is the reduction of variance. Deming, who is frequently credited with Japan's turnaround in manufacturing during the 1950s and 1960s, used statistical methods for identifying and reducing variance in manufacturing processes.

Clearly, quality takes on different meanings in different settings. When evaluating a manufactured product, one must decide what weights to assign to variables such as performance, features, reliability, durability, serviceability, and/or aesthetics. Deciding to purchase a washing machine will produce a different mix of criteria from that of choosing an automobile or a set of bone china. (For discussion of this concept see Garvin, 1988, pp. 49–50.) On the other hand, if one is evaluating a service, the assessment of quality will probably be shaped by the knowledge, skill, attitude, appearance, and timeliness of the providers as they interface with the needs and expectations of the receiver of the service.

From all these considerations, certain generalizations applicable to education emerge. First, quality is a receding horizon. There are no static, acceptable norms of performance. Second, in spite of theoretical considerations, if quality is to be improved, it must be defined with enough specificity so that its attributes are at least suggested, if not clearly delineated. Third, quality improvement is inexorably bound up with assessment and feedback.

The tension between the traditional and the egalitarian definitions of quality discussed in Chapter One is inescapable. Several authors have tried to find an acceptable middle ground. For example, John Gardner (1961) tried to avoid the egalitarian pitfall by insisting that quality (or "excellence," as he called it) is needed both by plumbers and philosophers. Yet when he proceeded to exemplify excellence, his examples were the traditional academic sort, and he never demonstrated how different but equal standards of quality could be used for other situations.

Such theories, which are safe as generalities, become dangerous when examined for specific details. Such an examination must respond to questions about the comparison of college degrees granted to the highly literate with those granted to the illiterate. Another issue to face is the comparability of student learning through sustained, intensive interaction with a qualified faculty member with student learning through essentially independent study with only occasional contact with a competent professor.

Alexander Astin approached the debate from a wholly different perspective in *Achieving Educational Excellence: A Critical Assessment of Priorities and Practices in Higher Education* (1985). He argues that neither traditional nor egalitarian definitions have driven the well-known rankings of institutions. Colleges and universities are judged to be excellent on the basis of four variables, all of which he deems to be inappropriate criteria of quality.

The first is reputation based on so-called beauty contests. Such listings usually are extrapolated from surveys in which presidents, deans, department heads, faculty, or professionals in selected fields are asked to rank institutions. Interestingly, ratings generated by such methods are extremely consistent over time and across groups. Astin discovered through multivariate analysis that the significant variables influencing the ratings are (1) undergraduate selectivity; (2) per-student expenditures; (3) the number of doctorate-granting departments; and (4) the number of doctoral degrees awarded. Obviously, all of these are proxy variables (that is, they stand for something other than what happens to students).

A second measure of quality is what Astin calls the resources view. Institutions with large endowments, highly paid faculty, and healthy research funds are considered excellent. Of course, this measure correlates highly with reputational indexes.

A third measure comes closer to focusing on outcomes. Institutions are rated excellent if they have low attrition rates and a large proportion of alumni who earn doctorates, make good salaries, and get listed in *Who's Who*. Again, these scales correlate positively with the reputational and resources views of quality.

The final approach Astin reviewed is what he calls the curricular content approach. This time he notes that all institutions rated as excellent have strong liberal arts emphases (even MIT). Not surprisingly, the same set of institutions come out on top when this index is used as when the reputational, resources, and successful alumni scales are used. This fact may suggest that these four variables are, indeed, appropriate proxies for quality. Nonetheless, Astin (1985, pp. 60–61) rejects all these approaches, preferring rather the "talent-development" concept of educational quality. This view focuses sharply on the impact institutions have on their students and faculty. "Its basic premise is that true excellence lies in the institution's ability to affect its students and faculty favorably, to enhance their intellectual and scholarly development, and to make a positive difference in their lives."

Such a definition seems consistent with American ideals

in that it allows for institutional and individual diversity by implicitly acknowledging the intrinsic value of all worthy endeavors. It supports the American dream of unfettered upward mobility since it provides for accepting students regardless of academic standing or ability. Further, it rightly suggests that quality knows no higher professions. All this is true and commendable, but we believe that Astin's definition still falls short of providing the focus necessary to identify quality undergraduate higher education, even though it may be adequate as an umbrella term judging the quality of all postsecondary education.

As suggested above, colleges and universities should focus on those few things that they do best: helping students develop the ability to receive and transmit information in spoken, written, or numerical form and to formulate and use abstract concepts. In accomplishing these principal purposes, collegiate institutions properly make use of many different techniques, including field work, collection of artifacts, and even remunerative work closely related to academic work. However, the basic techniques should continue to consist of reading and writing, numerical calculations, and closely evaluated practice in developing and using concepts. These techniques are best developed through sustained and intensive interaction between teacher and student, as well as closely supervised independent effort, so that constant evaluation is done by informed individuals who help students perfect their cognitive skills.

In view of these considerations, the following definition seems appropriate and workable:

> Quality undergraduate education consists of preparing learners through the use of words, numbers, and abstract concepts to understand, cope with, and positively influence the environment in which they find themselves.

The Decline of Undergraduate Education

A helpful preamble to any discussion of declining quality is the concession that the quality of higher education has never been as good as its apologists claim nor as bad as some educational reformers fear. Instruction in the past was frequently dull and pedestrian, and the requirements for a degree all too frequently consisted of a mishmash of courses not held together by any particular logic. Furthermore, comparing test scores across generations or across cultures is suspect because of shifting population mixes. Further distortion of comparisons derives from the facts that America educates a much broader cross section of its society than it did in previous generations and a much broader cross section than other cultures do today.

Some have suggested that while quality has actually improved, the rate of improvement has not kept pace with rising expectations. Similarly, others have opined that our perceptions are distorted because the slope of improvement in a more mature American system is not as steep as the slope of improvement in other countries. Therefore, quality of U.S. education may appear to decline when, actually, it is improving. Such considerations may, indeed, apply to manufactured goods, but there is sufficient evidence to suggest that in general the quality of undergraduate education in America actually has declined over the last twenty-five years.

The reasons for qualitative decline in undergraduate education are many and complex. While those reasons relating to topics covered in later chapters of this book will be dealt with later, three general forces that seem particularly potent need to be addressed at this point. The first of these was the commendable effort to enroll in colleges major segments of youth without previous access to higher education; these included members of minority groups, the economically disadvantaged, and women. In many cases, minorities and the economically disadvantaged had experienced serious educational deficiencies in their elementary and secondary education, so they arrived on campus unable to cope with the traditional course of higher education. In order to serve these students, institutions not only created varieties of remedial services but also began to modify requirements. Academic credit was often awarded for courses with high school–level content. Since the number of credits needed for graduation remained constant, in effect the required length of college-level experience was shortened. At first, such credits were counted as electives, but high school–level courses soon began to appear on the lists from which students could select their general education requirements.

Throughout the 1970s, the academic aptitude of entering college students declined, as did their preparation in basic subjects such as English, mathematics, and history. However, even as those deficiencies became apparent, colleges and universities reduced requirements in English, mathematics, foreign languages, and especially science. A general tendency developed to allow students to devise

> their own degree programs out of bits and pieces of academic work gathered from scattered off-campus courses, independent study and practical experience. A great deal of education was happening without carefully designed programs, without depth or breadth of learning, and, as indicated earlier, without benefit of libraries, laboratories, the cultural ambience of campus and the participation of fully qualified faculty. In their preoccupation with the market, some institutions all but abdicated their professional roles as designers of the curricula and as arbitrators of standards. And many gave up their traditional concern for the all-around development of the human personality in favor of counting disparate credits that may or may not add up to education in its traditional meaning. The result was a serious weakening in liberal education including reducing emphasis on reading, writing, speaking, foreign languages, mathematics, history, philosophy, natural sciences, and other subjects essential to producing well educated men and women [Bowen, 1980, p. 223].

The decline in collegiate graduation requirements was especially vexing. Particularly glaring was the precipitous decline of general education begun in 1960, which led the Carnegie

Foundation for the Advancement of Teaching to label this important component of the collegiate experience a "disaster area" (1977). That decline was especially significant with respect to the larger number of poorly prepared students who began to enter college at just about the time general education was deteriorating. Today, the apparent failure of secondary schools to prepare students, coupled with the collegiate retreat from general education requirements, almost inevitably produces millions of degree holders who simply are not educated in the historical sense of that term. In general, today's students can be defined as relatively less able, relatively less successful in academic work, relatively less financially comfortable, and relatively older than earlier generations of undergraduate students.

In 1980, Howard Bowen pointed out that a significant slippage in educational quality had occurred as higher education sought to serve these new groups of students. He believed that bringing them into college was probably wise even though the results were not completely satisfactory and the qualitative results have not yet matched those of traditional higher education.

Concomitant with the admission of poorly prepared students, the softening of requirements, and the awarding of credit for non–collegiate-level experiences, another movement was under way that was hardly noticed at the time but was substantial in its final results: the systematic shortening of the school year. When the governor's office in Missouri studied the calendars followed by that state's public institutions, they discovered that the number of days spent in class had decreased by as much as 15 percent over a twenty-year period — from 175 to 150 days, a cut of five weeks per year. Certainly no one would claim that increased time on any task is a panacea; however, an additional twenty weeks of instruction during the course of a four-year program ought to make a difference. A college president who served during the early 1970s (when major cuts in the calendar were being made) suggested that cost was the primary consideration. He recalled an informal session during the annual North Central Association convention at which presidents calculated how much money they could save if they shortened the calendar by two weeks but left tuition and room charges the same.

In general, institutional worry over enrollments and finances was a powerful force causing quality to deteriorate. In order to attract students, requirements were modified, the amount of classroom contact was reduced, grading standards were eased, academic credit was more easily granted, and new programs were created and advertised even though institutions lacked the expertise to offer them. Some of these changes were defended in the name of social ameliorism and educational reform, but actually were motivated by an economic need to increase tuition revenues or enrollment-driven appropriations from the state.

Many colleges and universities have engaged in (or are tempted to engage in) a variety of questionable academic practices because of financial problems. For example, there appears to be a growing tendency for institutions, especially low-quality institutions, to create and to advertise zealously presumably attractive programs, even though the institution might not have requisite intellectual resources to offer them. Related are unrestrained efforts to recruit foreign students, with only casual attention to either immigration forms and procedures or the student's ability to engage in academic work. To these difficulties should be added the proliferation of degree programs that require minimal formal class contact and the generous awarding of academic credit for military service, work experience, and a variety of experiences whether they provide a consistent educational pattern or not.

For example, some programs in business administration or public service award a degree by first granting the equivalent of three years' academic credit on the basis of a portfolio listing presumably relevant experiences and then requiring completion of only one thirty-week academic year, with one three-hour class each week. In one unaccredited institution, a Ph.D. was awarded on the basis of a previously acquired master's degree, a paid position in an educational institution, one five-week summer session, a thesis written under the direction of some local acquaintance, a two-week summer session to integrate experiences, an oral examination, and participation in graduation ceremonies.

Hundreds of such institutions offer whatever programs

a group of potential students seem to desire, wherever they desire it, and whenever it is convenient for the students' work schedules. The motivation for such activities is subject to question in institutions that have eliminated $1 million or more of annual operating deficits through offering off-campus programs that are less expensive to run and yield high net tuition income. The secret (or not so secret) ingredients for these programs consist of part-time cheap labor in the form of adjunct professors; many self-education services, labeled "independent study"; and low-cost or free physical facilities, such as a grade school building on Saturdays, an office building, or even the homes of students or adjunct faculty. The rationale to justify such programs uses the rhetoric of need fulfillment, service, democracy, or breaking the rigidity of traditional academic programs. Thus, the shortened doctoral program responds to the traditional criticisms of doctoral education, namely the high specialization and the extended time that are frequently required to earn the degree. The once-a-week program leading to a bachelor's degree in public service is explained as being an educationally valid way to accommodate the work needs of students, and the one-year bachelor's program in an institution in a ghetto is described as a black response to black needs that have not been served by traditional institutions.

The threats to quality in these programs are obvious. Meeting an instructor once a week or once a month, regardless of the qualifications of the instructor, at least makes a plausible (if superficial) treatment of topics. Expecting fully employed individuals to spend much of their study time by themselves is to risk very superficial study and to eliminate the powerful educational force of steady, consistent interaction with other students. Additionally, the use of distant, part-time faculty minimizes the amount of formal and informal monitoring that on a campus generally ensures reasonable fidelity to the tasks of education.

A more benign result of inordinate worry over enrollments and finances was the elimination or downgrading of entrance requirements to little more than high school graduation. Today many private and state institutions will accept virtually all students who apply if they have a high school diploma or a general equivalency diploma (GED). Actually, this practice is in effect a restoration of the situation before 1960, when most institutions accepted all or a great majority of the high school graduates who applied. For example, before World War II, the great state universities of the Midwest, such as the University of Illinois or Ohio State University, accepted all citizens having a high school diploma; and the incipient national institutions, such as Harvard, accepted two-thirds of the students who applied, with a substantial majority of those coming from New England and the New York metropolitan area. It has been claimed that such open admissions policies were compensated for by high attrition rates, but there is no good evidence for this hypothesis. Interestingly enough, multiple indexes of quality for those institutions at that time do not differ markedly from the indexes reported for the same institutions today.

Not all institutions, of course, engage in such activities. Those who do are often either private institutions of all sizes with a precarious tuition-driven budget or public institutions seeking to increase full-time equivalent student bodies for the sake of increased appropriations.

A third general threat to quality must be mentioned even though its potential negative consequences have started to emerge only recently. This phenomenon is the continuous increase in tuition and fees at the prestigious pace-setting private colleges and universities. During the 1970s, it became general practice to increase tuition and fees at approximately 2 percent above the annual increases in the inflation rate. The mean increases in tuition rates at all private colleges and universities have been 8 percent or more from 1985 through 1988, well above calculated inflation rates, and most forecasts predict similar increases for the next several years (personal talks with university administrators, for example, Vice-Provost Raymond Bacchetti of Stanford). Such increases make very possible a future in which these high-quality institutions will simply be too expensive for all but the children of the very affluent. The first qualitative injury would be symbolic but nonetheless real, because these quality-conscious private institutions have been in the forefront in maintaining academic and intellectual freedom, improving the condition of the professoriate, and occasionally demonstrating a direction in which true educational reform might move.

Institutions at Risk

The traditional concept of academic quality does not seem to be seriously jeopardized in well-established, financially strong colleges and universities, although some have experienced deterioration. Grade inflation has existed for decades in Ivy League institutions, and an increased need for remedial work is found in senior, research-oriented universities. However, in three types of institutions, academic quality matters are of critical significance.

The publicly supported two-year community college clearly must struggle to maintain academic quality. Academically, community college faculties are less well prepared than those in four-year institutions; the master's degree is the typical degree in academic subjects; and no degree is required in many of the vocational fields. The typical student is less able than those of four-year institutions although considerable overlap exists both in high school academic records and measured test performance. The substantial majority of students who enroll as freshmen in a community college either do not finish the first year or do not re-enroll for a second year, and only approximately 10 percent of students who enroll as freshmen subsequently receive a bachelor's degree from any institution. Although most community colleges have some form of general education requirements leading to an associate degree, only a minority of students fulfill these requirements, because they find the work either too difficult or irrelevant to their vocational plans (Cohen and Brawer, 1982, pp. 32–36).

If, as Astin (1977) argued, there is considerable educational significance to residential collegiate education, the commuting nature of community colleges denies students that significant factor. Since these institutions were designed for commuters, the typical student commutes to campuses in time for classes and departs immediately after the last class is over. Of course, a few students participate in clubs, student government, and athletics, but the majority seem to rely exclusively on classrooms for educational impact.

Further, if there is validity in the historic contention that collegiate education derives from intense research and scholarship, the community college again seems to be deficient. It is often claimed that since community college faculties do not do research, they are able to devote more time to teaching. However, there is no evidence to suggest that these instructors do, in fact, spend relatively more time on teaching or that quality classroom teaching and research are incompatible.

There has never been a culture in community colleges that expected research and scholarship; perhaps as a legacy from their secondary-school origins as junior colleges. The normal graduate education of community college teachers leading to a master's degree does not provide much training in research. Furthermore, administrative leadership frequently does not place high value on research, scholarship, and intellectuality.

The difficulty community colleges experience with respect to a somewhat narrow view of intellectual or academic quality is revealed in the purposes for which they exist. There are four or five generally accepted statements of purpose: to serve as transfer programs containing the first two years of a bachelor's degree; to provide general education, technical-vocational education, and adult and continuing education; to serve as a community cultural center; and to provide counseling to help students make difficult personal, academic, and career decisions. Achievement of these purposes varies. Among students who do transfer to four-year institutions, after a difficult transfer semester or term, performance is comparable with that of the students who spent all four years in that institution. However, across the country, such a small proportion of students do transfer that it is difficult to establish whether subsequent successful performance is attributable to the two-year institution or to the intellectual, personality, or motivational traits of the individual students.

General education courses in community colleges do not seem to be any better or worse than similar courses in four-year institutions. However, a rather common practice is for institutions to offer several levels of general education courses, some of which are distinctly remedial (that is, at a high school level).

Technical-vocational programs and adult continuing education programs vary so much that it is difficult to make general qualitative judgments. There are engineering programs stressing reasonably basic science and mathematics; straight skills courses, such as gunsmithing; courses in modern language; and courses stressing purely avocational themes.

A different approach to purpose may be inferred from what the institutions actually do. A community college serves as a total institutional counseling and advising effort, which quickly shows freshmen whether a baccalaureate degree program is appropriate for them. In California, for example, an estimated 80 percent of high school graduates enter colleges or universities, with the largest proportion entering two-year community colleges, yet the vast majority of those who enter complete neither an associate degree nor a bachelor's degree. They experience a college or a university and decide that it is not for them. Burton Clark (1960) labeled this phenomenon a "cooling-out function," and a reasonably strong case can be made that, although expensive, cooling out through experience is more consistent with democratic ideals than cooling out through examinations, which is the process used in other industrial democracies. Also, those students who do not earn degrees may still acquire marketable skills during the time they spend in the institution.

Another inference is that two-year public community colleges, as colleges, serve as a safety valve for lower-class feelings and aspirations that lead them to want a collegiate experience. At the same time, the total collegiate system, with its elite institutions, allows the middle and upper-middle classes to maintain positions of preference. In effect, the American system offers every high school graduate the opportunity to enter higher education, but it is structured and conducted so that less able individuals do not persist to an academic degree.

An additional function in this connection is that the community college also serves as a second chance for underachieving children of the middle classes to enter academic routes leading to positions of preference. These individuals, not admissible to four-year institutions on graduation from high school, still can enter two-year colleges and, after a time, mature sufficiently for entry into baccalaureate degree granting institutions and professional schools. The validity of this point of view is suggested by the strong support given two-year community colleges by academic and political leaders throughout the country. The academic leadership seems to see the two-year institutions as a means of caring for students with whom senior institutions cannot be bothered; the political leadership seems to see the two-year college as a relatively inexpensive way of accommodating the expanding educational aspirations in the nation. The truth of this assumption is certainly subject to debate.

A still different view of the purpose of two-year colleges is found in statements that announce the two-year college as a major new social institution capable of serving communities in an almost infinite set of ways. The significance of this view is reflected by the language used in asserting that a revolution is under way in the United States that can be serviced and given focus by two-year institutions:

> Everywhere, men and women are beginning to realize that the education that they received in the past, regardless of how little or how much, cannot sustain them for long in a time of rapid change. They sense that the world in which they live is no longer the world they have known, that the nation is undergoing deep and ever-accelerating changes, and that even the community or neighborhood in which they live no longer offers the comfort of continuity. They recognize that unless they take preventive action, they will become [as] obsolete as last year's headlines. They are discovering that if they wish to remain in touch with the reality of an ever-changing, ever-new present, they must change themselves — that the only way to survive in a world where so much is new every day, is to develop a process of continual self-renewal. They are demanding opportunities for renewal and leadership to show them the way [Gollattscheck and others, 1976, p. 2].

Clearly, the two-year community college is different from the traditional institution that awards bachelor's degrees, and many of its functions are qualitatively different from the functions of a four-year institution. It is also clear, as evidenced by enrollment trends, that these institutions are increasingly popular.

However, perplexities remain that at least should be examined, even if they cannot be resolved. Should academic credit signifying progress toward an academic degree be awarded for courses in elementary reading in an institution where over half of the students read at below the fifth-grade level? Some will say yes, and some will say absolutely no; some will insist that academic credit be awarded only for cohesive courses in the traditional arts and sciences.

Should four-year institutions be forced to accept transfer credit from community colleges as some state legislatures have mandated? In the past an informal technique was used by the credentialing and award-granting system of covertly accepting some kinds of academic credit, but rejecting other kinds. A better approach than mandated transfer would be to use the traditional transfer process and have the four-year institutions establish clear guidelines on which credits would be acceptable. A similar result could be achieved through the use of standardized examinations to validate what credit would be acceptable, although community college leaders have generally opposed this solution.

One possible compromise would be to award academic credit only for certain kinds of programs, while awarding a credential or certificate for nonacademic work. Some notable community colleges, such as the Kansas City Metropolitan Community College system, do differentiate between college-level and non–college-level courses. Breneman and Nelson (1981, pp. 211–212) suggested a plausible way to resolve the dilemma of credit for nonacademic work:

> [We suggest] an educational division of labor among institutions in the 1980s that would result in the community colleges enrolling fewer full-time academic transfer students of traditional college age and retaining a dominant position in those activities that four-year institutions have not undertaken traditionally and are likely to do less well. To a con-

siderable degree, this rough division of labor reflects tendencies and dependencies already underway: four-year residential institutions are working very hard to maintain full-time undergraduate enrollments, while community colleges continue to evolve away from the junior college emphasis on transfer programs toward service to new clienteles. Of course, this division of labor among institutions will never be absolute, nor should it be. For some undergraduates the community college will still be the best option, just as the university will be better for some older students returning to school part-time.

A second compromise could be achieved through public appropriation, with money supplied for only certain kinds of programs, but with institutions free to offer whatever other services they wish, provided they can be financially self-sustaining. This approach is increasingly being used.

A second kind of institution in which academic quality can be seriously threatened is the small, privately supported liberal arts college, perhaps 100 years old or older, that historically served young people who were from its own vicinity or who were members of the sponsoring church. Typically, students at such colleges were prepared to become public or parochial school teachers or clergy. As long as these schools operated on low tuition (made possible by the inadequate compensation of the faculty) and as long as there was a sustained market for their products, they could maintain a posture of reasonably high quality. However, as the cost of salaries and other goods and services began to mount and the number of tuition-free or low-tuition public institutions began to increase, these schools found themselves with serious enrollment and economic problems. Their former clientele could no longer afford their increased tuition, and the institutions lacked sufficient reputations to attract students from outside their region or denomination who would and could pay tuition and fees. That situation, which had begun in the 1960s, was exacerbated in the early 1970s when the need for elementary and secondary school teachers began seriously to soften. Often these institutions then found themselves accepting virtually every high school graduate who applied and offering whatever kinds of programs their leaders thought might attract and hold students.

By the early 1970s, some of these institutions began to experience such deficiencies in quality that, by the end of the decade, they generally were not much more selective than were publicly supported two-year community colleges. As enrollments dropped and tuition income decreased, these institutions first had to limit the number of faculty and decrease the faculty of many departments to only one or two instructors. When that strategy proved to be ineffective, low-attraction fields — such as most foreign languages — were eliminated or were taught by part-time instructors who could be recruited locally. Library holdings were allowed to deteriorate, as were laboratory equipment and other educational materials. When even those measures proved to be insufficient, many such institutions turned to creating new programs in the hope of attracting enough new students to provide a reasonable cash flow. Thus, some institutions began to offer weekend college work for groups of older women, while others began to contract with businesses and industry to offer specialized programs such as bachelor's degrees in business administration, even though the institution may never have had experience with professional degree programs in business. Unfortunately, the weaker and more threatened these institutions became, the more new programs — often inadequately supported and monitored — were developed to gain additional tuition revenue.

Such deviations from recognized good educational practice spread to encompass almost every dimension of these institutions. Additional examples include expecting a faculty member trained in history to teach literature and a general course in social science as well; employing as part-time instructors local individuals who had a native facility in a foreign language but no formal teacher training; and sending students to nearby community colleges or state colleges for courses it cannot offer itself.

One dramatic illustration of this phenomenon is the story of LaVerne College. With an on-campus constituency of 700 students, this college tried to serve over 10,000 students in locations across the United States through over fifty different programs. The off-campus programs lacked adequate administrative support, supervision, or coordination; and they used whatever part-time faculty could be recruited locally, essentially leaving them to conduct their own affairs. The regional accreditation organization finally forced LaVerne College to restructure its programs under the serious threat of withdrawing accredited status (personal conversation with the president of the college). However, most of the several hundred liberal arts colleges undertaking such efforts continue to survive the periodic accreditation visits and to keep their status as accredited institutions.

Although financial difficulties during the late 1970s and early 1980s led institutions to take steps that threatened quality, earlier periods of financial stress did not cause such actions. During the depression of the 1930s, salaries of full-time professors were cut, but, as a general rule, full-time faculty were not replaced by less well trained, part-time faculty. Although admission standards in most institutions in the 1930s were usually nothing higher than high school graduation, institutions did not attempt to solve the problem of decreases in enrollment by modification of admission standards (such as accepting high school juniors or seniors or recruiting older people), nor did institutions generally modify curricula seriously to shape them to the unique needs of many different groups of people. During the 1930s, there were weaker and stronger liberal arts colleges and some variation in curricular offerings; however, generally these institutions gave serious attention to teacher preparation, as evidenced by participation in the North Central Association Study of Liberal Arts Education. They tried to develop demanding programs of general education, as shown by their participation in the Cooperative Study of General Education, and, as a group, they produced a disproportionate number of future scholars and scientists (Knapp and Greenbaum, 1953).

The third type of institution in which academic quality is likely to be in jeopardy is the relatively new, privately supported, tuition-driven institution created since about 1970 to serve some of the presumed new clientele. These include humanistically oriented liberal arts colleges (for example, New College of Sausalito); law schools designed for part-time students with courses taught by part-time faculty (for example, John F. Kennedy University); for-profit educational brokering services that will create a program, develop a curriculum, and employ a faculty for any subject for which there appears to be a tuition-paying market (for example, the Institute for Professional Development); and freestanding doctoral programs in psychology taught by part-time faculty members recruited from private practice (for example, the California School of Professional Psychology). These types of institutions were typically created in the wake of the nontraditional movement and used the rhetoric of social service to rationalize their activities. In theory, the claims made by many of them were plausible; nonetheless, in aggregate, their practices and processes leave considerable concern for the quality of education received by their students.

Such institutions typically have little financial reserve and rely on tuition for all expenditures, including capital ones; hence, they do not impose rigorous admissions standards. Often the physical plant is rented space originally designed for other purposes. Their library holdings are limited, and they expect their students to use the library facilities of other institutions. Their faculties are, for the most part, part-time instructors who do little more than teach formal courses, often held at night and meeting far less frequently than courses in established institutions. Their students are also part-time, attending class at night after a day's work so that fatigue often may dull their educational efforts. Their student-support services often are minimal, and, even when services are provided, they are rarely used because of the students' busy schedules. All too frequently, in order to attract working students who want a degree but have limited time, graduation requirements are modest, and considerable credit is given for prior experience and for less-than-normal actual classroom contact with professors. These institutions have received considerable attention from regional accreditation organizations, which have been uneasy regarding many of their practices, but, even by 1989, accreditation teams are still unable to find a way to deal with many of them.

THREE

The Undergraduate Curriculum and General Education

Traditionally, sending young men and women to college has served many purposes, only a few of which are addressed by the formal curriculum or reflected in published mission statements. For example, colleges perform a custodial function, in that they provide an appropriate place for the young until adult society is ready to receive them. A college can also be viewed as a screen which, through a variety of mesh, selects people for advanced training or for positions of responsibility in adult society. Stated differently, collegiate education serves as a conduit for talent, strongly influencing subsequent occupational opportunities and choices. In addition, undergraduate education is intended to provide the young with the idiom, metaphor, allusion, and rhetoric needed for a common universe of discourse. In a related sense, undergraduate education can be viewed as the appropriate context within which individuals, during their late adolescence, can react to a variety of influences as they develop a coherent sense of their own identities. Finally, the totality of the undergraduate experience facilitates the development of the social skills necessary for success in modern, complex bureaucracies.

45

To some extent, the quality of the undergraduate experience has traditionally been measured by how well it addresses all these considerations. To us, these are still valid and important outcomes; however, laudable as they are, these are not the primary purposes for which colleges were established. The raison d'être for higher education is reflected in the formal curriculum. For it is here that students are systematically guided in their quest to understand, cope with, and eventually control their environment through the use of words, numbers, and abstract concepts. This chapter will focus on the formal curriculum, how it has been viewed and developed, and how its quality can be assessed.

Since World War II, there have been two periods when generalized agreement existed among faculty and students as to what did or did not constitute curricular quality: (1) the general education movement that flowered during the late 1940s and the 1950s and (2) the move toward selective admissions that occurred during the 1960s. An understanding of the impact of these two movements is facilitated by a brief look at the educational situation before the war.

Pre-World War II Curriculum Development

The undergraduate curricular situation before World War II consisted of some features common to most institutions and some experimentation in programs in liberal arts and sciences. The distribution system required that students take a specified number of courses in each of the domains of science, social science, and humanities. In addition, students usually were required to take English or rhetoric, one or two years of a foreign language, and physical education. In the undergraduate professional schools — such as agriculture, engineering, commerce, home economics, or education — students concentrated on technical and professional courses, with some modest requirement that they take one or two courses outside the professional school in such fields as literature and music. Courses were taught by an increasingly professional faculty; the desired theoretical norm was a faculty in which all (or most) professors held doctoral degrees, but, in fact, less than 25 percent of all faculty members at four-year colleges in the nation held such a degree. Courses in small and large institutions were increasingly developed as part of sequences in a disciplinary major, although they were also used as a means of satisfying general education requirements.

Some of the curricular experimentation predicted the shape of things to come. At Columbia College, John Erskine developed a general education course based on the great books of Western civilization, which would serve as a harbinger of the major concern with general education after World War II. Stringfellow Barr revolutionized St. John's College by installing a completely required curriculum based exclusively on the great books of the Western tradition. At Wisconsin, a two-year experimental college was created with the first year concentrating on Greece in the Age of Pericles and the second year on the United States during the 1930s. At Bennington College, Sarah Lawrence College, and Stephens College, serious experiments were carried out on a completely free elective system — however, the student's selection of courses would be made only after intensive consultation with an adviser. Antioch College made cooperative work-study central to its curriculum, and Swarthmore developed a widely known honors program that allowed approximately half of the juniors and seniors to put together an individually tailored curriculum that culminated in comprehensive examinations conducted by external examiners.

In general, collegiate curricula before World War II were not particularly demanding, except in some of the professional fields. Colleges and universities were not particularly selective with respect to students, often accepting all high school graduates who applied and whose pattern of high school courses was reasonably academic. The "Gentleman's C" had not yet been discredited, and social and athletic events were deemed as being perhaps more important than the academic curriculum for a college education. Fraternities and sororities had reached their zenith in campus life, and the football weekend had paramount significance. The big dance, with music provided by big name bands, focused student interest and whatever finances they could accumulate. Missing classes was accepted behavior, as was concentration on single-textbook courses.

The Rise and Fall of General Education

The general education movement, which began before World War II but flowered afterward, was probably the most systematic and far-reaching effort to establish curricular quality and integrity from approximately 1930 to the present. Academic leaders saw general education as the part of undergraduate education that ensured a breadth of educational experience and prepared students for their nonvocational lives as self-actualizing individuals, effective family members, productive citizens, and leisure-enjoying human beings. It consisted of different types of programs put together after intensive faculty study and effort, and it came to be the curricular expression of which knowledge the faculty believed was worth knowing.

The idea of general education caught the fancy of the postwar educational community. Its objectives were given national visibility through the publication of the *Report of the President Truman Commission on Higher Education* (1947). Its presumed outcomes were studied and publicized by the American Council on Education Cooperative Study of Evaluation in General Education (Dressel and Mayhew, 1954a), and new program developments were publicized by the highly active Committee on General Education of the Association for Higher Education. Dressel and Mayhew (1974) have estimated that perhaps 250 to 300 institutions were adopting new programs each year for three or four years during the early 1950s.

An important characteristic of these general education programs, regardless of the format adopted by different institutions, centered around a consistent set of shared intellectual beliefs. In all these programs, the individual, rather than the discipline, was the principal focus of curricular development. A frequent graphic metaphor was a circle, which symbolized the person. The circle was divided into quadrants labeled humanities, natural science, social sciences, and communicative arts. In one way or another, all courses tried to achieve some degree of interdisciplinary quality. Some institutions created new courses such as humanities, drawing on the history of Western civilization, music, philosophy, and the arts. Others sought to com-

bine disciplinary courses in such a way as to produce interdisciplinary insights. All these programs sought to stress rationality; virtually all elevated critical or analytical thinking as a transcendent outcome; and all were preoccupied with the Western
intellectual tradition and struggled mightily to project a contemporary synthesis of that tradition. Although all expressed
a concern for affective qualities and values, typically the concern
was put into effect through rational rather than emotional means.

The determinants of quality were reflected in the rhetoric
of the general education movement where the operative words
were academic rigor; comprehensive examinations; interdisciplinary; philosophically based; critical, analytical, or rational
thinking; achievement of specified educational objectives; and
applying academic concepts to the solution of human problems.
While the form of general education programs differed somewhat
among institutions, the essence of what general education was
attempting to achieve was revealed in the program at the College of the University of Chicago and the rationale developed
by the faculty of Harvard College.

Over a thirteen-year period, the University of Chicago
developed a prescribed four-year curriculum consisting of interdisciplinary courses taught by faculty not preoccupied with
research demands. Elaborate syllabi were used, and students
were required to examine original sources instead of relying on
single textbooks. Instructors did not assign grades, but grades
were determined by an impersonal university examiner who was
responsible for creating comprehensive examinations for each
of the fourteen year-long sequences that students were expected
to master. While students could elect a few specialized courses,
those could not replace the specially designed courses that expressed the general education ideal. The curriculum, as it became crystallized by 1947, consisted of a series of one-year
courses.

Several elements made the Chicago program a significant
prototype that affected education throughout the country during the 1950s and early 1960s. First, it was a prescribed program based on a firm faculty agreement on which skills undergraduates should master. Second, it was taught by a faculty who

considered the College the most important element of their professional lives and whose attention was not diminished by other university obligations. Third, the quality of syllabi was extraordinarily high. Each syllabus resulted from intensive faculty collaboration, and each guided students through a richness of original sources. The clear quality of the Chicago documents symbolized the high regard in which the faculty held the curriculum. Compared with the attractively printed and illustrated Chicago syllabi, course outlines from other institutions looked primitive and fragmentary. Finally, and especially important, was the stress placed on mastery as demonstrated through the use of comprehensive examinations.

The influence of the Chicago general education program on the national movement was profound. The program at Chicago was explained and praised by individuals who had been part of that program, rather than by the publication of a book (as Harvard subsequently exercised its influence). At small institutions (such as the Pennsylvania College for Women, subsequently named Chatham College) and large institutions (such as Michigan State University) participants in the Chicago program began to emulate Chicago's use of a core of required courses deriving from the great books of the Western tradition, separate faculties, and comprehensive examinations to establish students' grades. For example, at Chatham College, the academic dean, Thomas H. Hamilton, and the director of testing had been closely involved with the College of the University of Chicago; at Michigan State University, the personal consultant to the president was Floyd W. Reeves, who had long served on the faculty at Chicago. The first director of the Board of Examiners at Michigan State University had been exposed to the Chicago way of thinking through workshops and participation in the Cooperative Study of General Education, which had its headquarters at the University of Chicago and was directed by Ralph W. Tyler, the University Examiner responsible for the system of comprehensive examinations. Although the program at the University of Chicago served as a model that influenced practice across the country, it actually lasted only a few years at Chicago.

Contrary to the Chicago experience, the proposed program of general education at Harvard College was never really implemented as planned. However, the theory of general education, which was developed by the Harvard faculty and published in a report entitled *General Education in a Free Society,* provided a theoretical rationale that would guide (or at least flavor) faculty discussions from 1945 onward. The list of objectives for general education published in that document, informally called the Redbook, began to appear in college catalogues and recommendations for curricular reform almost immediately.

The intellectual achievement of the general education movement began to deteriorate by the late 1950s, and, by the late 1960s, the movement was in full retreat. The reasons for the decline may be summarized quickly. New interdisciplinary courses were extraordinarily difficult to teach for professors who had been narrowly focused on their disciplines. One solution was to create a separate faculty that would develop and teach new courses on a full-time basis. However, few institutions had the resources or the will to take this approach, thus leaving individual faculty torn between giving attention to their own disciplinary courses and giving attention to the new interdisciplinary ones. In such a struggle, the disciplinary bias inevitably won out. The relative success of the two approaches is well illustrated by two cases. At the University of Minnesota, faculties in the College of Science, Literature, and the Arts were expected to offer general education courses. Michigan State University, however, created a Dean of General Education who was given a budget and a full complement of faculty positions. The Division of General Education at Minnesota lasted only a few years, whereas it lasted almost forty years at Michigan State.

Philosophically, the general education movement was based on the intellectual hegemony of the Western tradition. During the 1950s, other traditions and cultures such as Oriental civilizations began to intrude, and it was found that those new influences could not be accommodated in any overriding synthesis.

Finally, the movement was dealt a death blow by two major external events. First, the successful Russian launching of *Sputnik* called into question America's presumed scientific and technological superiority. The immediate response was to restore both to secondary schools and to colleges and universities a disciplinary rigor that was seen to be antithetical to the inter-disciplinary approach of general education. Second, and even more significantly, was the sudden shortage of college faculty that began about 1960. Scarcity gave faculty the power to insist on teaching whatever courses they wished, and often they did not wish to teach self-developed courses in general education that required a major effort to become acquainted with several disciplines.

The Rise and Fall of Selectivity

The second qualitative peak was of a different order and reflected the triumph of the disciplinary approach over the in-terdisciplinary. This shift attempted to ensure curricular quality through selective admissions.

Historically, institutions have selected students for entry into college with different techniques at different times and with variations in different regions of the country. Before the emer-gence of secondary schools, students were selected exclusively by means of an examination, which frequently was administered orally to determine the student's competency in Latin and Greek. Gradually, as the number of prospective students increased, oral examinations became impossible; written examinations replaced them to such an extent that, by 1910, a body was created to standardize entrance examinations for those students applying to a small number of Eastern seaboard institutions.

As secondary schools evolved and as their standards be-came higher, colleges and universities, particularly in the Mid-west, began to use academic performance in secondary schools as a criterion for admissions. Thus, the college admissions picture before World War II was somewhat mixed, with the private Eastern institutions tending to stress performance on the SAT and rank in secondary school class. A few states (such as Florida, Iowa, and Michigan) had various statewide testing programs; applicants to public institutions in those states had to submit test scores and academic records from high school as evidence of their ability to handle collegiate work. However, most of the state institutions and the private institutions in the Midwest and South still required only a high school diploma for admission.

There was a myth, particularly in senior state institutions, that a relatively open admissions program was justified because the rigor of the freshman year would screen out students who could not perform. However, it is difficult to tell whether that degree of deliberate institutional selectivity through attrition was carried on at all. Overall, college dropout rates remained substantially the same in the prewar years and in the several decades afterward. Institutional record keeping was primitive; even during the early 1950s, public institutions could not present evidence of the reasons that different students dropped out.

Actually, acceptance into colleges and universities just before and immediately after World War II was a matter of self-selection. Institutions accepted virtually all individuals who applied, who had a high school diploma, and who had reasonably high scores on any required admissions tests. Students lacking aptitude and achievement in secondary schools simply did not apply to college. This nonselectivity characterized even those institutions that ultimately became highly selective.

However, by the beginning of World War II, an ethos and a technology of selectivity had emerged, especially along the Eastern seaboard, which was used nationally as soon as conditions arose that allowed selectivity. The first and most significant of these was the creation of the Educational Testing Service (ETS) in 1947, which assumed the technical testing work of the College Entrance Examination Board, the Educational Records Bureau, the Cooperative Test Service, the Psychological Test of the American Council on Education, and the Graduate Record Office of the Carnegie Foundation. Under the terms of the agreement among these groups, each agency was either paid to terminate testing activities — as in the case of the American Council on Education — or was convinced to purchase testing services — as in the case of the College Entrance Examination Board. The ETS immediately moved to improve the quality of testing and to conduct considerable research on how best to select students for collegiate work. As ETS became operational, institutions in the Midwest and Far West began to join the College Entrance Examination Board and to use the SAT and various other testing instruments in their admissions efforts (later, many of them would use the ACT program, instead).

The need for such services was underscored when, in 1954, the registrar of Ohio State University examined the 1950 census figures and predicted there would be a tidal wave of college applications by 1960. He concluded that institutions would need some mechanism to select students for the limited college spaces available. Ronald Thompson's (1954) predictions proved to be in the right direction, albeit highly conservative. Desire for admissions to college increased substantially, and various institutions responded differently to that increase. For example, private institutions did expand capacity somewhat, but they also sought to limit enrollment by requiring higher test scores and secondary school grades.

During the early 1960s, directors of admissions would report each year with pride that the SAT scores of entering freshmen had increased by a certain amount. A few well-known institutions became so attractive to applicants that they could choose to accept only the upper 1–5 percent of high school graduating classes. Harvard was one institution whose dean of admissions actually warned the faculty that Harvard could become so selective that it would eventually destroy its base of support as future corporate executives, lawyers, doctors, and engineers were denied admission, and their places were taken by future professors and other intellectuals. In his farewell speech to the faculty, Dean Bender argued that Harvard should enroll students with many different talents, not just those with academic talent. He opined that football talent, dramatic talent, journalistic talent, and managerial talent were equally needed if Harvard was to prepare people for successful life in a diverse American society. Harvard and a few other institutions actually attended to such warnings and sought to add other elements to the admissions equation; nonetheless, the process still placed heavy stress on high school grades and test scores.

Similar selectivity began to take place in public institutions as they began to use grade-point average and test scores to limit enrollments. Those applicants who did not meet prevailing standards were accommodated in the nonselective community colleges that states began to create during the 1960s in response to the increased demand.

Many institutions, however, continued the practice of admitting virtually any student who applied and had a high school diploma. Two-year, publicly supported community colleges in many states were required by law to accept nearly all applicants, and a substantial majority of private institutions expanded their physical plants through increased enrollment, which they preferred to maintaining a small enrollment through heightened selectivity. In those institutions, the 1960s saw a doubling of enrollment, and the resultant doubling of tuition provided many private colleges and universities the first relative affluence they had experienced in their 100-year histories. Nevertheless, the spirit of selectivity prevailed even in those institutions that, in fact, were unselective. Institutions joined the College Entrance Examination Board or adopted the ACT Program as a symbolic gesture that they were becoming more selective. The pervasive doctrine was that high grades were required if students were to enter increasingly selective graduate and professional schools, and high performance in such schools was essential to obtain teaching posts in prestigious institutions, residencies in major teaching hospitals, junior partnerships in major law firms, or clerkships to senior judges. Some institutions, such as Harvard, Carleton, Oberlin, and Stanford, became so selective that they would accept only 10–14 percent of the students who applied.

The intellectual basis for the victory of selectivity was the virtue of meritocracy and the essential nature of a status system. Thus, institutions were categorized as "big league," "minor league," "bush league," and "academic Siberia," depending on the degree to which they could be selective both with respect to students and to faculty. The impact on the curriculum was reflected in expressions such as, "increased proliferation of specialized courses," "increased rigor required for work in a major," "increased use of quantification," and "enhanced valuing of the concept of academic excellence," as defined by professors offering courses for graduate students as the first preference, while, at best, tolerating undergraduate students seeking other than disciplinary and intellectual goals.

A serious deterioration of the emphasis on merit and achievement began between 1968 and 1970, although there had been earlier events anticipating that decline. One of the earliest indications of a weakening of standards was the inflation of academic grades, which seems to have taken place as the result of two quite distinctive forces. The first occurred as a by-product of high selectivity. The historic use of the grading curve ensured that a certain proportion of students would receive low grades and a certain proportion would receive high grades. As the measured academic ability of students in selective institutions began to rise, it began to appear unfair to penalize a high-ability student with a C grade simply because of the superior performance of that student's peer group. It was argued that, in highly selective institutions, virtually all students should be expected to achieve at the A or B level, and institutions began to use new grading systems in which the grades of D and F were eliminated, so that students would receive grades of A, B, or C or No Grade.

The other factor that may have contributed to grade inflation was the student demand for relevance during the era of campus dissent. Some argued that eliminating vulnerability to failure would encourage students to explore new subjects and might ensure greater rapport between students and faculty. One technique was the Pass/Fail or $+/-$ system with the implicit understanding that virtually no one would receive a failing grade. As a result of these forces, modal college grades moved from a C to a B; in some programs and institutions, the modal grade became an A, and a grade of B was viewed as a signal that the student might be headed for academic difficulty.

The second indicator of retreat from meritocracy was the decline of selective admissions, which started as many institutions began to experience enrollment problems during the 1970s. In effect, this phenomenon was a return to earlier practices of admitting all applicants who had graduated from high school, but it also could be considered an absolute qualitative deterioration. However, in contrast to the earlier era when students with poor academic records did not apply to colleges, during the late 1960s, many high school graduates with poor academic records did apply to college. The result was a precipitous decline in the measured academic aptitude of college applicants, which came after several decades of rather steady increases in ability. On the SAT 200- to 800-point scale, measured quantitative aptitude declined from a high of 502 in 1963 to 470 in 1977, and verbal scores declined during the same period from 478 to 429; similar patterns of decline characterized other large-scale ability-testing programs. The long-term significance of this fact cannot yet be assessed. If the academic ability of college freshmen declines and, at the same time, college grades go up, these twin developments permit the inference, at least, that there has been a deterioration in the quality of colleges and universities.

Curriculum Reform in the 1960s and 1970s

The retreat from general education and the decline in selectivity and measured evidence of academic performance are facts. However, before the significance of these facts can be gauged, other curricular elements of the late 1960s and the 1970s must be considered. The philosophical roots of these were discussed in Chapter One; in the context of this chapter, these reforms ultimately resulted in a growing anti-academia trend, as reflected in such commentary regarding the substance of higher education. The curricular beliefs of advocates of non-traditional education are difficult to isolate because so much of their writing stresses only egalitarian themes, such as the need to remove barriers to traditional college education. Apologists argue that many different groups of people have needs, situations, or conditions not suited to traditional modes of education, but they also should be served in ways suitable to them (for example, the aged, the incapacitated, the incarcerated, or even the emotionally disturbed). They further point out that several barriers prevent such people from obtaining needed educational services: geographic, financial, transferability questions, and the irrelevance of orthodox definitions of education. Actual specifications of curricula, however, are often exhortative, such as encouraging provision of curricula for the alienated

students who really do not want to be in college or for those
who had had unsatisfactory educational experiences. Other curricular advice from reformers is instrumental, urging joint student and faculty program design, use of a broad mix of educational resources, use of adjunct professors, and major emphasis
on independent study and learning. Actual curricular substance,
however, remains obscure and must be inferred.

Cutting through the nontraditional rhetoric yields these
essentials: content of the curriculum was whatever an individual
wished to study; sequence should be determined situationally
(that is, whatever is most convenient to the student); and credit
should be assigned for whatever kind of experience appears to
modify human behavior. In curricular terms, this emphasis was
generally played out in several innovations dubbed experiential learning, affective-based curricula, cluster colleges, competence-based education, individualized self-paced instruction,
cooperative education, and innovative flexible schedules.

An essential component of the nontraditional movement
is the stress on experiential learning and the awarding of academic credit for such experiences. Statements about experiential learning tend to be exhortative: "if an individual's tastes in
leisure include bridge, or citizen action for equal rights, or new
trends in diet and meditation, there should be readily available
opportunities for both improvement of the individual's competence and reconsideration of his or her outlook" (Keeton and
Associates, 1976, p. 7). In criticism of formal, traditional higher
education, Keeton and Associates (1976, p. 14) wrote, "The
Achilles' heel is that credit hours do not signify directly what has
been learned or achieved, but represent a time-served measure
that correlates only roughly, and in unknown ways and degrees,
with what has been learned." Through inference, then, academic
credit would be granted for military experiences, for foreign
travel, for sequences of activities designed to serve as preven-
tative medicine, for library browsing, or for whatever other experience an individual had undergone that would modify behavior in desired directions. This position is epitomized in the
following quotation: "Above all we must cultivate a new spirit
that accepts the educative value and worth of all experience,

not merely that which is devoted to scholarly study or which is guided at every step by professors" (Keeton and Associates, 1976, p. 10).

Replacement of Cognition with Emotion. A second type of reform, which is a natural corollary of experiential learning and which is symbolic of rising anti-intellectualism, was the suggested substitution of feeling and emotion for cognition as a way of organizing the undergraduate curriculum. Affective or emotional concerns had long been attended to by collegiate institutions through a variety of extracurricular activities, such as homecoming weekends and songs praising the alma mater. However, by the late 1960s and early 1970s, explicit curricular concern for feeling and emotion was being urged, especially in some of the experimental colleges. The catalogue statement announcing the opening of Kresge College (University of California, Santa Cruz, 1970) captures the intent: "Santa Cruz' sixth liberal arts college will explore educational innovation through a human relations approach. Just as Man's natural environment is a result of a delicate balance and interdependency, so the excitement and creativity of a learning environment is a result of open, direct, and explicit relationships" (p. 41). Essentially, the curriculum at Kresge was to be individual feelings and self-expression, and one of the major pedagogical tools was to be use of T-groups, defined as sensitivity-training groups of persons who would meet together for the purposes of exploring mutual feelings and interactions. Surely, 18-to-22-year-old students have real developmental needs that can be responded to through the collegiate curriculum. However, this response can occur in a variety of ways short of turning the classroom into a T-group.

Colleges Within Colleges. By 1960, it became apparent growth in enrollments would be so large that many institutions would appear, at least, to be indifferent and impersonal in their dealings with students. In order to prevent this, throughout the country a third innovation was undertaken to create colleges within colleges, or to develop large institutions consisting of many small autonomous units. Frequently, there was also an attempt to give each of these subunits a distinctive characteristic. For example, Stephens College of Columbia, Missouri, created a house plan that consisted of a hundred students and five faculty members who would use a single residence hall for learning and for living. Faculty members had offices in the residence hall and most courses were taught there. The University of the Pacific created three cluster colleges, each consisting in theory of 250 students and a resident faculty, with the program being offered in each of the specifically designed residence units. The University of California, Santa Cruz, was designed to become a 20,000-student university divided into separate colleges of between 700 and 1,000 students, each with residence, instructional, and library facilities. At the University of Michigan, an experimental college was created in the belief that a smaller, more coherent situation would be a desirable alternative for students proceeding through the large, departmentalized College of Science, Literature, and the Arts. Western Washington State University created a new college immediately adjacent to the main campus that consisted of small, 50-individual-capacity residence units designed to be used for both learning and living purposes. Michigan State University created several large cluster colleges that would house students and offer a partially prescribed curriculum taught by the resident faculty who spent full-time teaching within the college. As these innovative curricula were undertaken, at least one—the University of California, Santa Cruz—enjoyed an immediate popularity with heavy enrollment pressures.

However, within a short time, these cluster or satellite colleges began to decline. They did not attract the number of students anticipated. And high attrition rates occurred among students who did enroll. Faculty members who were encouraged to attend to both college concerns and departmental disciplinary concerns chose their disciplinary interests to the detriment of the unique qualities that were supposed to characterize the various subunits.

Competence-Based Instruction. A fourth innovation that has obvious applicability to some sharply defined programs and that can still be found in some quarters is competence-based instruction. In general, the competence-based approach assumes that the purposes of a course can be stated in quite specific terms describing human behaviors, that the development of those behaviors can be facilitated by quite specific learning activities, and that the demonstration of those behaviors can be measured with some precision. Ideally, the total faculty of an institution or of a subordinate school, college, or division could get together and agree on a large array of specific behaviors that the organization values and wishes to produce. Once such agreement has been reached, it is assumed that each faculty member will then reorganize his or her share of the program in such a way as to contribute to the development of some of those behaviors. Clearly, the competence-based approach assumes a high degree of faculty cooperation with respect to the total curriculum. "There needs to be a great deal of coordination among faculty, between faculty and assessors (teachers and assessors are often different persons in competence programs), and between the administrators of the program and the practitioners in it. The amount of emotional and intellectual interdependence among faculty that is fostered by competence-based education sharply exceeds that of other interdisciplinary programs, themselves usually demanding in these respects" (Grant and others, 1979, p. 227).

The concept of competence-based education has been publicized widely and supported financially by foundations such as the Fund for the Improvement of Post-Secondary Education. It usually has been practiced, however, in relatively unknown institutions such as Alverno College, Antioch School of Law, College of Public and Community Service of the University of Massachusetts at Boston, Florida State University, Mount Hood Community College, and Seattle Central Community College. Moreover, "competence-based programs have had a high mortality rate. Perhaps because of their very demand, they have not proved particularly attractive to students; and in institutions where the faculty have no power to resist imposed change (such as well-established institutions with tenure), it has been difficult to win the loyalty of faculty to a competence-based approach. Thus the programs at Florida State University have come to a virtual standstill, and a substantial segment of the

Alverno College faculty has resigned, while those remaining have protested to the college's Board about the competence approach and its manner of implementation" (Grant and others, 1979, p. 14). Because of these tendencies, the likelihood of the competence-based concept spreading to all American higher education appears remote.

Self-Paced Learning. A similar fate for similar reasons can be predicted for a fifth, and related, innovation, which was partly curricular and partly instructional. This was the movement toward self-paced learning. This concept assumes, as does competence-based education, that the desired outcomes of collegiate courses can be specified with some precision. It assumes that faculty members can and will create a rather structured sequence of activities and measures of performance that students can follow at their own pace, going on to a next phase only after clearly demonstrating achievement of a prior, specific learning phase. It further assumes that students will work individually, using a variety of resources such as texts, articles, pictures, television tapes, and computers, and that the faculty member's role will be designer of the sequences, and information resource whom students will use as needed. Several researchers have shown that courses can be so organized and that student outcomes can be measured (Dressel and Mayhew, 1954a). However, the approach has not been accepted or used widely by faculty members other than by those few who gained some reputation from having devised such courses.

Off-Campus Programs. Another major curricular thrust of the 1950s and 1960s consisted of a variety of efforts to include in a systematic way some off-campus experience as an integral component of an undergraduate program. The two most widely adopted systems were providing students with (1) an overseas experience or (2) a system of cooperative education that allowed students to alternate between on-campus academic work and off-campus work experience related to their academic programs. The number of institutions making these efforts increased rather rapidly during the 1950s, when overseas programs were inaugurated at a rate of 15 to 20 each year. Cooperative education programs grew from 43 programs in 1953 to 61 in 1960, then to more than 200 by 1970. Advocates of these programs have been lavish in praise of their value for student development, and they predict continued expansion into other institutions.

In a few institutions that have made major financial and administrative investments in a system of cooperative education (for example, the University of Cincinnati, Antioch College, Northeastern University, and the University of South Florida), the curricular significance has been great, because considerable attention was given to articulation between an academic program and work experience. In a few other institutions (for example, Oberlin, Smith, Stanford, or Lake Erie College), a substantial proportion of students go overseas for experiences directly related to their home-campus academic programs. However, a strong impression persists that, on most campuses claiming cooperative education, the program is either a relatively small effort for particularly appropriate vocational curricula, or it is the primary means of securing or financing part-time work for students (work that is linked only rarely and accidentally to an academic program). Similarly, the number of students participating in formal overseas programs remains quite small, with a far greater number of students who gain overseas experience doing so through special travel programs. The cost of starting and maintaining a well-integrated cooperative education program or a comprehensive, academic overseas program is simply too great for most institutions to assume.

Academic Calendar Changes. A seventh innovation, presumably having curricular implications, consisted of the many attempts during the 1960s to change academic calendars and to break the temporal lock-step of undergraduate education. In the historic temporal arrangement, about two-thirds of all institutions used a semester system, one-third used a quarter or term system, and all institutions assumed that normal student progression toward a degree consisted of continuous enrollment during each academic year until the required credits had been accumulated.

Beginning in about 1960 and supported by impressive educational rationale, institutions began to experiment with new calendars. Some, such as the University of Pittsburgh and the state institutions of Florida, adopted the trimester system intended to equalize enrollment throughout the calendar year, thereby providing for more cost-effective use of the physical plant. Other institutions that had been on the semester system moved essentially to the quarter system (for example, in the 3-3 system at Dartmouth, students enrolled for three three-month segments and took three courses in each segment). Other institutions created an interim term between the fall semester and the spring semester. During the interim term, which extended over Christmas vacation and throughout January, students were expected to undertake different kinds of educational experiences, such as off-campus fieldwork or interdisciplinary team-taught, problem-oriented, on-campus activity. Other more radical changes were tried, such as Colorado College's adoption of a modular system in which intensive courses were offered for short periods (such as three weeks) followed by one-week periods for relaxation.

Two decades of temporal experimentation showed that some new calendars simply would not work. For example, the trimester system did not generate substantial summer trimester enrollments, and the interim term became little more than an extended intersession break. The most lasting effect was that institutions that maintained a semester system began fall semester earlier so that the end of the semester ended simultaneously with the beginning of the Christmas vacation. This practice eliminated the lame-duck two or three weeks in January, typical of the previous semester systems. An unanticipated outcome of this decision was the gradual shortening of the semester from seventeen or eighteen weeks to as little as fourteen or fifteen weeks. This probably was caused, in part at least, by the lack of air conditioning in campus buildings during the summer. Also, as noted in Chapter Two, shortening the semester was sometimes a conscious attempt to save money.

Virtually none of the major curricular experiments of the 1960s and 1970s became established parts of the mainstream of undergraduate curriculum in the way that general education did in the 1950s, although many of those experiments produced positive changes. As noted earlier, the major reforms suggested during the 1960s focused more on structure and time arrangements than on the actual content of courses.

The Return to General Education

By the late 1970s, some institutions attempted to restore intellectual cohesion to the undergraduate curriculum and to enhance its academic rigor. For example, the Harvard Faculty of Arts and Sciences approved a new set of graduation requirements to ensure that all students would gain insight into all the major domains of knowledge. Stanford University reestablished a Western Culture requirement and required that all students take specifically approved courses from the seven domains of knowledge. (In 1988, after an extended and highly publicized debate, Stanford enlarged the options in its Western Culture requirement to ensure that women and third-world cultures were represented.) Spurred on by mounting trade and federal deficits — grim reminders that the country was losing its economic preeminence in the world — and reacting to the focus on individual competitiveness which was a major theme of the Reagan administration, foundations and associations began turning out a flood of reports suggesting ways for improving education at all levels. By 1986, nearly all the national education organizations had published reports that differed in emphasis, but in general called for a return to the old definition of baccalaureate education. All the reports reflected a remarkable consensus regarding the problem, its extent, and (to a lesser degree) the steps that should be taken to improve the situation.

Involvement in Learning (Study Group on the Conditions of Excellence in American Higher Education, 1984) reflected the tone of many of the similar efforts to follow. This report was published by the National Institute of Education (the research arm of the U.S. Department of Education) and was the first federally funded study of postsecondary education in fifteen years. The report concluded that "The college curriculum has become excessively vocational in its orientation, and the bachelor's degree has lost its potential to foster the shared values and knowledge that bind us together as a society" (p. 10).

The report identified "three critical conditions of excellence — (1) student involvement, (2) high expectations, and (3) assessment and feedback" (p. 17). "Highly involved students demonstrate their commitment in a variety of ways: by devoting considerable energy to studying, by working at on-campus rather than off-campus jobs, by participating actively in student organizations, and by interacting frequently with faculty members and student peers" (p. 17). Institutions are urged clearly to communicate college-level learning objectives since "student performance clearly rises to these expectations, and students respond positively to reasonable challenges" (p. 20).

Among the report's twenty-seven recommendations was the suggestion that universities establish "clearly and publicly stated high standards of performance" against which student performance can regularly be assessed through essays, interviews, portfolios and tests" (p. 39).

Just before his appointment as Secretary of Education by President Ronald Reagan, William Bennett, then chair of the National Endowment for the Humanities, issued a report under the egis of that organization entitled, *To Reclaim a Legacy* (1984), which echoed a common theme encountered in most such studies: "If the teacher is the guide, the curriculum is the path. A good curriculum marks the points of significance so that the student does not wander aimlessly over the terrain, dependent solely on chance to discover the landmarks of human achievement" (p. 6).

In 1985–1986, former U.S. Secretary of Education Terrel Bell, under whose tutelage *A Nation at Risk* (National Commission on Excellence in Education, 1983) was completed, chaired the National Commission on the Role and Future of State Colleges and Universities, the report of which was entitled *To Secure the Blessings of Liberty* (1986). To the 372 institutions belonging to the American Association of State Colleges and Universities, the report stated, "Nothing short of a creative state-by-state effort to strengthen education at all levels, comparable to the Marshall Plan in scope, cost, and dedication, can ensure the preservation of our democratic legacy for the twenty-first century" (p. 4.).

Two of the questions discussed in regional seminars involved in preparing the report were "Are there certain general learnings that a college-educated person must have?" and "What should be the proper role of general education in the curriculum of state colleges and universities?" The report never answers those two questions. It does, however, make the observation, "Perhaps no concern about higher education has attracted more attention than the quality of undergraduate education. Most frequently the concern is expressed in terms of deficiencies exhibited by many college graduates in their communication skills, their ability to solve quantitative problems, their knowledge about the world around them, and their competence as critical thinkers" (p. 34). The report charged institutions with allowing quality to slip and suggested a partial solution: "in many states, faculty members, administrators, and trustees at public colleges and universities have permitted their responsibilities for establishing admissions policies and academic standards to erode to the point where such policies are now being shaped in the political arena" (p. 34). "The Commission recommends that state college and university faculties . . . develop coherent plans for determining when, where, and to what extent each student should demonstrate progress toward an agreed-upon set of bachelor's degree-level skills; and paralleling such measures, design instructional strategies to correct deficiencies and to assist students to achieve at higher levels" (p. 16).

The main issue dealt with in that report was the tension between access and rigor, reflected in the observations "Without quality in education, the nation loses its strength" and "Without equity in education, democracy ceases to function" (p. 9). On balance, the report tilted toward the access side of the equation, insisting that "All individuals in our society who aspire to earn a bachelor's degree must have the opportunity to attempt to fulfill that aspiration" (pp. 14, 43).

The report by a seventeen-member commission appointed by the fifteen-state Southern Regional Education Board (1985) tilted the other way: "Access should be a highly significant social and economic force, but it will not be unless it is access to quality education" (p. 2). "As the public perceives a widening gap between the relatively few colleges with high standards and those with lower ones, students who attend the latter institutions, in effect, do not experience genuine equality of opportunity" (p. 5). The disagreement was only one of emphasis, however, since both reports insisted that ways to harmonize access and quality must and can be found.

John Ashcroft, the governor of Missouri and a former member of the business faculty at Southwest Missouri State University, chaired a task force for the National Governors' Association and wrote a chapter for the association's 1986 report, *Time for Results: The Governors' 1991 Report on Education.* The report urges governors and legislatures to use financial incentives as a lever for getting institutions to assess student progress and report results publicly. Presumably, the National Governors' Association intends to monitor results from the member states in 1991. (The specific recommendations of the report are summarized in Chapter One.)

The Association of American Colleges released its critique of the undergraduate experience in a report entitled, *Integrity in the College Curriculum: A Report to the Academic Community* (1985). The report appeals to college presidents and academic deans to join with faculty members to "lead us away from the declining and devalued bachelor's degree that now prevails to a new era of curricular coherence, intellectual rigor, and humanistic strength" (p. 7.) The panel's ideal minimum required curriculum would reflect nine "experiences" essential to a "coherent undergraduate education" (p. 15). This particular formulation has received more attention than any of the other recommendations coming from the various commissions. In addition to individual institutions that have used it as a framework for reviewing curricula, the report of the Southern Regional Education Board (1985) recommended these nine categories of purposes to its member states and institutions: (1) inquiry, abstract logical thinking, critical analysis; (2) literacy: writing, reading, speaking, listening; (3) understanding numerical data; (4) historical consciousness; (5) science; (6) values; (7) art; (8) international and multicultural experiences; and (9) study in depth (pp. 15–24). The commission of this board eschewed "simply strengthening distribution requirements or adding multidisciplinary general education courses," believing that would "substitute coverage for teaching and learning" (pp. 24–25). They assigned particular blame for the current morass to recalcitrant faculty curriculum committees that too frequently acquiesce to the ambitions of every faculty special interest (p. 10). Other associations also issue reports stressing stronger liberal arts background in rather traditional ways.

Notable works by single authors who echoed the same concerns include Alexander Astin's *Achieving Educational Excellence: A Critical Assessment of Priorities and Practices in Higher Education* (1985) (discussed in Chapter Two); Derek Bok's *Higher Learning* (1986); and Ernest Boyer's *College: The Undergraduate Experience in America* (1987).

As the 1980s drew to a close, the National Endowment for the Humanities issued another report, this time authored by Chair Lynne Cheney, *50 Hours: A Core Curriculum for College Students* (1989).

As the title of Cheney's report suggests, the recommended antidote for such shortcomings is a fifty-hour general education core consisting of eighteen hours of "Cultures and Civilizations," twelve hours of foreign language built on two years of study of the same language in high school, six hours of mathematics, eight hours of the natural sciences, and six hours of "The Social Sciences and the Modern World" (p. 17).

The overall picture of undergraduate education at the end of the 1980s can be summarized quickly. General education still seemed to be in disarray in spite of the fact that 95 percent of all institutions had appointed committees to respond to calls for reform. Little substantive disagreement exists among administrators, faculty, and national reports about the changes that need to be made, but little actual movement has taken place. The reason appears to be more political than philosophical. For over two decades, departments have shoehorned courses into distributional systems of general education in order to (1) ensure credit-hour production that will justify faculty positions in the department, (2) expand the requirements for the major (that is, require all students in their department to satisfy that part of the general education requirement by taking their course), and/or (3) to expose more freshmen to the subject matter so that more can be recruited into their specific major. To date, most curricular committees and faculty senates have not given up the perceived benefits of the current general education systems.

Part Two

*An Agenda for
Strengthening
Academic Quality*

FOUR

Reforming
the Curriculum

Trying to define curricular quality is a bit like trying to define pornography: As conventional wisdom has it, it may be hard to define, but we recognize it when we see it. The underlying premise of regional accreditation site visits and program review is that experienced academics can, by examining catalogues and resources, visiting classes, and talking with students and faculty, judge whether a program is of high or low quality. A norm of academic quality is also implied by standardized tests, by research regarding the impact of the college experience, and by rhetoric used to discuss curricular decline in the various commission reports cited in Chapter Three. Clearly, a broadly accepted understanding does exist concerning the general characteristics of quality undergraduate education, even though that understanding has not been clearly defined.

Historically Accepted Standards of Curricular Quality

The report of the Study Group on the Conditions of Excellence in American Higher Education (1984) judged that excellence in undergraduate education required the following:

73

1. That institutions of higher education produce *demonstrable improvements* in student knowledge, capacities, skills, and attitudes between entrance and graduation
2. That these demonstrable improvements occur within *established, clearly expressed, and publicly announced and maintained standards of performance* for awarding degrees based on societal and institutional definitions of college academic learning and
3. That these improvements are achieved *efficiently,* that is, that they are cost-effective in the use of student and institutional resources of time, effort and money [pp. 15–16].

Admittedly, demonstrable improvements, established standards, and efficiency seem extremely elusive and difficult to define; nevertheless, they still remain ideals toward which all institutions can strive. In one sense, these terms are defined by examples within the core activities of collegiate institutions (which go back to the Middle Ages).

First, one generally accepted principle is that the curriculum should consist of a logical and consistent pattern of courses that have a cumulative impact on students' intellectual development. Of course, different patterns may be used, but each should reflect logic and consistency. According to this standard, a curriculum consisting of year-long sequences in English, history, philosophy, mathematics, biology, chemistry, physics, and political science would be considered an appropriate pattern of courses, whereas a curriculum consisting of short-courses of one term or semester that provide a sampling of thirty or forty different subjects in four years would be judged deficient.

This standard does not suggest that there is one ideal pattern of courses or administrative or logistical arrangements. Indeed, no persuasive evidence has emerged that a prescribed curriculum, a distributed curriculum, a free-elective curriculum, a curriculum consisting of disciplinary courses, or a curriculum consisting of interdisciplinary courses is either distinctly better or worse than the other options. Of course, any of these systems are subject to abuses that would make the configuration ineffective. The impact of undergraduate education seems more related to an aggregate of personal, emotional, and intellectual experiences than to the presence or absence of specific courses or some specific organization of courses. Having said this, we can safely observe that faculties of institutions or subordinate schools, colleges, divisions, or departments probably should consider major changes periodically, although even a significant change may not be demonstrably more effective than that which it has replaced. The discussion of change, however, enables faculty members to think and talk about the purposes of undergraduate education. Such conversation contributes to a valuable sense of community, stimulates reflection on individual educational beliefs and practices, and may contribute to the desired logical coherence.

Second, any selected logical and consistent pattern of courses should expose students over time to several intellectual traditions. An undergraduate program that ensures that students have some in-depth exposure to the humanities, social sciences, natural sciences, and modes of communication therefore would be viewed as appropriate, whereas a curriculum that permits students to study only one domain would fail to meet this criterion.

Third, an undergraduate program should expose students over time to many different ways of knowing—from revelation to the driest sort of empiricism. Accordingly, a curricular program that exposed students to visual arts, music, theater, history, political science, economics, chemistry, biology, physics, and mathematics would provide a needed balance, whereas a program that totally concentrated on interpersonal human relationships would be deficient.

Fourth, an effective undergraduate curriculum should have a reasonably high degree of verbal, numerical, and conceptual sophistication. The undergraduate program that primarily develops even a high degree of technical competence (for example, the technical skills of nursing) would be open to serious criticism under this criterion. Most existing nursing curricula, however, go considerably beyond developing technical competence.

Fifth, the undergraduate curriculum should be designed to develop an intellectual base on which more mature study can be undertaken. The clearest example of this criterion would be the requirement of a logical, coherent, and consistent major that develops the sophisticated insights needed to both apply the knowledge of the subject and build on it.

Quality also involves how people are grouped and how they interact. In 1936, Rashdal observed that the essence of the medieval university was that it made possible a life of study, whether for a few years or during an entire career. The university accomplished its goals by bringing, "during that period, face-to-face in living intercourse, teacher and teacher, teacher and student, student and student. It would be a fatal error to imagine that either the multiplication of books or the increased facilities of communication could ever remove the need of institutions which permit such personal intercourse. The university, therefore, must have a local habitation; if it embraces colleges in different places, there are virtually two or more universities in that one. Increased facilities of communication can never unite by the true university bond the inhabitants of distant towns; indeed it may be questioned whether the highest university ideal can be realized with the fullest perfection, even in a single modern city, the largest type, especially where it does not possess a distinct university quarter" (p. 463).

Although many students enrolled as undergraduates in colleges and universities today are commuters, a residential situation (or a simulation of a residential situation) would seem to be helpful for improving educational quality. Education is a social and gregarious activity, in which many of the important outcomes are generated by sustained and reasonably intimate interaction between student and student and between student and faculty. This interaction is most likely to transpire in a residential situation and is least likely to happen when students remain on campus only long enough for their formal classes. Astin (1977, p. 249), using his own and other data, suggests that "In almost every respect, residents benefit more than commuters from their undergraduate experience. Residents not only show greater changes in personality and attitudes but also become more involved in campus life. Most important is the increased chance of persistence, which in turn maximizes the chance of implementing career plans. Residents are much more satisfied with their undergraduate experience than are commuters."

A different sort of qualitative consideration is the manner in which educational programs are created. Courses and programs that stress quality should conform to several rigorously imposed criteria. Is the field or subject intellectually alive and growing? Does the field or subject attract people to specialize in it? Does the subject attract capable students and can students be placed in relevant positions after graduation? Does the field attract financial resources so that it may continue to flourish? Programs should be produced through the interaction of an institution's history and tradition, the informed beliefs of faculty, student interest, and society's need and demand for graduates. Allow any one of these factors to dominate, and educational distortion results.

A campus culture of quality is also essential if excellence in the classroom is to be realized. Recently, a faculty member in a regional state university characterized his institution as an educational factory. Such an attitude reflects acceptance of what Gardner (1961) called "amiable mediocrity." That is not the attitude encountered in those places judged as maintaining quality over time. Quality requires a highly trained faculty possessing deep, relevant insights into the subjects they teach. It also requires highly motivated and adequately prepared students to cope with the sophisticated words, numbers, and concepts used to penetrate the essences of those subjects. It requires adequate and stable finances to support the extended time needed by faculty and students to generate an excellent educational experience (it requires not great wealth, but sufficient resources and the prospect for continuing resources to ensure a stable environment). The final necessary components are shared pride in the concept of quality and an unabashed quest for ever-increasing levels of quality.

Some Preliminary Considerations

While it would not be appropriate to prescribe specific courses or patterns of courses as a way to ensure quality, improving the curriculum does necessitate coming to grips with some important specific issues.

The first issue relates to the central purposes of higher education and how those get translated into programs and activities. A critical perspective for those concerned with improving the quality of undergraduate education should be parsimony — a realistic view of what higher education is and what professors and higher educational institutions can really do. The major shortcoming of the nontraditional doctrine of the 1970s was the limitless goals set for colleges and universities based on a criterion of satisfying any human need or demand. That doctrine led institutions to offer courses and programs even if they did not have the needed personnel and resources to implement the programs effectively. The more realistic view being urged here was well expressed by Barzun (1981, p. 35), who commented on the errors of overly expanding collegiate-based activities. He pointed out that colleges and universities in the past could have taken a more intellectually healthy route.

> [They should adopt] simpler ways, intellectually sounder or more in keeping with [available resources]. Simplicity would have meant not just giving up grants and foundation playthings such as institutes and centers for immediate social action, but also many ornamental activities, including public sports. Some of us who urged the move at the time were ridiculed as "scholastic and monastic." But we accept the phrase as tersely descriptive of a still desirable correction. "Monastic" here has of course nothing to do with religion or asceticism or the model of coeducation and cohabitation now a part of campus life. It betokens merely the mind concentrated on study in a setting without frills. To rediscover its true purpose is always in order for an institution or any other being, and doing so entails scraping away all pointless accretions and is always a painful act; but it is least painful after a catastrophe such as happened during the late sixties.

The fact that Barzun caused apoplexy among so many by suggesting that public sports should be a candidate for elimination suggests that some, at least, have added entertainment to instruction, research, and public service as the central focuses for higher education. Our doctrine of parsimony would lead to a radical redefinition of competitive athletics and their appropriate place in the educational scheme. The current problems of collegiate priorities are obvious and widespread.

A more realistic approach would lead institutions concerned with improving quality to reduce the number of programs offered and the number of courses that support those programs to an absolute minimum. The courses listed in catalogues to support degree programs may range within a single institution from only required courses to a much wider selection. Of course, if only 100 percent of requirements is offered, then a student pursuing that program must take every course taught in that field. Although such a program is lean, it may be preferable to the other extreme — an ill-defined smorgasbord of choices. Since adding courses to a curriculum increases neither the number of hours a student must complete to graduate nor (in all probability) the number of hours required in a particular field, the net effect of such profligacy is to dilute the focus of the program and to force faculty to teach on the periphery of their training. In *Quality Education for Less Money* (1974, p. 25), Meeth joins several other writers and economists in suggesting that private colleges will not compromise quality by reducing offerings in each discipline to as little as 130 percent of the requirements for a degree; others have set the target at 150 percent. Whatever percent is seen as appropriate, institutions should enforce limits to prevent resources from being squandered in one area that could more properly be used to shore up other deficiencies.

A more realistic perspective would also accept that there are a number of quite desirable human traits and attributes that either are not the responsibility of colleges and universities or are likely to be so highly developed by the time individuals reach college that collegiate experiences will probably not modify them dramatically. The latter category includes such traits as honesty, a sense of justice, fundamental ethical principles, and even individual attitudes toward the dignity of human beings. Such underlying values are of course susceptible to modification if sufficiently precise and intensive interventions are used. Certain techniques can, for example, modify such a deeply embedded personality trait as authoritarianism. However, the needed therapeutic intervention requires considerable clinical competence — a competence not likely to be possessed by most college professors.

Concern is periodically expressed that collegiate institutions should assume responsibility for values. However, the interest wanes when the complexity of the needed technology is realized. The complexity of serious efforts to modify fundamental values is illustrated by Richard Morrill in *Teaching Values in College* (1980), a quick reading of which should reveal that expecting college professors to make such an effort would distract them from doing what they are actually prepared to do. Certainly faculty and administrators should model ethical behavior and clear values; also, a certain amount of exhortation in courses and through symposia and the like is appropriate. However, wholesale expenditures of time and resources to modify the basic attitudes of college-age young people would probably not be efficacious. Similarly, colleges and universities probably can do very little for substantial numbers of students with respect to marital adjustment, personal cleanliness, personal habits, personal adjustment, political affiliation, style of parenting, and (except in certain religious institutions) religious belief and affiliation.

A second issue derives from the cycles of criticism targeted at traditional educational methodologies. Here a salutary perspective would be cautiousness with regard to pronouncements insisting that historically accepted concepts and methods of education are bad or irrelevant. Actually, the principal reason that significant, pervasive reforms have not taken place in established four-year institutions may be that traditional styles and techniques have validity based on the collective judgments and perceptions of experienced academics. The traditions most frequently criticized with respect to undergraduate education are the four-year degree program that measures academic credit by hours spent in class, formal courses meeting regularly each week, lecturing, and letter grades for academic subjects; organized courses intended for those who are eighteen to twenty-two years old; and admission to college predicated on demonstrated academic performance and measured academic aptitude or potential. In the aggregate, these elements are viewed as academic lock-step to be avoided at all costs. Yet the same elements can be judged positively as providing needed structure, intensity of experience, routine, and dividing of complicated intellectual tasks into manageable units. The Monday, Wednesday, Friday class meeting one hour each day, for each of which two hours of preparation is assumed, functions reasonably well for many academic disciplines; whereas a much more intense experience such as a seven-week single course plan or a much more casual plan of classes meeting only occasionally tends to leave students intellectually and emotionally exhausted or frustrated because of lack of graduated evidence or progress.

Although all educational practice should be periodically assessed, that assessment should not start from the premise that the practices are probably deficient; rather, the opposite premise might well be assumed. Thus, disciplinary courses have persisted, while interdisciplinary courses have difficulty surviving because both faculty and students feel more secure in the comfort of disciplinary structure. Courses stress transmission and elaboration of information because that is what professors can do best, and it is what students fundamentally wish and expect. Many faculty and students do not relate intensively to each other on a personal level, in part because they represent two distinct and different generations. The three hours of formal class, coupled with the occasional conference between a faculty member and an individual seeking specific help could very well be the optimum personal contact between a faculty member and student. Faculty members, obviously, should be encouraged to respond to real student needs, but they should not be expected ordinarily to involve themselves in the intimate details of their students' lives. It is intriguing that many of the reformers would probably not wish deep personal involvement between themselves and

the professionals who serve them — physicians, lawyers, clergy-
men, and tax accountants — and yet they urge professors to
become deeply involved in their students' total lives.

A calmer educational rhetoric is especially needed, as well
as a more rational marshaling and presentation of evidence or
indication of the lack of relevant evidence. It is not verifiable
that formal, organized, and credentialed education stifles human
growth and creativity, and that those traits may be most successfully cultivated and cherished in the romantic setting of complete freedom. Certainly structure can become oppressive and
routine can be deadening, but those facts do not invalidate all
structure and routine. No productive research group could expect to uncover brilliant insights without careful preparation and
the meticulous attention that routinely must be paid to detail.

A third issue has to do with the definition and integrity
of the baccalaureate degree. What is needed is a clearer notion
regarding what should constitute a bachelor's degree in arts and
sciences. As a result of many forces and developments, the
bachelor's degree has become readily obtainable through virtually any conceivable aggregate of courses and experiences.
Doubtless this laissez-faire attitude toward the meaning of an
academic degree evolved over 300 years with such landmark
decisions as requiring Latin alone in place of the previously required Greek, Latin, and Hebrew; elimination of curricular
prescription; allowing modern languages to be substituted for
classical languages; the gradual elimination of foreign language,
mathematics, and English requirements; and finally simply accepting whatever an individual student had done or wanted to
do. The contemporary situation should be reversed, with institutions and other concerned agencies insisting on at least some
structure to a program leading to an academic degree.

One possible structure on which to base a definition of
the bachelor's degree would be division of the required curriculum into four approximately equal parts: (1) a major or concentration in either an academic discipline or in a collegiate level
vocational and professional course; (2) contextual or cognate
courses related to the major but to be taken from other disciplines; (3) basic courses providing college skills and insights judged

essential for anyone receiving an academic degree; and (4) liberalizing or broadening subjects that students would choose in order to broaden their intellectual outlook. All four components should be present in any baccalaureate degree. Academic quality would be expressed to the extent that courses in any of these four segments meet the criteria that have historically defined the nature of collegiate level work — yet some of the rigidities of the past would be eliminated. By requiring four different sorts of course experience, this structure would prevent technical, vocational, or professional curricula from being overly specialized or technical to the exclusion of other important educational values. The structure is also a way of responding to every student's need for exposure to the liberal arts and basic sciences.

The problem with current formulations is not that colleges offer vocational preparation; they have always done that — from the preparation of bureaucrats for the medieval church and government to the preparation of social workers today. Rather, the problem has been that the lack of effective controls has allowed technical and vocational programs to crowd out concerns for general education and, at the same time and partly as a consequence, to self-destruct with respect to academic and intellectual integrity.

What is needed is a sharper distinction between undergraduate courses that lead to an academic degree and other kinds of services that an institution might be able to provide. Much confusion concerning the curriculum (especially in the public, two-year community college) stems from an effort to assign academic credit for courses ranging from remedial writing courses, through highly applied courses in the building trades, and on to academic courses clearly parallel to those offered in four-year institutions. This suggestion may seem to run counter to the American tradition of including many programs within the boundaries of higher education. Existing tradition has provided great flexibility by allowing students to start a program in agriculture, then shift to a program in chemistry, and possibly actually to receive a bachelor's degree in education, without losing an exorbitant amount of academic credit. Further, the argument is constantly advanced that the historic glory of higher education in America has been that, over time, it has embraced many new specialties, such as agriculture, home economics, engineering, business, education, social work, journalism, pharmacy, nursing, police science, and theater. If these specialties are appropriate, so the argument goes, why not add other courses and specialties as social needs arise (for example, real estate, fashion modeling, circus performance, jewelry making, and life insurance selling)? One answer could be that these concentrations might be appropriate, but that courses in them ought to be worthy of academic credit. However, another response could be that there should be some meaningful distinction between what is collegiate level work that will lead to an academic degree and what are other sorts of education, training, and behavior modification. The ability to make this distinction for operational purposes will obviously rest on informed judgment, just as awarding a doctoral degree, in the final analysis, is based on the judgment of others who hold doctorates. The collective faculty wisdom should express judgments and make decisions regarding courses, programs, and activities; however, to protect this judgment from the charge of capriciousness, it should rest on some defensible criteria.

Consider a program in carpentry, offered by a community college in cooperation with the Carpenters Union, which is intended to provide workers for an expanding home-building industry. In some respects, it might be argued that carpentry does conform to the above-mentioned emphasis on words, numbers, and abstract concepts. Successful carpentry certainly requires some mathematical awareness: at least some arithmetic ability and some geometry. There is a necessary technical language with which to discuss problems and solutions. Further, successful carpentry also requires an ability to conceptualize a finished project and to understand how details contribute to the realization of that concept. In addition, carpentry requires definite manual dexterity and the ability to make distinctions with respect to woods, tools, and other needed materials. Moreover, there are levels of skill proceeding in a hierarchical order from the simple and rudimentary to the complex and sophisticated. In addition, there are ethical elements, such as care for the quality of a finished product. Yet a program in carpentry alone would not be considered appropriate as an academic program worthy of an academic degree. The reason is a matter of relativity. An academic course or program involves relatively complex theory, relatively sophisticated and complex language, a theoretical base that is expanding and changing, and an understanding that requires multiple and complex relationships with other domains of knowledge. Compared with carpentry courses, academic courses place more emphasis on developing broad understanding and less emphasis on honing highly specific skills. It is conceivable that a program in carpentry could be organized and taught so that it would conform to the most rigorous canons of academic quality. However, such a program would far transcend the purposes of a carpentry program set up to develop skilled workers.

A fourth issue relates to the often unrecognized difficulty associated with achieving some quite proper academic goals. The appropriate attitude should be an unwillingness to offer programs that are doomed to mediocrity because of lack of resources. Fluency in one or more foreign languages is one of these desirable goals for every educated individual that, unfortunately, is very likely unachievable and therefore should not be considered in most institutional planning or efforts. Three arguments can be made for retaining the objective of foreign-language fluency: (1) most U.S. students are much less proficient with foreign languages than is desirable; (2) facility in the use of foreign languages quickly makes available to individuals rich new cultural resources, and (3) facility with foreign languages, which serves to open up new cultures, might produce some greater degree of tolerance for civilizations other than those of North America. However, foreign-language fluency can never be achieved for any but a tiny proportion of the population for at least two reasons. First, the sheer size and self-containment of the United States is such that most of its citizens lack the motivation to become proficient in a foreign tongue. Second, probably in response to that lack of imperative, foreign-language requirements in secondary schools and colleges have been far less stringent than would be essential to develop true linguistic facility. Thus, during the 1930s and 1940s, a time of much more stringent language requirements than the 1980s, the usual requirement was two years of a language in high school and two years of a language (usually a different language) in college. But two years of exposure to two separate languages did not develop sufficient linguistic insight to ensure retention or even expansion of facility in reading, speaking, or writing. Since that time, requirements have been steadily reduced so that secondary school requirements were virtually eliminated, and collegiate requirements decreased first from two years to one and then were eliminated. During the 1980s, a few institutions attempted to reestablish a requirement but still only at a level likely to produce superficial knowledge. If an institution sets genuine foreign-language facility as a goal for its students, then the requirement should be a minimum of two years of a language in secondary school followed by at least two years of collegiate courses in the same language, or, in lieu of such preparation, two years of college instruction plus a year spent in the country where the language is actually spoken. This assumes that the target language is in the same language family as English; if not, two years of high school and four years of college-level study would be required. Departure from that level of intensity in any significant way would seriously erode the quality of the resulting linguistic proficiency. (See Cheney, 1989, pp. 29–31, for a discussion of this issue.)

A perplexing issue also requiring patience and commitment involves the importance of intellectual dexterity with numbers and other abstract symbols. In a society dominated by science and technology and likely to be highly dependent in the future on computers, the need for mathematical ability is obvious. The issues to be resolved, then, are which skills are most needed for everyone and how they can be developed. It has been urged that all students should have four years of mathematics in secondary school followed by more mathematics in college. Unfortunately, such a recommendation runs counter to the rather deep-seated fears and feelings of antagonism regarding mathematics that exist in the larger society. Also, the shortage of qualified people willing to teach mathematics at the secondary level presents a real problem in implementation. In view of these obstacles, what is desirable and probably achievable is for institutions gradually to increase mathematics requirements and, at the same time, to work with secondary education so that the mathematical sophistication of high school graduates will increase gradually. At the same time, colleges should stop giving academic credit for courses that are clearly high school level or simply reviews of elementary school arithmetic.

Also, some educational leaders may argue that a deep understanding of the nature of science is imperative for all educated individuals, not only because of the value of science for its own sake, but because science plays such a significant role in the order of life. This ideal is reflected in collegiate curricular discussion in which scientists criticize courses about science, or even courses in the history of science, on the ground that only direct exposure to physics, chemistry, or biology can produce the level of understanding and sophistication desired. Ideally, having all students take real science courses in the major scientific fields might be a desirable goal. However, to achieve such a goal would probably require considerably more high school science than students are currently receiving. Given the role and condition of American secondary education today, the same sort of gradualism suggested for mathematics also may be needed with respect to science.

In the ideal future, one might hope that equal stress could be placed on language facility, quantitative facility, scientific literacy, and facility with the use of abstract concepts, but as of 1989 verbal skills remain the most important for all people. Individuals can survive and function at some minimal level in American society without any more mathematical ability than it takes to balance a checkbook and prepare an income tax form. However, they simply cannot function effectively without language skills. By all reckoning, the greatest challenge facing higher education today is to develop among students facility in the use of the English language.

In many respects, the essence of undergraduate education is literary, that is, learning through the use of various kinds of literature to cope with various complexities in life. This is a trait that legitimately can be sought in almost all college-level courses and lies clearly within the competency of the faculty. From facility with the English language come the most essential skills and competencies. These include the abilities to read or hear instructions, to give instructions, to transmit complicated information clearly, to obtain information on which various sorts of evaluation can be made, and to organize and reorganize information in search of alternative beliefs about reality. Further, it is through language that the various acts of citizenship are learned and practiced. Gathering information about social issues, analyzing social events, discussing political matters, and preparing to vote on the basis of knowledge all require literary skills, which can be developed best through an intensive program of reading, writing, and speaking over several years.

It may sound extreme, but a strong case can be made for the idea that for all college students of whatever age or whatever background, most of the essential value of collegiate education can be obtained from well-prepared, informationally enriched courses in literature, writing, speaking, and history plus a few other courses dealing with substantive matters. Of course, many theoretical arguments can be raised against this stark outline. Those who contend that there are hemispheric differences in the brains of various individuals may contend that a literary slant favors one cerebral organization or cognitive style over another. Others may argue that because of life experiences and educational backgrounds, some people cannot cope with so much language. The only response is that the argument advanced here is with respect to the essentials needed by all people, regardless of what their background, lifestyle, vocation, or calling might be. Clearly, people will differ with respect to verbal facility, but all require some degree of verbal sophistication to cope with U.S. life in the twenty-first century.

Language ability is also the route to several other legitimate outcomes of undergraduate education. One of these is the acquisition of a growing store of knowledge about a variety of complicated subjects. After promoting language facility, probably the most important thing colleges and universities do is to transmit to students considerable knowledge, along with an understanding of that knowledge and an ability to apply that knowledge in new situations. The more knowledge that colleges supply to students, the more knowledge they will be able to recall and use (granting that there will be a certain amount of forgetting). Some contend that a collegiate institution should not be concerned with a student's acquisition of knowledge, but rather, with the student's skills necessary to acquire knowledge when needed. However, the highest level of acquisition of knowledge is research and scholarship, the first step toward which is the individual's learning as much as possible of the relevant subject matter. It is, after all, from the deep awareness of knowledge that questions for proper inquiry emerge. Whitehead (1951, p. 45), commenting upon secondary education, pointed out that "there is such a thing as pushing on, of getting to know the fundamental details and the main exact generalizations, and of acquiring an easy mastery of technique. There is no getting away from the fact that things have been found out, and that to be effective in the modern world you must have a store of definite acquirement of the best practice. To write poetry you must know metre; and to build bridges you must be learned in the strength of materials. Even the Hebrew prophets had learned to write, probably in those days requiring no mean effort. The tutored arts of genius is — in the words of the prayer book — a vain thing fondly invented."

At least three other desirable attributes are important and achievable objectives of collegiate education; (1) a reasonable understanding of, and an ability to cope with, the complex bureaucracies through which contemporary society is organized; (2) a reasonable sense of the main elements of American society and the ways in which it differs from other societies; and (3) a modicum of skill with a computer, which is easily developed by simply making the resources accessible.

Some Worthwhile Strategies

Even though each has its own unique emphasis, a remarkable consistency can be observed among the various reports urging a return to quality in undergraduate education. Depending on how discriminating one wishes to be, some 200 separate recommendations for improving the undergraduate experience can be extracted from these documents. Not surprisingly, some are broad and general while others are very specific; a few are mutually exclusive. Many of the recommendations reflect historical precedence or research, and others are more on the order of folklore. Few of the radical reforms of the 1970s appear on the lists, and few of the suggestions could be called revolutionary or untried, at least in some setting at some time in this century. It is our impression that the discontinued reforms were abandoned for social or political reasons, not because faculties concluded that they did not work. In other words, there would probably be little debate over the absolute efficaciousness of most of the suggestions. Some recommendations relate to faculty development, campus life, institutional or governmental policies, interinstitutional cooperation, and other topics taken up elsewhere in this book. At this point, six recommendations which would have a definite impact on the curriculum will be discussed. Five of the six are advocated in recent reform literature; all appear to be reasonably consistent with the principles advocated in this book and well within the potential of current college and university faculties. By no means is this an attempt to be exhaustive; rather, it is an effort to introduce a reasonable sampling of specific approaches we think merit consideration.

The Study Group on the Conditions of Excellence in American Higher Education (1984, pp. 20, 39) stressed the need to set high expectations as a way of improving quality. They urged institutions to be "less grandiose in their statements of goals and far more specific about their objectives" by defining "the knowledge, capacities, and skills we expect students to attain." People do generally respond to their environment. If the environment is laissez-faire, they respond casually and without commitment; on the other hand, if it is an environment in which expectations are clearly high, most people work harder, and, incidentally, gain greater personal satisfaction. Some evidence suggests that students feel college is less demanding than they expected or think it should be. Several reports have urged that assessment approaches be developed so that student progress can be regularly measured and certified, and the Southern Regional Education Board (1985, p. 3) suggested a method that could raise expectations, ensure satisfactory student progress, and result in a more productive upper-division learning environment. "Students should be expected to qualify for study at the next educational level, with qualification depending upon satisfaction of clearly stated performance criteria at major entry and exit points, such as high school graduation, college entry, promotion to upper-level undergraduate study, and college graduation."

A properly conceived advanced-standing requirement whereby students must be formally admitted to junior status could represent a clear symbol of high expectations. Such a requirement should probably include multiple measures of performance as measured by nationally normed tests, as well as locally developed examinations, writing samples, portfolios, and interviews; the final judgment should be rendered by faculty. In addition to verifying writing proficiency, these measures could assess mathematical ability and critical-thinking skills, along with less quantifiable traits necessary for pursuing certain fields of study (for example, the demonstrated empathy needed by psychology and counseling majors). Two of the benefits of a program would be a positive kind of anxiety on the part of freshmen as they looked forward to the hurdle and a more homogeneous upper-division environment that would facilitate teaching to higher-order thinking skills such as analysis, synthesis, and evaluation. It also avoids the practical problem with senior examinations, which are part of some graduation requirements. Few institutions are willing to deny graduation after four years of promotion and presumed satisfactory performance in courses. Additionally, such a qualifying test for junior status provides a middle ground for those institutions that are forced to accept all or nearly all applicants and yet wish to maintain appropriate standards for the baccalaureate degree. States that require institutions to accept transfer credits would probably allow the same standards to be applied to transfer students who are entering a new college in their junior year.

The most obvious danger of such testing is that the procedure would lower rather than raise expectations. This could happen if the institution lacks the courage to fail anyone or if the test is so easy that it is of little challenge. In the latter case, bright high school students could pass the test and demand junior standing. Logistics are another concern. Considerable faculty time would be required although probably not as much as it would appear on the surface. In a typical institution, the sophomore and transfer students who went through the process would fall into three broad categories: the hopeless ones who should be told to pursue some other avenue of career preparation; the obvious successes who should be patted on the back and told to keep up the good work; and those who are marginal and need remediation and some sort of probationary status. Problems concerning teaching to the test and the distortion of the goals of lower-division instruction will probably not be significant, particularly if local faculty participate in constructing evaluative procedures.

Efforts to increase the amount of writing required of students is a second strategy that should clearly be central to any effort to improve undergraduate education. The report of the Association of American Colleges (*Integrity in the College Curriculum . . . ,* 1985, p. 25) reflected a common conclusion: "Writing across the curriculum is a common sense concept that expresses what an undergraduate education should offer in the realm of training for literacy: many opportunities to write in all courses, serious attention to written work by instructors in all courses, a variety of writing experiences — short papers, long papers, quick papers, unhurried papers, reports, critiques, narratives." Surveys suggest that in many institutions students do very little substantive writing after they finish a basic writing course. Training and encouraging faculty to incorporate frequent written assignments into their teaching will require attention to the nature and length of such assignments, the ways to provide appropriate feedback, and techniques for grading papers.

The ready availability of computers may serve to improve students' writing skills. For most students, word processing takes the drudgery out of editing (of course, dogged editing of one's own efforts is essential to developing a clear writing style). Word processing also allows students to focus on a particular problem (for example, transitions, paragraphing, or punctuation) without retyping the entire document.

Northwest Missouri State University installed a network of computer workstations in each residence hall room and each faculty office in the summer of 1987. Two years of experience with the system reveals that, in addition to increased use of the library's electronic card catalogue by all students, 95 percent use word processing and 82 percent use electronic mail. Also, anecdotal evidence suggests that faculty members are giving more writing assignments and requiring more editing of unsatisfactory prose. With or without computers, all faculty must be urged to accept responsibility for helping to ameliorate the pervasive lack of writing skills among today's undergraduates.

Another closely related suggestion is to require each senior to complete and orally present and defend a thesis before a group of peers and faculty. The project would focus on some aspect of their major from a historical, social, ethical, economic, or political perspective. Such an exercise would test the cumulative impact of the student's undergraduate experience on their intellectual development and provide valuable feedback to faculty.

Quality might be improved also if freshmen were given a basic reading, listening, or seeing list of works with which they must be familiar before graduation. The list could be a general list for the institution, specific to major fields of study, or both. Whichever method is used, the list should probably be annotated and updated frequently. Also, seminars and discussion groups to review the listed works would be particularly beneficial.

These suggestions would combine to help create a culture of quality on campus. In far too many institutions, an anti-intellectual atmosphere denigrates or trivializes serious scholarship.

Two other changes bear consideration even though they are not central to campus culture: remedial instruction and time on task. As noted earlier, most institutions find it necessary to offer some remedial instruction, if only in the form of a basic writing or math refresher course, and acknowledge that the practice must continue until secondary schools do a better job of preparing students for college work. Most agree, however, that academic credit should not be awarded for such activity — certainly remedial courses should not be substitutes for core curricular requirements. The University of Missouri, Kansas City, has refined an approach to remediation that appears to be more efficient and effective than the traditional practice of offering separate courses on particular topics. Use of "supplemental instruction" provides remedial help for students in the context of specific courses. For example, in addition to the regular sessions of a chemistry course, supplemental sessions are held to review materials presented in class and to teach note-taking techniques, test-taking skills, and other remedial topics (such as how to organize and write lab reports or how to use the textbook as a learning tool). These sessions are usually taught by graduate assistants or senior level students whose performance was outstanding in that particular class. Supplemental instructors work closely with the professor teaching the class and also receive special instruction on how to conduct their sessions. Follow-up studies have shown that students participating in these sessions have a dropout rate 10 percent below those of equal academic ability who did not take advantage of the additional help. Also, the average grade of those participating in these sessions was one letter grade higher than what would have been predicted.

The quality of effort students invest in learning is obviously an important consideration. C. Robert Pace (1984) has studied this aspect of student behavior and has concluded, "Quality of effort is the best predictor of students' progress toward the attainment of important educational goals. Granted all the elements that account for the selective distribution of who goes where to college, once the students get there what counts most toward their attainment is not who they are or where they are but what they do. It is the quality of effort they put into capitalizing on the resources and opportunities for learning and development that exist in the college setting that makes the difference. . . . The more students put into their college experience the more they get out of it" (p. 96).

Pace, among others, has commented on the quality of effort students spend in college, but the quantity of time also merits some attention. As noted in Chapter Two, during the 1960s and 1970s, many institutions shortened their school year by as much as 15 percent. In many cases, gradually moving back to 170 days per academic year would add the equivalent of one semester to the undergraduate experience and still allow the fall term to end before Christmas. Although we certainly agree that the amount of time spent is not as important as the quality of time, the issue here is not quality of time, because we are assuming that all other variables remain constant. The suggestion is that students will learn more if faculty have more time to present necessary material and students devote more time to its assimilation, mastery, and critique. We realize that the suggestion of adding one or two weeks to each semester will not generate enthusiastic responses. To be successful, many courses would need to be revised, not simply lengthened. Those in leadership positions would need to exert their influence so that the final days of the newly lengthened term would not degenerate into the fun and games that have increasingly characterized the end of term in some schools in the K-12 sector. But we are persuaded that this proposal deserves close scrutiny. The increased costs might well be minimal, since faculty members typically have nine-month appointments but only teach about eight months. Lengthening the academic year would also allow the addition of strategically placed holidays to create one or two three-day weekends — increasingly rare in colleges and universities — where both students and faculty could rejuvenate themselves from the rigors of academic life. If the collegiate years are as critically important as conventional wisdom judges them to be, then they should be pursued on a timetable that enables these experiences to be assimilated and enjoyed.

In summary, adequate standards exist for assessing quality in undergraduate education. Also, some rather clear, straightforward, and tested methodologies have been advanced for reversing the slide that has taken place in recent decades.

FIVE

Streamlining Extracurricular Services

Virtually every study of the impact of college on students underscores the out-of-class collection of experiences as being the most potent educational force affecting student development. In light of this finding, some attention must be paid to the various out-of-class organizations and services that contribute to that powerful impact. These services, in organized form, have been called student-personnel activities, student services, or campus life services. Whatever the name and however organized, these activities typically include counseling, student activities, residence halls, discipline, special services, and student government; sometimes they also include admissions, health service, campus security, financial aid, placement, remedial clinics, and even intercollegiate athletics. Some critics of managed student services have faulted their inability to demonstrate a contribution to the educational experience. For this reason, the focus of this chapter will be on organized student services and activities.

History and Philosophy of Student Services

It is obvious that the out-of-class life of students can be divided into those events that just happen and those activities that are organized by the institution. Both kinds of activities can be enormously important to student development. As students interact with each other in the context of an educational environment, they develop a number of skills and beliefs essential for adult living as well as for academic survival. Skills of personal relationships, courtship, sexual behavior, and in some institutions cohabitational living are still developed, for the most part, not in classes and clinics, but through more informal means. Skills of study and academic survival, including academic gamesmanship, are probably learned more frequently from peers than from faculty and counselors. Voluntary organizations such as Greek letter societies are frequently responsible for shaping and forming both relatively "good" and relatively "bad" attitudes and values. A fraternity can produce considerable social competence or gross antisocial behavior.

Also, many of the skills needed to cope with the educational bureaucracy probably are developed most effectively through interaction with peers. Learning the procedure to obtain a loan and to select courses is done informally. Thus, we are persuaded that the environment and special circumstances of an institution have far more impact on students than the collection of services an institution chooses to offer. For example, single-sex colleges or military academies as institutional types affect their students more than any particular genre of student service.

Organized student activities began, as did so many other developments in higher education, at the end of the Civil War when higher education entered its century of explosive growth. Before the Civil War, when institutions were typically quite small, presidents and faculties assumed full responsibility for the total life of students in their custody, although students themselves took the lead in creating some activities (such as social clubs and athletic teams). As institutions began to grow and as faculties became professionalized with respect to their academic disciplines, other agencies were required to administer the proliferating range of collegiate activities taking place outside the classroom. Thus, there emerged deans of men and women, directors of admissions, residence hall advisers, and directors of intramural athletics. The expansion of such positions slowed considerably during the depression of the 1930s, when institutions could not support activities that generated little or no tuition or appropriation income. However, at the end of World War II, an enormous expansion occurred, which was later called the student-personnel movement. This expansion included (1) a generation of theorists searching for a rationale to accommodate a diversity of activities, (2) graduate training programs to produce appropriate practitioners, and (3) claims by student-personnel professionals of responsibility for virtually every activity on campus, except classroom work, financial affairs, and supervision of the physical plant.

The proliferation of activities stemmed directly from post–World War II needs and conditions. The need of veterans for counseling and advising led to counseling centers. Students needed housing as enrollments grew beyond the absorptive capacity of local communities. Increasingly heterogeneous student bodies produced a need for remedial services. The influx of foreign students also produced the need for appropriate support services. Additionally, expanding enrollment pressures generated a need for more systematic admissions techniques. An emergent philosophy expressed a point of view demanding growth. This point of view stresses the individual students and all elements of their lives and circumstances (Delworth, 1980).

The zenith of the student-personnel movement was reached during the 1950s when theorists claimed responsibility for an enormous range of activities. These included interpreting the institution to parents and students; selecting, admitting, and orienting students; administering and interpreting diagnostic services; administering career guidance and postgraduation placement services; providing mental and physical health assessment and remediation; and administering discipline. Additionally, the staffs of student services would coordinate record keeping, financial aid, and the assemblage and distribution of information to be used in improving instruction and the curriculum. Further, they would assume responsibility for maintaining student group morale and for supervising housing, food services, and extracurricular activities (including the student's social and

religious life). Finally, they would promote international understanding, the application of creative thinking to the solution of
social programs, and a fuller realization of democracy (Delworth,
1980, pp. 26–28).

No sooner had the zenith been reached, however, than
decline set in. New conditions, including student demands for
freedom and a lower legal age of adults (from twenty-one to eighteen), eliminated many of the disciplinary and supervisory functions adults had previously exercised over students' lives. Also,
the success of the professional-academic revolution ensured the
hegemony of academic affairs on campus and a corresponding
decrease in both resources and respect for nonacademic matters. "In the eyes of many student services professionals, the functions they perform are too often valued by trustees, administrators, and faculty as a somewhat distant second to the primary
functions of teaching, research, and service. They sometimes
feel that others perceive them engaging in a nebulous array of
vaguely supportive activities, or performing expensive babysit-
ting, which, at best, keeps potentially troublesome students
quietly occupied, and, at worst, provides the opportunities for
fomenting trouble through such outlets as inflammatory student
newspaper articles or invitations to highly controversial figures
to speak on campus" (Delworth, 1980, p. 47).

These views contrasted sharply with the rationalistic views
of Robert M. Hutchins, former president of the University of
Chicago. He saw no need for faculty members to waste time
on improving the conduct and the health of students. He believed,
"Undoubtedly, fine associations, fine buildings, green grass, good
food and exercise are excellent things for anybody. You will note
that they are exactly what is advertised by every resort hotel"
(Hutchins, 1936, p. 29). Accordingly, he rejected the need to
educate the whole person, believing that education was the
single-minded pursuit of intellectual virtues.

By the end of the 1980s, a movement seemed to be developing to seek some middle ground. While few were advocating
a return to the philosophy of in loco parentis, there seemed to
be a spreading perception that a more managed, structured environment was needed. Responding to this need, the American

Council on Education chose as the theme for its November 1989 meeting "Educating One Third of a Nation: What Works," which focused on campus climate, teaching, learning, and the curriculum.

The Temptation to Attempt Too Much

Of the two major categories of managed student services, only one is controversial and impinges on qualitative question. The first category is the purely administrative or custodial services that include record keeping, providing food and lodging, and maintaining a reasonable level of orderly conduct on campus. Examples of these types of services are residence hall management, campus security and health services. The second category consists of services with presumed educational significance and includes counseling services, remedial services, living arrangements for educational purposes, and student organizations designed to facilitate achievement of clearly educational objectives.

Before attempting a critique of the second category, we will explore several somewhat transcendent issues because their resolution will have a direct impact on the kind of services institutions choose to provide.

The first issue (one which is all too frequently ignored in the advocacy literature regarding educational services) is establishing priorities in the face of finite financial resources. No one can seriously dispute the potential value of teaching adults to read, counseling individuals regarding sexual problems, providing free lectures and concerts, publishing a campus newspaper, providing free day-care centers for children of college-attending mothers, offering counseling services regarding death and dying, or providing students with a variety of role models (including authors, dancers, painters, or successful older women in residence). Yet, institutions with finite resources would not be able to accomplish worthy institutional goals if they attempted to provide all desired services. Given the sobering significance of computers as intellectual tools for problem solving, which of the following activities should have a higher institutional priority:

establishing a network of computer terminals so that all students
may learn to use the computer as an aid in coursework and
problem solving or establishing a network of individuals responsible for training students in interpersonal relationships? Both
are certainly desirable, but, at some point, a hierarchy of priorities must be established at any collegiate institution.

Related to the broad issue of priorities is the issue of what
kind of service should be provided various special groups of
students and how intensive that service should be. A defensible
case can be made that some college students have intellectual
deficiencies that need to be removed before asking those students
to cope with academic work. Deficiencies in reading, writing,
mathematics, and study skills can, within reason, be eradicated
by a college or university. Four years of remedial reading probably can help some students who would otherwise drop out or
fail. Likewise, there are some students with distinct psychological
problems who could be helped to persevere to a bachelor's degree
if they had the support of a therapy session once a week. However, is there a limit to the intensity of effort beyond which
responsibility to help such students transcends the proper expenditure of institutional funds? Put another way, should there
be some limit as to how much effort an institution should expend on individual students?

During the 1950s, Michigan State University maintained
remedial clinics for reading, writing, speaking, and arithmetic.
Some students with deficiencies were assigned to those clinics,
although not all who reflected need could be accommodated.
An examination of the impact of those clinics suggested that
they helped students stay in school a little bit longer, but did
not seem to increase graduation rates. A writing clinic, for example, appeared to help students pass courses as long as they
were participating in the clinic. When they stopped attending
the writing clinic, however, academic failure and dropping out
seemed to follow. The policy question for Michigan State University was sharply stated: "To ensure the academic survival of
deficient students, should remediation be provided as long as
necessary, even though continued remedial training might mean
reduction in resources for academic and research activities?"

Another comment is warranted here about nontraditional education for new kinds of students. A series of similar rhetorical questions as those asked regarding traditional students can sharpen the focus of these issues. Should a collegiate institution at public expense employ counselors to help prison inmates overcome rage and hostility in order to cope better with academic work? Is a university obligated to fund periodic home visits to a physically incapacitated seventy-year-old woman to assist in her academic work? Should it assign counselors to go into remote areas of a state to organize a support group for students and to meet with them regularly to discuss their problems, goals, hopes, and fears? Should it provide a bookmobile to bring library holdings to isolated communities? Finally, does a collegiate institution have an obligation to fund an effort especially designed for students lacking the emotional stamina to do academic work on their own? As is true for a myriad of services, there can be little dispute as to the social worth of these activities, but are these services the responsibility of a collegiate educational institution?

One of the major activities in student services that developed after World War II involved the use of residence hall advisers to organize residence hall student government, plan residence hall social and cultural activities, and participate with faculty to create a new entity called residential education. The use of residence halls as centers for learning and living reached its zenith with the creation of the cluster colleges, house plans, and experimental residential colleges. These groupings were intended to be relatively small groups that would provide primary group support for students and bring learning and living into a natural balance. For some students these worked, at least for a time. The concept, however, never was adopted into the mainstream of higher education practice for at least two major reasons: most residence halls were not designed for these purposes, and neither a majority of faculty nor a preponderance of students really embraced the idea as something they wanted. Students prefer to live with close friends, and friendship and major field of study are not necessarily coterminous. Furthermore, students become attached to a particular residence hall or room and may be reluctant to move just because they change fields of study.

Another issue is how much service to students should be provided by professionals as opposed to how much students should provide for themselves. During the expansionist period of the student-personnel movement the implicit assumption was that as needs arose, professional services should be made available. Thus arose a plethora of advisers for student government; sponsors for clubs; leaders for black residence halls; survival counselors for black students in engineering programs; directors of centers for women's affairs; veterans' counselors; and counselors for problems related to draft registration. A different point of view, early expressed by a nineteenth-century president of Harvard, Charles Eliot (Morison, 1930), held that students should be almost completely free to make whatever decisions they wish to make and that they should be expected to provide or not provide whatever services they wish. Thus, if students wish, they can organize student government; persuade faculty members to sponsor activities; organize, within limits, their own living arrangements; and recruit their own campus speakers. Furthermore, exercising freedom to succeed or fail may be educationally potent and valuable, and excessive administrative interference in student affairs may deprive students of valuable learning opportunities.

This point of view was exemplified by the University of Illinois in the 1930s. The university maintained a dean of students responsible for discipline, a housing office responsible for certifying housing quality, and an intramural athletic staff responsible for providing athletic equipment. Modest academic advising for those in academic difficulty was provided by the offices of the deans of the several schools and colleges. The student union and a campus newspaper were run by the students, and various religious centers were run by denominations. Many fraternities and sororities run by students—usually without supervision—provided considerable student housing. Other housing was available at privately owned rooming houses and two, small, university-operated residence halls for 300 female students. Although more services were provided by some of the smaller, privately supported institutions during that era (especially by those affiliated with religious denominations), a general pattern prevailed in American higher education in which formal programs for intellectual and professional development were stressed and most other matters were left to the students themselves. Of course, conditions have changed so much that this specific laissez-faire approach may no longer be valid. Perhaps institutions have been forced to assume more responsibility because of the increasing heterogeneity of college student bodies, the reduced socializing effectiveness of the church and the small-town community, the propensity of American families after World War II to move frequently, and the change in secondary schools from a college-preparatory to a comprehensive-service emphasis. However, we still must ask how many new responsibilities colleges and universities legitimately can fulfill and still meet their historical objectives.

The Essential Context

Clearly, the range of possible services is so broad that it is unlikely any institution, regardless of wealth or inclination, can address them all. In order to prevent student services from becoming an unlimited sinkhole into which limited resources are poured, institutions must review the essential collegiate values that form the basic rationale for the university.

First among these attributes is a climate in which ideas are believed to be important in and of themselves. Obviously, ideas that will lead to action of some sort are not to be discouraged. A university is an instrument of society that trains people in the skills of a vocation, citizenship, and the art of successful living as determined by that society. Accordingly, the university will assume that many ideas are of worth simply because of their relevance or their practical purposes. However, a university should also foster another attitude toward ideas. It should be a place where the abstract refinement of a concept is held to be as worthy as building a house or auditing a set of books. Further, the university should possess an atmosphere in which students and faculty feel a desire to invent, explore, and discuss ideas. The source of these ideas need not be primarily verbal. Ideas first expressed in sound, color, or line are to be valued, as well as those exposed through verbal or numerical symbols. In addition, ideas need not all be highly serious. The campus should not make people ashamed of the pursuit of the light and fanciful any more than it should discourage the pondering of questions on the nature of humankind or the significance of justice. The notions from one of Gary Larson's "Far Side" cartoons may have as appropriate a place in the collegiate environment as do the massive interpretations of God by a Buber or a Maritain.

Second, the campus should provide conditions and should sponsor a spirit in which leisure is enjoyed and respected. It is not the goal of a university to keep its students and faculty at assigned work all the time. Furthermore, to attempt this impossibility would be foolish. Rather, the university should accept leisure as essential in the lives of people and should provide ways for its creative use. One can contrast a desirable use of leisure to simple time-killing or to filling leisure hours with activities that anesthetize people to the reality of experience. The university should reject neither television, consumption of food and drink, nor complete idleness; indeed, these can be used appropriately as leisure activities. The university should, however, seek to have its students and faculty select wisely from the many leisure activities available so that they might enjoy them as complete and worthwhile experiences.

Third, the university should create a climate in which academic work is viewed as having essential value rather than as a tedious means to some pragmatic end. Again, the university does not reject its responsibility to prepare its students to do the many things which they and society need. The university should help students keep in mind the need to become effective teachers, skilled draftsmen, and accurate accountants. However, if these ends are the chief motivating forces in the academic program, even a successful university will not be a great or vibrant institution. The sheer esthetic pleasure of working a statistics problem or the complete personal involvement in preparing a research paper should be cultivated. This abstraction perhaps can be clarified by examples. The course in Functional English is generally regarded as primarily a hurdle to overcome on the road to a degree or as preparation in skills needed for other courses; as such, the course is not as consistent with the ideal as is the same course viewed as a tough, demanding but nevertheless pleasurable experience. Perhaps pleasurable is the wrong word; courses may prove vexing to students, but, if accomplishment of long, hard assignments is viewed as a worthy goal, the ideal will have been realized at least in part.

Fourth, the university should be pervaded by a spirit that encourages people to accept the uncertainties of life. The spirit of the frontier—where there are many difficulties, where the possibility of failure is always present, and where human emotions are always taxed—is the spirit being sought. Human beings are always faced with uncertainties, and uncertainties are never comfortable. People can respond by seeking to find some more clearly understood way, or they can develop a resilience of character that allows them to live without knowing how the story will end. It is the latter, almost stoical, ideal that should characterize the university. In pursuit of this ideal, the university should be a place in which students and faculty can see their most vital beliefs scrutinized and still not flinch, a place in which changes of vocational plans are regarded as simply one more uncertainty, and a place in which theory can be followed to the furthest limits of human comprehension. The university should be a place in which teacher or student can ask Why? until the question forces the discussion to basic presuppositions.

Fifth, the university should be a place in which intellectual and creative effort is valued for itself. It should foster the belief that the artist should be more than tolerated. The artist should be encouraged to pursue efforts even though the resultant abstractions seem to distort traditional concepts of beauty and even though the effort seems to profit no one, not even the artist. The university should encourage students to investigate the most esoteric subjects if those subjects seem to have genuine appeal for the student. In short, the university should encourage students to value the experience of creative effort and to value a similar quest by others. This prescription obviously is not easy;

it is difficult, for example, to accept endless theorizing about personality structure when the theory has little obvious relevance to actual human behavior. To encourage a college sophomore to delve into religious questions that have perplexed centuries of theologians may seem like a waste of time. Allowing students to proceed down alleys, even though the professor knows the alleys are blind, calls for a high faith in creative effort. Yet, all these activities must be pursued if the goal of a vigorously alive collegiate enterprise is even to be approximated.

Sixth, the university should be a place in which both cognition and affection are viewed as effective and valuable forces; there should not be a preoccupation with conscious reason alone. The university should accept and teach its students to respect feeling as much as rationality in its role as one kind of human response. It should accept the reality that students and teachers do become angry with each other and the value of the expressions of sheer joy that can come from a pleasant afternoon at a football game. It should accept the feelings of uncertainty that envelop students who see basic religious beliefs seemingly challenged by the findings of science — even when these feelings are expressed with great emotion. The university should accept emotional responses to modern poetry, whether the students like or bitterly dislike contemporary writing. It should, however, also encourage its students to use both reason and emotion as tests to validate each other.

Finally, the university should make a significant difference in the lives of its members. Whether one likes the particular outcomes of any particular institution is relatively unimportant. What is significant is that students and the community should be distinctively different simply because the university exists. We are not referring here to the increased purchasing power that a university education brings or to the increase in the number of people listed in *Who's Who in America*. We suggest neither that students should more uniformly accept the beliefs of their professors nor that the larger community should be a macrocosmic version of the university. We do mean that both students and the community should be more willing to consider ideas, to enjoy leisure, to accept academic effort, to encourage creativity, to communicate with each other more freely, and to accept the uncertainties. If colleges and universities can even approach this ideal, they shall indeed have achieved the purpose for which they exist.

The Quest to Find an Appropriate Balance

Undergraduate students are emerging adults seeking to develop, each in his or her unique way, and yet all students have many needs in common. What institutions can do best (after providing emergency medical care and the necessary services of housing and food when appropriate and after ensuring that reasonably competent advising is available to all) is to provide as rich an array of activities and services as resources allow. This point of view is different both from the view of the 1950s with its emphasis on the planned development of the whole student and the radical egalitarianism of the 1970s with its intent to meet whatever need any member of society felt should be satisfied. We acknowledge that institutions have limited resources and limited competence and that these resources should be used for developing the intellectual abilities of their students. Nonetheless, we are convinced that some allowance should be made for institutionally sponsored, sharply focused student development activities. In terms of a general point of view regarding student services, however, we believe that the laissez-faire approach has much to commend it.

Of the wide variety of student services that are now either provided or urged, the most relevant and promising for matters of educational quality are academic advising and orientation to college life and academic affairs. Whether one adopts a developmental theory or the direct empirical approach of asking students and former students what they need most, the opportunity to talk with a mature adult about concerns emerges as a strong correlate of success in college. Jacob (1957) remarked that, except for a few institutions, most colleges and universities in the 1950s had little impact on students. Those few represented quite diverse curricular arrangements, from pure instrumentalism to pure rationalism. The one element they had in common was deliberate provision for sustained and intimate advising to such a degree that whenever a student needed adult support, it was there.

As to how advising should be provided, there are a variety of approaches; some are appropriate for one type of institution or faculty but not for others. In general, however, students occasionally need help in four areas: (1) accurate information regarding course schedules, degree requirements, and the day-to-day mechanics of college life; (2) career guidance; (3) emotional support as they confront the normal stresses of late adolescence; and (4) help with learning how to solve problems in their own lives. Helping students learn how to solve problems in their own lives is a direct extension of teaching and central to our definition of quality undergraduate education. Yet, few faculty members take the time to provide such advice or direction.

For institutions such as community colleges, state colleges, and smaller liberal arts colleges, making advising a part of the contract for all full-time faculty members and then enlisting and training them to do the job would be most worthwhile. Also, it is important not to provide too many trained professional counselors, since their very presence is a temptation to faculty to abdicate their own roles. Furthermore, what most students need falls more into the category of common sense than it does psychology. Their basic need is for a caring adult to listen to them and tell them the obvious. At Stephens College, during the period of its greatest influence, all teachers and professional administrators were expected to advise a proportionate share of the total student body. All were trained through advising seminars and an advising handbook, and all were required to see advisees at least six times in an academic year. It was this system that most enabled the college to attract a national student body to a rather uncomfortable, Midwestern town thirty-five miles from the nearest trunk railroad, and to graduate well over 70 percent of its entering students — a rate nearly 50 percent higher than similar public institutions. By standards such as the SAT scores of students, Stephens was not selective, but its advising provided an essential service that produced good results.

Finding a solution to the advising dilemma is more difficult in research universities and prestigious colleges whose faculties see their discipline and their research and scholarship as the most important activities and availability to undergraduate students an unwarranted drain on their time. A pluralistic approach would seem workable that includes departmental responsibility for advising declared majors, investing considerable resources in advising publications, involving faculty in living units when possible, and creating opportunities for intense advising for at least some students through such devices as overseas campuses and residence halls devoted to a single interest (for example, language houses). If institutions are willing to invest enough resources in such efforts and to ensure diligent coordination, the advising needs of many undergraduate students can be satisfied.

Greater attention to orientation to life in an academic institution also deserves emphasis. As a general rule, residential institutions could well provide up to one week of rather intensive orientation for freshman students. During that period a great deal of attention should be given to the skills needed for academic survival, wise selection of academic programs, learning about advising resources, and, of course, provision for social life and recreation. Commuting institutions, of course, cannot mount such an intensive effort, but can, with imagination, organize worthwhile orientation programs of at least several days. During a two-day orientation, there would be time for some personal advising and a reasonable variety of group activities that could acquaint students with the academic nature of the institution and thus would lead logically to the selection of a program at the time of registration.

A variation available for some institutions to help students is summer orientation programs of perhaps five days for each of perhaps six to eight different groups of students. Students would come to campus on Sunday and leave Friday afternoon. During those five days, a variety of activities can be undertaken, but, ideally, the principal emphasis is on academic careers, academic choices, and academic survival. Orientation also represents the best opportunity administrators will have to influence students through exhortation during their four years of college. A well-prepared presentation to freshmen regarding campus ethics and the need for serious attention to studies will have more impact during freshmen orientation than a similar address at any other subsequent time.

One may wonder why it is necessary to discuss such simple suggestions, but frequently (especially in large institutions), the significance of orientation is not recognized and no major efforts are made to provide orientation sessions. Orientation frequently stresses the social, recreational, or bureaucratic to the exclusion of the academic and intellectual. Of all the possible uses of resources for student services, creating a well-organized orientation program that leads directly into a consistent and intensive advising effort is more likely to produce greater student retention and better academic performance than any other combination of activities. Even high school students committed almost from birth to attend college appear to have little understanding of what college is all about, what programs are available, what the realistic requirements are for various professions and vocations, and especially how to work independently. Asking only that new students appear at a scheduled time for registration is asking students to make grievous errors. However, if those same students can be provided with several days of intensive instruction about the specifics of a realistic collegiate program, the likelihood of wise choices is enhanced. If every student has one professional person to whom he or she can go as questions arise, the chance for survival is higher still.

A related activity is remediation for academic and intellectual deficiencies. Many students enroll in college unable to read, write, study, or calculate effectively, and, if an institution accepts them, it may have a moral obligation to help them to rectify their deficiencies. However, two issues should be faced. The first issue is which intellectual deficiencies can be overcome reasonably quickly, and the second is whether a collegiate institution should use its resources for the sustained remediation needed to overcome deeply rooted problems. Certainly, some reasonably able high school graduates with moderate academic success may read too slowly, have poor study and writing skills, or need some refresher work in mathematics. These problems can be alleviated by ten to fifteen weeks of remediation. Almost all first-year law students at Stanford find that a writing course helps them with their academic work. Similarly, Harvard had a basic writing course for years. An institution that is reasonably secure financially may create supplemental courses such as those described in Chapter Four or may even offer a limited number of remedial courses in reading, writing, study skills, and mathematics for perhaps the 10 to 15 percent of its entering freshman class who need such help. Curricular planners at such a school may assume that remedial effort in some skills could require a term or two; however, if, at that point, some students still could not cope with a normal academic program, a decision would have to be made about whether those students really belonged in that institution.

In a limited number of instances, a somewhat longer remedial period might be appropriate, as in the situation of southern black students who enroll in an engineering program but lack both the skills needed to cope with mathematics and the basic sciences and appropriate black role models. For such students, a two-year program might be created that includes a considerable amount of advising, specially organized courses in mathematics and natural sciences, an opportunity to earn money through cooperative work, and an opportunity to meet black engineers. This approach has been offered by the University of Houston and apparently has reduced black attrition rates and increased grade point averages. However, even in such situations, in the absence of external sustaining funds, one or two years at the most should be allowed. At the end of two years, if a student still cannot cope with collegiate level work, he or she may be dismissed from the program and advised to consider the alternatives.

The essential message advanced here is rooted in the belief that the basic academic skills needed to cope with academic work of reading, writing, and mathematics are, for the most part, developed over a long time and that a fundamental deficiency in any of them in a student who is eighteen to twenty-two years old is not likely to be remedied in a relatively short time. For admitted students who, after they have been admitted, are found to read at the fourth or fifth grade level, both the institution and the individual are served well if the student seeks the assistance of another school that specializes in inculcating basic skills. Remediation can build on a foundation of basic skills to improve the speed of reading, retention, writing mechanics, and knowledge of basic arithmetic rules and procedures. This sort of objective makes remedial seminars a legitimate collegiate activity and, in the long run, contributes to academic quality.

Once again the issue of academic credit must be faced. Many public community colleges offer a variety of other English courses in addition to the traditional college-level freshman course in composition. Some of these courses seek to develop a rudimentary understanding of simple English usage. Whether the level is simple or quite advanced, similar academic credit is equally awarded. Some argue that, if academic credit were not awarded in even marginal courses, students requiring such basic instruction would probably not attend the community college, and, even if they did, they could not obtain financial aid. In addition, often public community colleges are reliant on public funds appropriated on the basis of enrollment in courses carrying academic credit. Hence these institutions are eager to increase those enrollments, even if doing so means granting academic credit for some courses that offer work at little more than the fifth grade level. There can really be only one intellectually honest answer to this problem: A college or university should differentiate between collegiate level courses and those below that level and should award credit only for those courses which meet collegiate standards. If students are so unmotivated to attend college that they will try to rectify serious intellectual deficiencies only if that effort is rewarded with collegiate academic credit, they probably will not persevere to completion of a program and should be allowed to find other avenues to maturation and development into adulthood. However, there can be no valid argument against community colleges' offering whatever courses students want and need so long as students pay the full price of such services through real tuition.

Other barriers to academic performance include problems of physical or mental health. For the public, two-year, commuting college, medical services should be available to take care of medical emergencies or to refer students to appropriate medical services. Residential institutions may feel the need for additional service on campus to provide some hospital-like care for students, as well as some limited, outpatient care. The rationale for such service is clear: the removal of relatively superficial barriers to academic performance. Helping students to get over the flu enables them to get back to their primary task, and administering flu shots provides some insurance against diversion from the primary task. The college or university, however, is not a clinic that can legitimately provide care for the chronically ill. Most institutions cannot provide major medical services; for these, students should be expected to seek outside help, usually paid for through health insurance.

Similarly, psychological counseling can help remove such barriers as fear of taking tests or inability to concentrate. Professional counselors can help sensitize faculty with respect to problems of mental health. These efforts are warranted to the degree that they contribute to academic quality. Long-term therapy, however, does not seem appropriate, even though at the end of four years of counseling a disturbed student may be able to cope with academic work better. Such extended psychological treatment for students should not be deemed an institutional responsibility.

Counseling centers may be used to sensitize all parts of the campus community to the various problems of mental health. Warnath (1973) strongly endorses this as an educational activity, arguing that a better mental health climate can thus be achieved and that this increased sensitivity contributes to the achievement of academic goals and objectives. However, too much achievement should not be expected from an intensive sensitization effort because college faculty members are trained professionals only with respect to the subjects they teach. Over time, some may develop a modicum of psychological sophistication and may help some students to overcome problems, but expecting a professor of French, physics, or engineering to take on the attributes of a clinician is unrealistic. Life on campus probably would be better if all professors were trained in a few counseling techniques such as listening skills, nonevaluative attitudes, and sensitivity to problems that transcend their knowledge or experience. But the cost of trying to ensure this condition is probably too high for the benefits obtained.

With respect to the many new types of students who — for one reason or another — have begun to enter collegiate institutions, new counseling needs have arisen, including marriage counseling; counseling for elderly people seeking to earn an academic degree; counseling to help cope with the death of a spouse, deal with Social Security problems, or adjust to retirement; new career counseling for military personnel planning for early retirement; and counseling for prison inmates who are about to be released and who are enrolled in academic programs. The advice given above is still applicable: Counseling services are warranted only to facilitate academic progress through dealing with relatively superficial barriers.

One type of activity is more properly called campus services than student services and is intended to enrich the social, cultural, and intellectual tone of a campus. These activities include lecture-concert series, traveling displays of art, visiting scholars, painters, poets, artists in residence, and the celebration of special events through artistic or intellectual statements of various sorts. Some of these activities have been so important that it has been observed that collegiate campuses have collectively become the major impresario of the arts in the United States. These events have had a long history deriving from debates, sermons, and declamations of college campuses in the early nineteenth century.

A clear logic supports a variety of such activities. They can contribute to the cultural level of a campus, break the monotony of academic life, provide students with varied role models, and bring intellectual content to the campus that otherwise might require specialized and expensive academic courses and programs. Although no scientific means are available to determine the actual impact of such events on members of the campus community, intuition suggests that they do make positive differences in the quality of campus life and should be given reasonable support.

However, with these events also, cost is a factor, and only a small proportion of institutional funds should be used, with the bulk of expense provided by individual payments. A variety of events, each attracting a small number of people, is probably better than a few blockbuster events demanding large attendance. Planning and organizing events for the most part is better done by small, decentralized campus groups than by a centralized campus office. Although some events have a legitimate institutional development purpose (for example, homecoming does attract potential donors) and some events can be offered as a service to the larger community, still the primary goal of these events should be to contribute to student development, especially cultural and intellectual development. Jerry Beasley, the president of Concord College in West Virginia, has instituted a lecture series that includes many speakers from Washington, D.C. Each spring, the following year's schedule (including topics) is circulated to the faculty, and they are asked to indicate which lectures are germane to their classes and will be required as part of a course. This approach ensures that students will have exposure to current issues and that speakers will be lecturing to a respectable crowd.

In summary, although each institution must set its own priorities as to the services and activities it can provide, some services appear to be essential for all. These include, in order of significance and importance, academic advising, limited remedial services, counseling, career planning and placement, intramural athletics, opportunities for students to form primary group associations, and a reasonably elaborate variety of interesting events and activities. If institutions have more resources than needed to achieve their primary mission, they may also provide somewhat expanded health coverage, overseas campuses, specialized living arrangements (for example, foreign-language centers), campus ombudsmen, artists- or scholars-in-residence, married student housing, and some form of religious counseling. Other services, while of potential value, are too far removed from central collegiate purposes to warrant institutional support and administration, although students may wish to provide or obtain those services for themselves.

SIX

Maintaining
a High-Quality
Professoriate

The American college or university theoretically provides an ideal setting for professors to be intellectuals. It provides a milieu in which people can share a common concern for the pursuit of knowledge. It provides professors regular remuneration, the security of tenure, and substantial academic freedom to be exercised during the large portion of their time available for intellectual work. All this is supposed to ensure that American higher education will remain the qualitative leader in the world. Yet some have begun to question whether this insulation from outside influence has become a shield behind which self-serving recalcitrance and mediocrity can flourish. The report of the Association of American Colleges (AAC), *Integrity in the College Curriculum* (1985, p. 9), made this indictment: "Presidents and deans must first confront the obstacles to faculty responsibility that are embedded in academic practice and then, with the cooperation of the professors themselves, fashion a range of incentives to revive the responsibility of the faculty *as a whole* for the curriculum *as a whole*" (emphasis theirs).

Regardless of how one might wish to distribute blame for the recently observed declines in quality in higher education, all agree that substantive improvement cannot be made without the involvement of faculty.

Faculty Characteristics

Generalizations about faculty are extraordinarily dangerous in a diverse system that includes open-admissions, two-year colleges; provincial, private liberal arts colleges; normal schools turned state colleges or universities; massive, flagship state universities; and highly elite, private universities possessing resources of $1 billion or more. Generalizations become even more hazardous in view of the rising tide of part-time faculty, many of whom draw on vocational experience rather than academic preparation for legitimacy to teach. Nevertheless, some common characteristics, expectations, and myths have relevance for academic and intellectual quality for at least the full-time, tenure-track college or university teacher in a two-year, four-year, or graduate institution.

American higher education is a pronounced status system, affecting the aspirations and self-identities of those who participate in it. In general, the high-status institutions that provide the highest salaries and the greatest freedom to professors are the flagship research universities and prestigious private colleges; the faculties are quite similar in these two types of institutions, despite differences in the sizes of the institutions. These institutions maintain light teaching loads and emphasize research and scholarship as the most appropriate professorial activity. Next, the rather large, comprehensive institutions seek to become members of the elite group by emulating their practices. Following these are the regional universities; private universities; state colleges; relatively small, invisible, private liberal arts colleges; and, lastly, private and public two-year institutions. Faculty behavior and prerogatives in the elite institutions are the norm toward which faculty members in lower-level institutions aspire—either by moving themselves into the next higher tier, helping to convert their institutions, or gaining for themselves the prerogatives of the elite faculties.

The role of a college or university faculty member is a peculiar blend of the ideal and the mundane. The ideal side is illustrated by the kind of life an ideal faculty member leads. Among the joys of such a life is the sheer fact of the campus as a desirable place to work. Wherever it is located, the college campus reflects a preoccupation with the best of human experience. There is also the pleasure of working with young people on the threshold of discovering self and the importance of ideas. In such a setting, ideas themselves govern the pattern of life as members of the college community offer one another stimulating opportunities to discuss an idea, not necessarily for any practical end, but for the worth of the idea itself.

In regard to self-direction, a scholar ideally is free to survey a subject and determine on which part he or she will concentrate for research and teaching. Colleges and universities cannot guarantee the personal security and inner tranquility requisite for high-order self-regulation, but they can set the best possible conditions within which it might be achieved.

Throughout life everyone is evaluated, and performance is judged. Part of the pleasure of the collegiate career is that professors, like people in other professions, are evaluated by their peers and colleagues (and not — as is usual in most vocations — by a superior whose judgment may be suspect).

Those are some of the ideals. Among the woes of such a life is that, after all, college teaching is a job, and all jobs have their dull sides as well as their bright ones. For every bright and promising student encountered, professors will meet dozens who seem concerned only with obtaining a degree with the least amount of work possible. Progress up the academic ladder to full professorship is slow, and professional recognition and promotion may seem not only far away, but also the result of campus politics rather than a reflection of demonstrated ability.

In this sense, academic life is in many ways more tension-producing than most other callings. Scholarship and teaching are each similar to acting in that one's entire personality is on public display and even the most secure practitioners of the art may have the uneasy feeling that their best efforts will not be enough. Another bother is the load of administration and committee work — such as schedules, budgets, equipment, and faculty promotions — all of which are necessary functions, yet take away from the hours available for classes and research. The professor is in many ways a solitary sort of person who chafes under the strictures of administrative regulation but who must accept those strictures as facts of academic life.

Contributions to Quality

Over time, college and university faculties certainly have contributed to the strengthening of academic and intellectual quality in American higher education. Although the initiative usually came from administrative leadership, faculties in the late 1940s and throughout the 1950s enacted graduation requirements designed to ensure that all students were at least exposed to the major domains of human knowledge. In research universities, faculty members produced such a volume of significant research that the United States became the research capital of the world, contributing to the technological triumphs of the mid-twentieth century. This flowering of research in many fields led to curricular enrichment as new courses and programs, such as Southeast Asian art, statistically based history, genetics, and computer science were added to college catalogues. By serving on test advisory committees, faculty members made certain that the various national testing programs reflected that curricular enrichment. The growth patterns of institutions such as Stanford, Carleton, and Dartmouth (which had been quite unselective and emerged during this period as highly selective, pace-setting institutions) reveal that the first and most important step was the wholesale recruitment of stronger faculties who were capable of doing significant research.

During the two rapid growth periods of the veteran era (1945–1952) and the 1960s, institutions generally were able to accommodate large numbers of students without serious dilution of the quality of faculties, as indicated by the percentage of faculty holding a doctorate or terminal degree. Cartter (1974, p. 17) remarks that data "suggested that the percentage of professors with the doctorate had increased in each four-year interval, for each type of senior institution" from 1950–51 to 1962–63.

Also, faculties surely have contributed in some measure to the overall success of higher education since 1950. In making those contributions, faculties obtained for themselves a variety of benefits and prerogatives generally deemed to be essential to sustained improvement of collegiate educational quality. First, the financial conditions of the professoriate improved substantially between 1958 and 1970. During the 1940s, the real purchasing power of the professoriate declined as compared with the other professions — actually declined to an approximation of 1939 levels. However, beginning in 1958, faculty salaries began to increase at about 7 percent each year, significantly ahead of rates of inflation. These rates of increase continued so that, by 1970, faculty salaries had, across the country, doubled in relation to their 1958 levels. After a period of relative decline during the 1970s, salaries began to increase again beginning in 1984 and continuing at least through 1988. Fringe benefits for faculty also steadily increased (starting from a typical package of Social Security, some form of retirement plan, medical insurance, and occasionally a term-life insurance policy) until, by the 1970s, fringe benefits were valued as a tax-exempt package equivalent to 20 percent or more of salary and often including catastrophic illness protection, health insurance, dental insurance, insurance for disability income, tuition assistance for children and spouses, assistance in obtaining housing, and several other small but important perquisites.

Second, the number of courses taught decreased, as did the student-faculty ratios. Before World War II, normal teaching loads in junior colleges and many liberal arts colleges ranged from fifteen to twenty-one class hours per week, taught in the form of five or six different courses in a semester or quarter. In major state universities, teaching loads for senior full professors usually ran between three and four different courses each semester or quarter and sometimes to as many as five courses. During the 1960s, however, course loads dropped to three or four courses per term in primarily teaching institutions and to one or two courses in the prestigious research universities. This decline in actual course contact was justified on the grounds that faculty members needed more time for research, scholarship, and the preparation of courses.

Third, the educational and research resources available to faculties improved as library holdings were increased, better and more complex laboratory equipment was installed, technologically sophisticated educational facilities such as language laboratories were created, and office space was expanded. As computers became significant tools, growing amounts of computer time was provided to faculty members. While some institutions were not able to improve the lot of faculty members, in many situations the professional life of faculty became more desirable with lighter face-to-face teaching loads, more adequate equipment, longer summer vacations with opportunities to earn additional income by teaching summer school, more frequent sabbatical leaves, and increased subsidy for professional travel.

Faculty and the Decline of Quality

Before addressing the possible ways in which faculties can be encouraged to assert a renewed concern for academic and intellectual quality, we need to explore the conditions that nurture academic quality.

Quality probably will be compromised when faculty members are superficially prepared in the subjects they teach and thus must rely primarily on their vocational experiences to comprise course content. Appropriate academic preparation must rest on a large and complex body of interrelated information, a large and equally complex range of generalizations to interpret the meaning of that information, still another large and complex series of interrelated but unanswered questions regarding additional information, and a range of ways to uncover answers to those questions. The possession of sophisticated insight into such matters requires that professors steep themselves in whatever subject they intend to teach. For example, a professor of school administration should not be expected to teach a specialized course in school law even though he or she might possess some awareness of legal issues and principles. Nor should a professor of entomology be expected to teach a course on human sexuality without adequate academic preparation. If institutional leadership can follow a simple rule requiring intensive academic preparation before allowing courses to be offered, the chances for enhancement of academic quality will be significantly higher.

Academic and intellectual quality are also most likely to be enhanced when a number of intensively prepared professors continue, over time, to deepen their understanding of the subject they teach and to offer a series of interrelated courses that, according to an explicitly stated logic or rationale, are intended to develop student knowledge, understanding of that knowledge, and ability to apply that knowledge.

A major faculty contribution to academic deterioration, although often accompanied by claims of strengthening quality, was the gradual elimination of graduation requirements that were designed to ensure that undergraduates received a core liberal arts education. Although faculty members earlier had approved strengthening graduation requirements, they seemed to become discontented with the results. As quickly as possible throughout the 1960s, dismantling of general education took place. At Stanford, requirements were virtually eliminated because a research-oriented faculty and students bound for graduate or professional school wanted nothing to stand in the way of increased specialization in academic work. At the University of South Florida in the 1970s, the highly structured College of Basic Studies was eliminated, and responsibility for undergraduate general education was assigned to increasingly specialized disciplinary departments. The result was the elimination of requirements that did not contribute to greater student specialization in their majors. Faculties do continue to discuss the purposes of undergraduate education in liberal arts terms reminiscent of earlier times, but often they cannot reach the hard decisions about actual graduation requirements.

Another clear manifestation of deterioration in quality is the previously discussed problem of grade inflation. Since the late 1960s, faculty members individually and collectively have contributed to this problem, and they seem to have done so for a variety of overt and covert reasons. In study after study, it has been shown that grades in virtually all types of institutions have been inflated. Of course, earlier grading systems were far from perfect, and unreliable and invalid grading occurs in almost every institution. However, the existence of a well-defined grading system did serve as a strong motivation for students to take academic work seriously. McKeachie (1963, p. 119) stated that grades are the most important motivational device: feedback for the student who is interested in learning; the key to graduate-school admission; and an eligibility requirement for participation in athletics.

Copperman (1978, p. 116), in an admittedly more strident tone, focuses on the impact grade inflation has on overall quality: "Grade inflation penalizes the superior, the talented, and the hard working and rewards the mediocre, incompetent and lazy. It produces a kind of intellectual fantasyland, where everybody is superior. It teaches America's brightest young people that there is no particular merit attached to hard work. It is a measure of the deterioration of our institutions of higher education."

In academic mythology, faculty members have been responsible for the academic quality of institutions. Through corporate decisions of faculties, curricular content is established and standards are created. Yet most college faculties do not participate in the academic governance procedures by which academic decisions are made. For example, one estimate in two large California institutions is that not more than 18 percent of the total faculty served on more than one board or committee for a five-year period. There appears to be in most institutions a relatively small oligarchy of faculty members who serve in senates and on committees and who, essentially, make the major institutional decisions. While this arrangement may be satisfactory in practice, it does remove from the active decision-making process the variety of opinion that would be found if the total faculty were involved. Possibly, a wider expression of opinion would produce a substantially different academic emphasis than the one generated by the small number of academic oligarchs who do, indeed, rule.

Several implications for quality arise from the status system outlined earlier in this chapter. The most important consequence is that different types of institutions have quite different missions, and they therefore attract quite different kinds of students. Faculty members, instead of identifying with unique institutional missions, seem to identify with the highest status roles, which may actually be antithetical to the goals of lower-level institutions. Seeing the light teaching loads in elite institutions, they demand the same for themselves, although they lack the talent or temperament for research and scholarship that are insisted on in elite institutions. Consequently, the emulation of elite faculties turns out to be a caricature rather than a faithful imitation.

This propensity is exacerbated by the common view of life provided through the socialization of graduate school attendance, whether the individual earned a master's degree before joining the faculty of a community college or a Ph.D. degree before becoming an assistant professor in an Ivy League research university. Although most instructors with advanced degrees never engage in serious research and scholarship leading to publication, graduate students often internalize the ideal of the graduate faculty member for whom disciplinary research is the highest form of academic activity. The community college instructor, the liberal arts college professor, the state university professor, and the academic star of a prestige department in a comprehensive university all expect to be given teaching loads that allow time for research, and they all insist on using disciplinary integrity as a criterion for judging institutional and curricular issues.

This phenomenon can be clearly seen in the creation of Michigan State University, Oakland, which was planned as a commuting institution to cater to the vocational aspirations of young people of the region, who typically came from families without college backgrounds. The first faculty consisted of relatively young scholars from Ivy League institutions who wanted to imitate at Oakland the traditions they had experienced as undergraduates and graduate students. The faculty endorsed propositions that required all students to learn either Russian or French, offered no mathematics below the level of calculus, and offered no remedial English composition in the freshman year. "Every student was to take a required curriculum of university courses, consisting of two year-long courses in Western institutions and in Western literature in the Freshman year, a year in non-Western studies, a year of science and mathematics, a four-semester sequence in social science, plus a foreign language, and one term of music or art" (Riesman and others, 1970, p. 31). The faculty seemed to have assumed that the freshmen would come from prestigious and demanding high schools that would have prepared them for such a rigorous curriculum. Instead, most freshmen had attended secondary schools of no particular distinction, and, even in those schools, they had ranked below the top 20 percent of their graduating classes. The attempt to transplant elite values and style to a nonelite institution produced immediate chaos when the faculty gave failing grades to three-quarters of the students at the end of the semester. Gradually, the faculty was forced to modify its expectations to avoid the closing of the institution because students refused to attend. Perhaps some of the high attrition rates in nonelite institutions are related to faculty styles patterned after elite faculties and inappropriate for the given student population.

Also, professors may have feelings about their marginal status that do not assist the active pursuit of learning. A former high school teacher, now in a community college, wants to be considered a real college professor but lacks the full credentials, the publication record, and even the freedom to create courses patterned on his own interests. Professors who teach teachers at state colleges that have been converted to comprehensive universities also may have marginal status as a result of institutional and personal realities. A catalogue tells them that they are university professors and that research and graduate education are important, but they possess neither the skills nor the interest to engage in such activities. The results may be insecurity and anxiety, which some professors seek to relieve through striking out at the system or organizing to defeat it. The most fertile fields for unionization are community colleges and state colleges in transition.

Faculty marginality also is reflected in a sense of alienation from the dominant established culture that identifies with strong business and materialistic values. This alienation is reinforced during times of financial squeeze or declining enrollments and is exacerbated by the disproportionate weight in institutional affairs of those faculty who entered the professoriate during the 1960s. A decline in financial support has led some toward militant unionism and others to engage in militant political action to safeguard their interests. Ladd and Lipset (1975) remark that class or vocational interests may, therefore, enhance the traditional adversary culture associated with higher education. One may even identify in this process a countercyclical trend in the academic community, whereby the more conservatively inclined teacher segment at schools that are less research oriented take on socially critical views in harmony with their support for militant unionism. The initially more liberal views of the younger faculty, reflecting the dominant orientations of the 1960s when they entered the profession, may be reinforced, rather than moderated, as these faculty suffer frustrations imposed by scarce financial resources (see Ladd and Lipset, 1975, p. 404).

Toward the end of the 1970s, permanent faculties had begun to age and many institutions began increasingly either to use itinerant, part-time faculty or to turn over rather quickly full-time faculty appointments at the lower academic ranks. The proportion of part-time faculty grew from 23 percent in 1966 to 41 percent in 1980 (Study Group on the Conditions of Excellence in American Higher Education, 1984, p. 11). The significance of this use of temporary, itinerant, or rapidly rotating faculty is underscored by Bowen (1980). He pointed out that, as colleges and universities began to employ part-time faculty, the teachers really did not become part of the collegial faculty responsible for educational policy. "Higher education has always used part-time faculty, and there is a place for them if used sparingly and wisely. They can lend flexibility and variety, bring practical knowledge and experience into the academic community, and make available the services of outstanding people who could not be employed on any other basis. But, in recent years, when the reason for using part-time people often has been financial, and when many of them could bring nothing to the academic community that full-time members could not supply, the increased use of part-time staff probably represented deterioration of quality" (p. 218). Not surprisingly, the Study Group on the Conditions of Excellence in Higher Education (1984, p. 36) judged that the addition of a single full-time faculty member is far preferable to the addition of three part-time faculty members.

There are several varieties of part-time or inadequately educated faculty that also may have consequences for quality. First, part-time faculty members in on-campus situations may be appropriately prepared but spend only limited time on campus to present their classes and hold brief office hours to advise students. Their courses may be well-prepared and professionally executed, but their contacts with students are so superficial and formal that they deny the student the growth that requires more continuous interaction. Similarly, an institution offering off-campus programs (for example, on a military base) may use its own qualified faculty to conduct evening classes, perhaps meeting once a week. Or institutions may staff their off-campus programs, as Nova University does, with highly qualified national lecturers, who hold full-time appointments elsewhere, and who meet their far-flung classes once a month for a period of four or five hours. In all these situations, the qualifications of faculty cannot be questioned, but there is a serious question about whether those instructors can spend the time needed for significant changes to take place in their students.

Increasingly, institutions are establishing off-campus courses and programs taught by faculty members who are not screened as rigorously as are on-campus, regular faculty members, and whose qualifications may be questioned. Thus, a resident director of an off-campus program may seek faculty whose preparation is somewhat related to program needs, but whose preparation is all too frequently only marginally relevant. A local businessman may be recruited to teach principles of economics, or a local school superintendent may be asked to teach educational organizational theory. Also, institutions are more frequently employing, both on- and off-campus, professionals (such as lawyers, tax accountants, medical doctors, or salespeople) on a part-time basis to teach specialized courses. These individuals may have had considerable, distinguished experience as practitioners, but such experiences do not necessarily equip them to engage in the complicated task of education.

Here exists a paradox that must be faced. Full-time college and university faculty members are assigned relatively light working loads in the form of classes that meet four to twelve hours per week on the assumption that teaching those classes is a highly professional activity requiring both a great deal of preparation and considerable additional professional effort outside class. Full-time faculty members testify that they spend fifty to sixty hours per week doing professional work, whether they are teaching in a research university or in a community college. There is also the assumption that professors become better teachers over time, and that this improvement in quality is rewarded by promotions, increases in salary, and periodic sabbatical leaves (designed to further improve academic performance). Higher education is often described as a labor-intensive industry for which mass-production methods are inappropriate. Consequently, a certain intensity is generated by the professional nature of the college teacher's role. If these assumptions and claims are valid, how can one justify the use of a local trial lawyer to teach a one-night-a-week course in American jurisprudence? The practice of trial law is undoubtedly a complicated activity in which lawyers might be expected to improve through experience, but is experience equivalent to educational sophistication?

To believe that college and university teaching is not a highly professional activity is to undermine the bases for faculty prerogatives. Thus, leadership of public, two-year community colleges claim educational superiority for those institutions on the grounds that faculty members are not subject to dilution of their primary teaching responsibilities by the additional pressure to do research and to publish. Implicit in these claims is the assumption that faculty members spontaneously improve their teaching abilities and the organization of their courses. But how can this claim and these assumptions be reconciled with the staffing formulas in some of these institutions — in which as many as two-thirds of the faculty are part-time, and many of these part-time employees lack adequate preparation in either education or the academic field? If full-time college teaching is not a demanding professional role, then all instruction could be provided more economically and more efficiently by part-time faculties. If full-time college teaching is professionally demanding, then the widespread use of part-time itinerant faculty cannot be justified.

Before leaving the topic of part-time faculty, we should note that the use of part-time faculty can also produce qualitative improvement (for example, when highly qualified individuals are retained for whom no regular position exists). However, whatever the justification, we believe that part-time faculty will not be as effective overall as faculty devoting full-time to the educational process of one institution.

Another potential threat to quality relates to future supply of professors. The drying up of academic positions during the late 1970s and 1980s denied secure academic appointments to the young assistant professors who, in normal times, would have been expected to be the scholars and intellectual leaders by the beginning of the twenty-first century. Of course, there likely will always be some room for appointments of junior faculty, and, in the 1990s, a large number of vacancies is projected as 500,000 professors appointed in the 1960s begin to retire. In 1989, the American Council on Education published a survey that projected that, by the mid-1990s, 49 percent of institutions will face shortages in computer science positions; 38 percent in business; 36 percent in mathematics; 27 percent in physical sciences; 26 percent in health professions; 18 percent in vocational-technical training; 17 percent in biological sciences; 16 percent in foreign languages; 11 percent in arts and humanities; and 10 percent in education.

Since World War II, two big increases in faculty appointments have occurred: the first at the end of the war to accommodate the veteran enrollment, and the second in the 1960s to accommodate the post–World War II increase in birth rates. Members of both of these cohort groups have by now gained permanent tenure and, with the federal government's abolition of mandatory retirement beginning in 1994, anticipated retirements may not materialize. In the 1980s, the prestige institutions across the country were reporting a tenure rate of between 70 and 80 percent (AAUP/AAC Commission on Academic Tenure, 1973, pp. 9–11). This fact alone makes an overall decline in scholarship plausible and could result in a decline in the new textbooks and other materials needed for education. Although an aging faculty might not decline intellectually, maintaining the continuity of intellectual effort is such a complex and delicate matter that these conditions may seriously unsettle the ecology of research, scholarship, and education.

A less widespread decline in quality of faculty happens most frequently in the relatively small, tuition-driven private institutions, but it could happen in tax-supported ones as well: An institution must make major cuts in faculty to avoid financial ruin. Many liberal arts colleges prospered during the 1960s and offered reasonably rich programs with a student-faculty ratio of ten or twelve to one. With the advent of financial adversity, institutions moved that ratio upward to thirteen or fifteen to one with scarcely discernible ill effects. They were still able to offer relatively broad, reasonable curricula with courses taught by fairly qualified faculty. However, when financial problems forced still higher student-faculty ratios, academic integrity was jeopardized. A liberal arts college of 800 students with a twelve-to-one ratio still has sixty-six faculty members, a number large enough to offer a rather varied program. When enrollment drops to 600 and the ratio increases to fifteen to one, twenty-six positions are eliminated. If enrollment drops to 500 and the institution is compelled to go to a nineteen-to-one ratio, an additional thirteen faculty members must be dismissed, leaving a full-time faculty of only twenty-six. In several extreme situations, institutions purporting to offer a broad program in liberal arts and sciences have reduced faculties to ten or twelve full-time people plus a few transient part-timers — certainly, this kind of faculty is not sufficient to accomplish their stated missions.

A final threat to the quality of faculty relates to the actual operations of institutions. Institutional policies and procedures may encourage anti-intellectualism rather than foster the pursuit of learning. Specifically, the common promotion process encourages rapid publication of often inconsequential material, rather than the protracted pursuit necessary for a major intellectual contribution. Far better for most faculty to stay abreast of what is happening in their field and to use that knowledge to update their teaching materials. It has been remarked that Immanuel Kant would not have survived the American tenure system, because he published nothing of consequence until age 57.

Moreover, American academics spend their professional lives in tightly constrained departments with little opportunity to interact easily and frequently with others in different fields. Many of these departments establish rather fixed standards to which all who would succeed must conform. The intellectual free spirit may not be welcome in some departments. In major research universities, faculty members are frequently distracted from a concern with learning by the quest for consultantships or research grants. The grant system adversely affects both the senior professors who must find grants and administer them, and the junior faculty whose financial security frequently depends on the annual renewal of external support.

Given these complex and frequently contradictory characteristics, we can see how faculty members may have unintentionally contributed to the decline in academic quality. They have often turned their attention away from those professorial duties that lie at the heart of quality undergraduate education.

Suggestions for Faculty Renewal

Solid evidence of decline in the quality of faculty as instructors is hard to find, and the severity of decline (if it is taking or has taken place) is neither well-understood nor well-documented. However, that situation precludes neither a search for ways to improve instruction in the nation's colleges and universities nor attempts to strengthen the role of the faculty in restoring quality.

Administrative leadership can play a role in improving faculty quality. Presidents, deans, and departmental heads can try to recruit and retain only truly qualified faculty through better search procedures and better review procedures for promotion and tenure. Administration officials can review the use of part-time faculty and take steps to improve the quality of part-time appointments. Organizational arrangements can be created to facilitate faculty participation in governance. The various processes of faculty affairs can be improved and made more sophisticated, and clearer statements of faculty rights, responsibilities, and conditions of work (as well as more precise methods of ensuring accountability) can be developed on the basis of growing experience.

Members of the Study Group on the Humanities (Bennett, 1984, pp. 25–26), which included several institutional presidents and deans, "believed strongly that presidents can be an effective force for curricular change only if they define their role accordingly. . . . David Riesman characterized a good president as having 'a combination of persuasiveness, patience, ingenuity, even stubbornness.'" Accordingly, presidents should constantly challenge faculty to rise above narrow departmentalism and reestablish the ideals of a liberal education in graduation requirements for undergraduates. By publishing and analyzing grading patterns, they also can lead in rectifying grade inflation.

But we also observe that administrators can and have fostered a variety of abuses. They may be so preoccupied with external constituencies that they leave faculties leaderless. They can be capricious in appointments, or they can refuse to share power with faculties and show marked distrust for faculties. Strong and effective administrators can generate a creative tension between themselves and their faculties from which can come effective academic decisions and practice, or they can generate constant confrontation destructive of a good academic spirit.

Administrators properly are concerned that faculty members develop, mature, and improve, and the institution should facilitate that improvement. Emphasis should be placed on the relevant traits of scholarship, the ability to communicate, the art of teaching, and academic good citizenship. To expect more from faculty generally is to expect the impossible and really to violate the social contract that has, since the twelfth century, prescribed what professors must do to earn social support and approval. These matters can and should be evaluated in a variety of ways, and the evaluations ought to be linked to positive and negative sanctions.

Individual faculty can be encouraged to modify and improve a limited range of teaching practices. Derek Bok (1986, p. 63) rightly observed that testing drives the study habits of students. Since students do adjust the way they study to their expectations of how they will be tested, a very important use of faculty-development resources is providing faculty with ongoing training on how to formulate questions that force students to use the higher-order thinking skills of analysis, synthesis, and evaluation. Another good use of resources is providing help to faculty on other topics that are generally applicable and may have a genuine impact on quality, such as effective ways to teach critical thinking, incorporate manageable writing assignments into nonhumanities courses, and perform an advisory role for students. Again, expectations should be realistic: a relatively small percentage of total faculty will participate in such in-service training (and those who do often are the best teachers to begin with), and rapid changes will not take place. Nevertheless, new instructors should be strongly urged to participate in such activities, and their future in the institution should be based in part on their eagerness to take advantage of such opportunities.

Some modest improvement in quality might occur if professional academics began to read some of the expanding literature about higher education and its processes. Of the almost 700,000 professors in the United States, the number reading books about higher education or joining associations concerned with the processes of higher education is relatively small. By 1980, Jossey-Bass Publishers had become the major publisher of professional books in higher education, with typical sales ranging from 2,000 to 5,000 copies. The American Association for Higher Education (AAHE) claims to be a major voice for individuals interested in the problems and processes of higher education. Yet this organization has fewer than 8,000 members, and participation in its widely publicized annual conference averages about 3,000 (remarks of G. K. Smith to AAHE Founders Reunion, Mar. 1989; *AAHE Bulletin,* 1989).

Further, changing several general public attitudes may improve faculty quality. First, professors should have a human image, rather than a romantic or heroic image. Faculty members are reasonably intelligent human beings who have learned to do some things relatively well and who possess traits that can aid in the development of students; they are not necessarily paragons of virtue. Perhaps criticism of faculties is so easy because the ideal images of faculties have been so exalted. For example, faculty members have been described as the agents through which divinity touches the soul and spirit of the young. They have been portrayed as shapers of character whose influence on youth will last a lifetime. They have been proclaimed as ideal role models of the examined life and as the personification of humanistic virtues. Radical egalitarian reformers see faculty members as so flexible and talented that they can quickly develop all the techniques and approaches of most of the helping professions. In addition, professors frequently claim for themselves the role of critic of society and all too frequently are accorded that role by elements of the larger society.

Of course, all these claims are hyperbole. Professors are people who have learned a great deal about something that humankind deems important and that can contribute to the development of youth. Historians, linguists, and philosophers are professors because of a traditional belief that history, language, and philosophy are important. As long as that belief is accepted, the most effective way to improve the quality of faculty is to encourage them to learn more about their subjects and to become more competent in transmitting that knowledge to students.

SEVEN

Fostering
Competent Teaching

The essential academic outcomes of higher education are produced through the subtle but powerful interaction of a limited number of elements. Collegiate institutions themselves represent one of these elements by symbolizing desired goals through structures and artifacts and by helping achievement of them through appropriately designed space and facilities. A second and most important element is the students, who, coming from varied backgrounds, nonetheless seek common goals and aid and reinforce each other in that quest. The third element is the curriculum or the collection of courses that provide to students those items of knowledge judged through tradition and through explicit decision as most likely to contribute to intellectual development. A fourth element is a collection of services and amenities specifically designed to enhance students' abilities to cope with the curriculum and to help them overcome barriers to intellectual development. The fifth factor is the faculty, which consists of a number of individuals possessing knowledge and skills that are most frequently conveyed to students through the act of teaching, usually in a situation involving a single teacher and a group of students.

In a sense, the relative influence of each of these components depends on the relative weight of other factors in the equation. Thus, in a small residential college that has facilities that allow groups of students to interact with each other intimately and for extended periods of time, there is likely to be less need for many sophisticated services because peers themselves can in proper situations serve each other in such matters as understanding the bureaucracy and developing skills needed to survive in the academic environment. On the other hand, in institutions catering to commuting students, less reliance can be placed on students and more must be placed on formal service arrangements.

Likewise, in institutions that have many well-prepared students and highly talented, experienced, and insightful professors, a formal, rigorously organized curriculum is far less necessary than in institutions that have many poorly or moderately prepared students and faculty members of mediocre talent and limited experience. In the romantically idealistic vision of Mark Hopkins sitting at one end of a log and a student on the other, no formal curriculum would be needed. The late Joel Hildebrand, renowned professor of chemistry at the University of California, Berkeley, frequently criticized formal general education requirements that were intended to acquaint freshmen and sophomores with the broad domains of knowledge of the humanities, natural sciences, social sciences, and communicative skills. Hildebrand argued that students should be taught the details of discipline first. Proper mastery of these details would allow them eventually to perceive the interconnection between domains of knowledge. This idea would undoubtedly work if every teacher of those details possessed the breadth of interest and perception that Professor Hildebrand daily demonstrated. Unfortunately, there are not many professors possessing the consummate wisdom and insight of a Hildebrand, so, for most professors, greater reliance must be placed on the formal curriculum.

An opposite notion underlies the general education movement: Students should first be exposed to the broad domains of knowledge and then elect the area in which they wish to specialize. In some respects, this phenomenon may be illustrated with two historical episodes. A tightly prescribed curriculum was the rule in American colleges during the seventeenth, eighteenth, and early nineteenth centuries, when teachers for the most part were relatively young and without a high degree of academic preparation. The prescribed curriculum began to deteriorate as the formal qualifications of faculty members began to improve during the decades after the Civil War. A second appearance of a prescribed curriculum in the form of quite specific general education courses enjoyed its most rapid growth between 1945 and the mid 1950s, a period of large veteran enrollments and a scarcity of well-qualified faculty. Given a situation in which most faculty appointed to cope with the veteran enrollment possessed a master's degree and some only possessed a bachelor's degree, a carefully structured curriculum seemed necessary. That type of structured curriculum began to deteriorate almost simultaneously with the increase in numbers of new faculty members having been well trained in graduate school and having received a doctoral degree.

This chapter is based on the assumption that most college faculties are men and women of considerable intelligence, adequate academic preparation, and reasonable (but far from outstanding) pedagogical skills. Contemporary faculties need some curricular structure, but probably do not need the structure presented by the staff-developed general education courses of the late 1940s and early 1950s. As a corollary to this assumption, we argue that if the formal academic qualifications of faculty members were to decline, the need for a carefully structured and crafted curriculum would increase.

There is little evidence of changes in the quality of college teaching since the advent in the late nineteenth century of the lecture-seminar-laboratory system. However, teaching is such an expensive part of college education and symbolically so central to that education, that specific attention needs to be given to the issue of whether teaching can or should be improved.

The Nature of College Teaching

A brief review of typical examples of college teaching since 1940 does not reveal significant change in any direction. One finds some horrible examples, some sublime examples, and a great many rather ordinary examples. One intellectually powerful but personally bland history professor sat at a desk in front of a classroom of fifty students and read his research notes from a stack of three-by-five cards in a rosary-like fashion—one bead of fact after another. Another, faced with 100 students, seated the ten men in the back row and arranged the ninety women in a rather precise order of pulchritude, from the first row to the next-to-the-last row. His teaching style consisted of slowly walking the width of the front of the room, rolling a pencil continuously between his hands, talking steadily, and observing carefully the beauty in that front row.

The lecture method has continued to predominate (for example, an hour lecture delivered in English to the three students enrolled in conversational French). One diminutive German scientist lectured from a raised dais so that he could dominate the class both physically and intellectually. In a course in humanities (which ought to develop student sensitivity to the good, the true, and the beautiful), the fifty-minute class hour was devoted to hearing three students read papers, seemingly copied from encyclopedias and dealing with historical figures of Western civilization. The only audible sound at the end of each reading was the scratch of the professor's pen inscribing the appropriate grade in the grade book. In one course in modern algebra, offered to thirty students, the professor spent the entire hour at the blackboard, back to the class, scrawling the proofs to three problems. Eye contact took place perhaps every five to seven minutes as the instructor turned quickly, gazed at the class, and queried, "Okay?"

A sampling of over forty classes taught in nineteen institutions revealed that lecture was the predominant mode, pedestrian dullness the predominant style, and student lassitude the predominant spirit. The two classes judged as outstanding were, nonetheless, lectures, but the lecturers had been able to discover techniques of gaining some student participation, even in 150-student courses (see Dressel and Mayhew, 1954b).

The age of innovation and reform during the 1960s and 1970s produced a few attempts to use technological devices and some techniques for ensuring participation, such as games. On the whole, however, classes across the country remained much the same. In widely proclaimed experimental colleges, lecturing prevailed but in a somewhat less organized style than in the more traditional institutions. Lecturing also prevailed in the nontraditional institutions and programs, although it took place much less frequently than in traditional institutions because classes met so infrequently. Here and there were such bright spots as use of television monitors linked to computers instead of the traditional blackboard to demonstrate problem-solving in a graduate school of business; a new approach to language instruction stressing small classes and much activity; and the videotaping of an entire lecture-course on the subject of women and the law.

Nor did the system change during the 1980s. The typical freshman college course consisted of thirty or more students in each class taught by means of lecturing. The same pattern was observed in church-related colleges, in many prestigious colleges and universities, and in a sampling of nontraditional programs. In some, lecturing was more precise than in others, but whether the courses were offered to students who were eighteen to twenty-two years old or to fatigued adults attending an evening course in a community college, the teaching was basically a single faculty member transmitting information, insight, and occasionally inspiration to groups of relatively passive persons.

Lest this review appear to be a caricature, we point out that occasional classes could be observed in which a lecturer held an audience spellbound or in which the lecturer was able to engage a full class in an active dialectic, and, in most classes students seemed reasonably satisfied with the instructor's performance and with their own achievement of rather idiosyncratic educational goals and objectives.

What can be made of all this? Although one can find quite elaborate lists of behavioral objectives for undergraduate collegiate education, what actually takes place in college courses is the attempt to transfer knowledge, as C. Robert Pace (1979, p. 173) has remarked. He believed "that the acquisition of knowledge is the primary, and certainly the most obvious aim of college courses and curriculum. Professors seek to impart knowledge of facts and principles, of generalizations and concepts, of ways of thinking about phenomena, of interpretations of data and meanings, of underlying assumptions, and similar information and processes related to the subject matter of their courses."

The same point is made somewhat differently by Russell Kirk (1965), who pointed out that the undergraduate liberal-arts curriculum is essentially literary, that is, most of the work done consists of reading and trying to comprehend ideas provided through written expression. Many will argue that such a conception of undergraduate education is excessively narrow, and that college courses should seek to develop ethical standards, psychological adjustment, better interpersonal relationships, a deepened sense of personal values, and sympathy for many different kinds of people. All of these are laudable and commendable elements of human development, but are college teachers and college courses appropriate instruments to facilitate achievement of such goals?

During the twentieth century, college teachers have been prepared for their role through graduate study of some discipline. Whether the degree earned is a master's or a doctoral degree, graduate students learn a great deal about some subject; doctoral students, especially, learn a considerable amount about doing research in a subject so that more knowledge can be obtained. Graduate students learn about teaching primarily from five to ten years of observing their own teachers, and they typically model their subsequent teaching behavior after the characteristics of their own teachers with whom they identified. In relatively few situations do graduate students take courses in the psychology of learning, in methods of teaching, or in the history and purposes of higher education. Graduate education essentially deals with the study of some subject in reasonable depth to prepare people subsequently to teach that same subject to others. The methods to be used in teaching those subjects will be developed by models, occasionally through teaching experience while still a graduate student, but usually through trial and error during the early years of a teaching career.

This kind of preparation appears to develop some basic ability on the part of college professors to perform their essential tasks. Those tasks include the selection of knowledge to be incorporated into a course, the organization of that knowledge, the transmission of that knowledge, and the rendering of assistance to students to enable them to understand better the complexity of that knowledge. College teachers do seem to affect the development of higher mental processes but usually in the context of a given body of knowledge. They also should, and frequently do, impose standards both by evaluation of student performance and by their own personal behavior and example. Additionally, college teachers living within the academic community have the power to influence through friendship and personal interaction. The traits needed for this activity are those developed throughout the teacher's lifetime. However, the quality of performance of each of these activities always can be improved. Better written materials can be found and organized more clearly. Techniques for the transmission of knowledge can be improved, as can problems designed to facilitate development of the critical thinking processes. Desired standards can be clarified so that students know what is expected. A variety of approaches to such improvement will be discussed later.

There are, however, many desirable activities that college teachers are not competent to perform merely by virtue of their academic preparation and emotional orientation. Perhaps 20 percent or more of college students experience a debilitating level of free-floating anxiety. Certainly, the student in the traditional college age group (eighteen to twenty-two years old) is trying to understand his or her own sexuality, emotional development, and changing relationships with others. However, college teachers possess only a common-sense ability to assist them with such matters, an ability acquired through the process of becoming an adult. The intensive study of French literature does not qualify a professor to deal with student loneliness; the mastery of U.S. intellectual history does not prepare a professor to help students deal with sexual problems; and a doctorate in physics is no preparation for professional involvement in group dynamics. In short, nothing in the formal education of college teachers prepares them to be psychotherapists, psychometricians, social workers, pastors, or learning theorists. Therefore, to expect college teachers to develop through practice into such specialists is inconsistent with the reasons that people become college teachers in the first place. They become college teachers because they enjoy the in-depth study of some subject that they believe will be valuable for someone else to learn. Occasionally, a college teacher will learn some skills by reading in the literature of developmental psychology or a professor will develop diagnostic and therapeutic skills as an avocation, but such exceptions have been rare in the past and will probably be equally rare in the future despite the exhortations of some educational reformers.

Prescriptions Without Value

Since 1940, the literature concerning collegiate education has been replete with the exhortation that teaching must be improved, although frequently the writer has failed to indicate the needed steps to accomplish this goal. When they are specific, criticisms of college teaching and suggestions for its improvement have taken one of three forms. The first is a kind of generalized anxiety and belief that college teaching is not as good as it might be, and that, somehow, it can be improved. Typical of the demand is the plea of Rosecrance (1962, p. 189): "The improvement of college teaching is central to the improvement of higher education and deserves more attention than it has heretofore received. Students come to college to learn from persons whose scholarship is greater than their own. They deserve the best that can be provided. The institution itself depends in great part on the quality of the faculty, and the instruction given by it."

This theme of discussing the significance and centrality of teaching and its poor actual state was found repeatedly in educational conferences throughout the 1940s and 1950s. W. Francis English, in 1955, quoted the educational editor of the *New York Times,* Benjamin Fine, as saying that no more than 10 percent of college professors do an adequate teaching job, and then English continued, as follows: "The charge is not new; the story of yellow notes of ancient vintage being the sources of uninspired, mumbling lectures is an old one. Unfortunately, it too often characterizes classroom performance, but there is no evidence that it predominates. There has been a great deal of inspired, adequate and solid teaching going on in American college classrooms. There needs to be more, and we hope it can become nearly universal. We must encourage it, talk about it, plan ways and means of bringing it about, and reward it when it happens" (p. 93).

A decade later, Bruce Dearing (1965, p. 116) would point out the irony in an extraordinarily wealthy and talented system of higher education in which the quality of undergraduate teaching was rarely praised. Instead, there was throughout the land a flight from teaching and an often expressed fear that the quality of undergraduate education was in decline.

A second category of criticism asserts that there is too much lecturing, that lecturing is not done very well, that the lecture does not provide adequately for individual differences, that too much use is made of teaching assistants, that a doctoral degree is a research degree that does not prepare people to be teachers, and that, therefore, teaching is somehow bad.

Throughout the forty years from 1940 to 1980, there were repeated criticisms that the Ph.D. was a research degree and therefore not entirely satisfactory as preparation for college teachers. Some critics argued that there should be a degree especially designed to prepare people for the role of undergraduate teacher. The obvious assumption is that somehow, mysteriously, formal instruction in pedagogy or an increase in understanding of the use of educational technology will result in improved instruction. During the 1950s, some institutions tried to create divisional Ph.D.'s, but these attempts did not last, primarily because faculties insisted that candidates for the divisional Ph.D. in physical science, for example, be required to take the same course required of those seeking a Ph.D. in physics and a Ph.D. in chemistry. During that same period, partly in response to Ford Foundation grants, some institutions tried to create an enriched master's degree designed for undergraduate teachers, especially at the lower-division level.

During the late 1960s and the 1970s, a few institutions experimented with a Doctor of Arts degree to prepare teachers of undergraduate education. This degree allowed students to study several related disciplines and to study the history and philosophy of higher education, as well as courses dealing with collegiate pegagogy. In a few institutions, the Doctor of Arts degree flourished, primarily as a part-time program allowing people already teaching in community colleges, for example, to acquire a doctoral degree. However, even apologists for the degree were unable to document widespread adoption of the degree, and the number of individuals receiving it remained relatively small compared with the thousands receiving the Ph.D. degree each year. Perhaps the Doctor of Arts degree could have assumed prominence if the whole decade of the 1970s had been characterized by a shortage of college teachers. However, the shortage disappeared by 1970, and the oversupply of graduates with doctoral degrees became serious by the end of that decade. That oversupply placed the Doctor of Arts degree in direct competition with the far more prestigious Ph.D. degree. Most institutions, given the choice of a Ph.D. or a Doctor of Arts for a new appointment, usually would choose the candidate with the Ph.D. — simply because, one suspects, of the great prestige of the American Ph.D.

The third category of criticism is that college teaching is deficient because it does not attend to the many facets of human development and is not based on psychological knowledge and research. Such criticism contends that college teachers should, but do not, attend to the developmental needs of college students, to the social and psychological dynamics of the classroom situation, or to traumatic behaviors (such as the use of grades as a force to motivate student behavior). Much of this criticism derives from psychological and psychoanalytic theory. For example, Joseph Katz (1962, p. 386) borrowed the concept of transference from the clinic: "Transference is a phenomenon that many teachers (and students) would rather not have exist. It introduces a bothersome element into the supposedly dispassionate intercourse of minds. Yet it is a potent vehicle for learning, mislearning, and not learning. Resistance to the teacher needs as careful attention in college learning as does resistance to the therapist in psychotherapy."

Proponents of these reforms either premise their arguments on the assertion that traditional modes of teaching are wrong and very likely destructive or on the premise that radically new approaches to teaching are necessary as new kinds of students enroll in colleges and universities. They argue from the premise that traditional colleges and universities must accommodate the quite different needs of these new students, who are described as less able, less achieving, less economically secure, and older than traditional students. Especially high on their list of priorities is for higher education to give explicit curricular and instructional attention to issues in human relations and the development of better personal skills. They argue that people express in all kinds of ways their feelings of inadequacy in their relationships with co-workers, family, and friends. Since participation in personal growth seminars and in interpersonal relations workshops is unprecedented, they conclude that the potential for helping all students, new and traditional, to improve interpersonal skills is very great. Although most of the research shows that college students do gain interpersonal skills throughout their college careers, their education in this area is more by accident or coincidence than by design, and it appears to be the result of group living and close acquaintance with a variety of people. Because strong trends toward nonresidential education may decrease even the present feeble attempts to help people improve their ability to relate to other people, these reformers argue that conscious attention must be given to both adequacy and excellence in the development of interpersonal skills.

Responding to such criticism would require setting significantly new goals and developing new competencies on the part of faculty. How they expect college teachers generally to develop responsible expertise in this essentially therapeutic activity is not mentioned; they only plead that it should be done. Apparently, they assume that disciplinary-trained faculty members can and will develop skills to formally conduct T-groups and sensitivity-training encounters in order to help college students realize that the development of feeling and emotion is a goal equal in value to that of obtaining knowledge and intellectual development.

Such psychologically based criticism is particularly vulnerable because few professors in the arts and sciences and in the most professional fields have relevant training or experience. Moreover, many lack motivation to achieve psychological insights beyond those that accumulate through years of teaching experience. To expect a professor of engineering, economics, French, or history to use role-playing, group dynamics, sensitivity training, or even nondirective teaching is to expect much more than many mortal men or women can demonstrate. If it requires a lifetime of study to acquire and maintain an understanding of American history, where is the time to become sophisticated psychologically and sociopsychologically?

These reformers essentially call for all professors to become learning psychologists. Their goals can be discovered through a discussion of individualized learning, mastery learning, and cognitive styles, since these are arenas in which their theories often get translated into prescriptions. The principles of individualized instruction are as follows: (1) The student must be an active rather than a passive learner. (2) The goals of learning must be clear and must be made explicit to the student. (3) The desirability of small lesson-units (frequently referred to as learning-modules) is closely related to the need for course objectives. (4) Effective learning requires feedback and evaluation. (5) Individual differences in rate of learning must be recognized and accommodated. Hence, all approaches to individualized instruction feature self-pacing, that is, permitting the learner to control the pace of the presentation. In moments of candor, the reformers may admit that college teachers may not possess some of the skills and understanding needed and that few teachers or counselors know anything at all about cognitive styles, despite the fact that research on cognitive styles has been going on for twenty-five years in some psychology laboratories. Yet they obviously want professors to cope with a variety of dimensions of cognitive style, such as field independence versus field dependence, scanning, breadth of categorizing, conceptualizing styles, cognitive complexity versus simplicity, reflectiveness versus impulsivity, leveling versus sharpening, constricted versus flexible control, and tolerance for incongruous or unrealistic experiences. In these approaches, the teacher assumes the role of manager: he or she prepares materials, diagnoses, prescribes, motivates, and serves as a resource for the student. The emphasis is on learning, rather than on teaching.

The concept of behavioral objectives has loomed large in educational literature since the end of World War II. There appear to be a variety of legitimate skills and objectives that college and university professors are competent to seek, and the necessary technologies are available for the achievement of these goals. For undergraduate students, these necessities would include skills of reading, writing, speaking, and calculating. In professional programs, the necessary abilities include the full variety of skills needed for professional practice, such as surveying, taking medical histories, developing a legal brief, or doing dental extractions. Beyond those skills, professors can probably consciously seek three major objectives with respect to courses taught: possession of considerable knowledge about the subject, in-depth understanding of the subject, and development and application of materials on the subject in emerging situations. College professors, over time, can develop ways of seeking to achieve those outcomes, but neither classroom time nor professorial background and experience will allow explicit effort to achieve more refined and elaborated kinds of behavioral objectives. Student achievement of those objectives usually will not come from explicit exercises to achieve each one, but rather achievement will come over time from a deepening of knowledge and understanding and from the ability to apply them.

Clearly, some comment regarding educational technology and quality of teaching is appropriate. Advocates of educational technology see its use as revolutionizing education through the use of radio, open- and closed-circuit television, videotapes, audiotapes, computer-based instruction, and the use of satellites to reach distant educational markets. They also see a fourth revolution in education as research on the uses of technology reveals that in many situations technology-based instruction produces measurable and significant changes in people. Entire courses can be videotaped and offered in remote areas. Computers can be programmed to interact with students — sometimes more effectively than a human teacher can interact.

However, for a variety of reasons, educational technology probably will remain in a supportive or enriching role relative to the classroom instruction in colleges and universities, rather than serving as a replacement for such instruction. First is the matter of sheer cost; while the cost of technology is decreasing, every comprehensive study of costs indicates that the total cost of instruction based on technology is higher than the total cost of traditional classroom instruction, and there is no evidence that the educational outcomes are great enough to warrant the additional cost. The use of technology is economically warranted where high-cost, technology-based instruction is mixed with less expensive instruction to yield a sustainable cost (for example, in a carefully conceived, computerized, simulation game of political processes). However, it becomes affordable only when linked with the most cost-effective, large lecture class to provide the basic information and understanding.

Technology can provide many critical services. Word processors can facilitate composition of papers; computers can solve problems and facilitate bibliographic searches; videotape recordings of teachers can show them ways to improve their performance; and a credit course delivered over open-circuit television can reach thousands of students in an urban area. However, even using those techniques places an economic cost and an additional burden on faculty members that they probably will not accept willingly. Eble (1972, p. 81) captured reality with these remarks: "Teachers will continue to do the easiest thing, both because of natural inclination and because of the many demands made on their time. Slide and computer freaks will continue

to put on dazzling shows; some of their expertise will rub off
on other teachers. But we have a long way to go before any of
the electronic media — even the tape recorder and the projector —
become natural parts of instruction."

Equally as demanding as the idea that professors should
develop many new skills not generated by their own academic
preparation is the doctrine of a systems approach to teaching.
In simple terms, this approach posits that instructors should
develop lists of quite specific behaviors that they wish to produce,
carefully select the teaching techniques most likely to produce
those changes, and skillfully prepare and use measuring instruments designed to demonstrate whether the behaviors have been
modified. This doctrine derived from theories developed by
Ralph W. Tyler (1932), and it is exemplified by the long list
of possible objectives presented by Bloom (1950). As a general
way of thinking about the task of instruction, the approach has
much to commend it. However, subsequent advocates seem to
imply that the act of teaching can become almost a science, and
that there are specific ways to develop each of a wide variety
of specific objectives. Planning for an hour of classroom instruction would involve specifying a substantial number of objectives
and a specific instructional intervention for each of them.

The variety of sources of radical recommendations for improvement of college teaching is great. Some derive from psycho-
analysis and would have professors use almost therapeutic methods. Others derive from behaviorist psychology and would have
professors function with the precision of a psychologist conducting a controlled experiment. Religion is the source of some, and
these suggestions would have professors assume almost a nearly
pastoral role in helping students deal with ethical dilemmas. Still
others almost derive from physiology and would have professors
tailor their teaching to affect a specific hemisphere of the brain.
All these approaches assume a willingness on the part of college faculty members, over time, to develop the requisite new
skills.

One of the most frequently urged administrative reforms
is modification of the academic reward system so that the act
of teaching is regarded as a high and valuable calling. The argu-

ment is made that the rewards of promotion, tenure, and salary increase are based primarily on research productivity; hence, faculty members are encouraged to devote more time to research and less to teaching. This argument is somewhat spurious, since most faculty members do little research beyond keeping up with their subject and preparing for their courses. Furthermore, the argument rests on the unestablished premise that research and teaching are incompatible. A reasonable argument can be made that, rather than being at odds, research, scholarship, and teaching are highly interactive activities—improvement in one is quickly reflected in improvement in another. Thus, the active and productive researcher is constantly gaining new insights with which to enlighten teaching, and the professor actively examining the frontiers of his or her subject is likely to be a more interesting teacher than the one who continues to reiterate knowledge obtained as a graduate student. In some institutions, a reward system that stresses research may produce an imbalance in the expenditure of faculty time and energy, but there is virtually no evidence that the time devoted to teaching in such cases is inferior in quality.

In addition to the predominant reward system, institutions frequently attempt to provide other administrative incentives to encourage greater attention to the skills of the college teacher. Some make titular or financial awards for outstanding teachers, while others provide released faculty time to improve teaching techniques. Many institutions have adopted systems of formal student evaluation of teaching, the results of which are reviewed by faculty superiors and placed in the faculty member's permanent file. It seems reasonable that the existence of these incentives may stimulate individuals to think more about their teaching activities and behavior. However, although most college teachers as undergraduates did not plan to enter college teaching as a career, they probably brought to teaching some pleasure in that work and desire to do it well. It is difficult to imagine a professor not responding emotionally to student evaluation that is either highly complimentary or sharply critical. College teachers generally rank teaching as their predominant activity and source of satisfaction. It is likewise difficult to imag-

ine a professor not experiencing feelings of pride after a successful lecture; a feeling that in itself can lead to attempts to improve
other lectures. In a sense, then, incentives may simply inten-
sify the urge for improvement already present in individuals.

During the 1960s and 1970s, many institutions made structural provisions to express a concern for the improvement of
teaching. Some created centers for the improvement of instruction that offered professors help in lecturing skills, test development, and the preparation and use of audiovisual aids. These
centers frequently are given budgets to allocate small sums to
faculty members to experiment with some new teaching device
or approach. The testimony of directors of such centers indicates
that they are used by some faculty members and that particularly
the grants for experimentation are judged as useful by recipients.
However, the relatively small size of the center staffs in large
institutions suggests that center services are used by only a
minority of active faculty.

Other institutions have created offices variously labeled
dean of undergraduate studies or dean of instruction, which are
assigned to give administrative attention to undergraduate teachers. These officers frequently have small budgets to be used to
stimulate development of new courses and to provide released
time for professors to develop new approaches. The participation
of these officers in high administrative councils probably ensures
that educational concerns receive executive attention, just as
fiscal concerns do. Still other institutions place retired professors
with great reputations in teaching positions on partial salary
to enable them to consult with active professors on the problems
and perplexities of teaching. Some institutions have developed
a program permitting professors to visit each other's classes and
to discuss pedagogical questions and issues. Testimony from such
institutions suggests that, over time, classroom visits cease
to be threatening and become helpful and even enjoyable. In
some institutions, there is a videotape service that allows professors to have their own classes videotaped and then examine
the recordings in hopes of improving performance. Other techniques to encourage professors to improve their skills include
creation of libraries of books on higher education and college

teaching and on-campus discussions with visiting professors who are known to be superior teachers.

Over all, these administrative and structural arrangements probably have been symbolically important. They are relatively inexpensive ways of emphasizing the importance of good teaching and probably have stimulated self-improvement efforts by some active professors. The continuation of these efforts can be recommended sincerely so long as educational leaders do not expect them to produce a radical transformation of the pedagogical climate.

Prescriptions with Value

Much more plausible from the standpoint of suggesting ways to improve college teaching are the common-sense recommendations advanced by Jacques Barzun (1981), Wilbert I. McKeachie (1978), and Kenneth F. Eble (1972). These recommendations assume that the primary concern of college teachers is intellectual development, although they recognize that teaching oriented toward intellectual development can produce an affect on emotions, personality, and deeply held values. They also assume that collegiate pedagogy will typically employ a limited number of instruments: lecturing, discussions, formal assignments, laboratory exercises, and tests and grading. Therefore, it seems clear that a major step in the improvement of the quality of college teaching would be to ensure that every college teacher had a reasonable and growing mastery of the appropriate subject matter, together with a true competency in the basic skills of speaking, listening, responding, testing, and grading. The burden of the message of the common-sense reformers is that the use of these skills can be improved. Eble (1972, p. 36) most clearly exemplified this general position: "Despite the vast collective experience teachers can draw upon, there are still genuine questions as to whether teaching can be reduced to any set of essentials. The individuality of the teacher and of the students, the particular characteristics of subject matter, the multiple goals of learning, the contexts of teaching and learning — all seem to defy any clear statement about how a good teacher should go about the task." He then enumerated the characteristics of a good teacher as humility, generosity, sheer energy, ability to perform, variety, enthusiasm, knowledge, honesty, and a sense of proportion. Eble's approach to teaching was captured by the title of one of his books, *The Craft of Teaching* (1976). In jargon-free chapters, he presented plausible praise for use of the classroom, lecturing, conducting discussions, using seminars, tutorials, advising, selecting texts, making assignments, administering tests, and assigning grades. In many respects, the best suggestion to improve college teaching would be a recommendation that all teachers periodically read Eble's *The Craft of Teaching* (1976) and Wilbert J. McKeachie's *Teaching Tips* (1978).

Rather than urging that college teachers undertake activities for which they are unprepared (and which they may not want), improvement in teaching can be attempted through policies and recommendations encouraging faculty members to do those tasks for which they are prepared. Improvement of teaching might be achieved through institutions demanding more rigorous academic preparation of those appointed to teach. This would mean that all institutions, including two-year colleges, would seek faculty members holding the doctoral degree, either in the arts and sciences or in professional fields. If institutions were unable to recruit applicants with doctoral degrees, they could seek those who had earned master's degrees in subjects they were expected to teach and who had completed at least one full academic year of course work above the level of courses they would be expected to teach. Following the logic of this recommendation, the Doctor of Arts degree holder, possessing a teaching major and a related teaching minor, would not be as attractive as a Ph.D. holder (because of the in-depth preparation in a single subject the latter has) but somewhat more attractive than the applicant who holds a master's degree in a single subject. The rationale for this is that effectiveness in a classroom is related to the depth and sophistication of knowledge of the instructor. The instructor's knowledge of a subject generates the enthusiasm that appears to be so critical for effective teaching.

Rigorous academic preparation, which is strongly desirable for full-time teachers, should be required also for the growing number of part-time faculty. One of the major weaknesses of the part-time or external degree programs is that the part-time faculty members too frequently have had less intensive academic preparation than the full-time faculty in the same institution. Students would be well served if institutions demanded that part-time faculty be appointed through screening procedures exactly like those employed for full-time faculty. The director of an off-campus program would not be allowed to appoint part-time faculty members whose credentials had not been carefully reviewed through established procedures on the home campus.

An important technique is repeated here because of its significance: development of the belief in all kinds of institutions that an important use of professorial time is to engage in some significant form of research and scholarship. If college teaching is to be improved, remedial action will come from the professors who seek a constantly deepening understanding of their subjects. This means that every single week, ideally, every professor should spend some reasonable amount of time in research and scholarship related to the subjects that he or she teaches. Eventually, this would mean that evidence of research and scholarship would be used in making decisions about retention, promotion, tenure, and salary increases.

It probably would be desirable, although not imperative, that graduate students receive some supervised teaching experience during their graduate study. Graduate students have been closely observing teaching for seventeen or more years, and this diffuse experience is probably more influential than a single semester or year of supervised teaching, during which most of the student's energy is still expended on graduate study itself. The real preparation for college teaching is a combination of those long years spent observing others, and the trial-and-error experiences obtained during the first five to ten years of actual teaching. Graduate students should also be allowed to take courses on the characteristics of college students, methods of teaching, or the nature and history of higher education. Knowledge about college students and college institutions might ease the adjustment of young faculty members. However, effective teaching is probably the result of the style of the college teacher, developed over time, and there are as many different styles as there are faculty members. Style is developed with experience and not through the superficial acquisition of a few skills or ideas learned in brief courses on psychology and pedagogy.

One effective way to improve the quality of college teaching is for faculty members to make more precise and rigorous demands on student performance. During the 1960s and 1970s, a great deal of attention was given to the allegations that materials assigned to students to study were frequently irrelevant to student interests and needs; that tests and examinations frequently required rote memory of information that would be forgotten immediately afterwards; that graduation requirements were frequently based on such noneducational reasons as departmental desire to increase enrollments; and that many course requirements demanded skills and traits not possessed by many new or nontraditional students. Using psychological theory more than empirical evidence, the radical reformers urged that students participate in developing their own work assignments and use their own satisfaction to evaluate their performance. Much of the essence of the nontraditional movement was to remove the rigor and the constraints of previously imposed requirements so that the nontraditional student could participate in ways particularly appropriate for him or her. However, we believe that the solution to inadequate test materials and assignments should be the improvement of their quality and precision, not their elimination. The answer to capricious graduation requirements should be to make them more defensible, rather than to remove them.

If a realistic view of teaching (as expressed earlier) is accepted, that acceptance dictates the direction of reform. If the professor accepts the fact that the primary objectives are knowledge, understanding, and the ability to apply it, then materials can be selected and assignments made that are clearly designed to facilitate achievement of those three goals. Similarly, if test questions are carefully designed to determine the student's knowledge, understanding, and ability to relate these findings to new situations, tests will have a powerful effect on student approaches to learning.

Several issues remain. Some urge a futurist posture with respect to college teaching, suggesting that significant changes will take place as a result of technology. However, despite the prophecies of aficionados of educational technology, no persuasive evidence shows that computer-assisted, individualized instruction is likely to replace classroom teachers or that videotaped courses will ever challenge the successful tradition of professor, classroom, textbook, and group of students. Similarly, it does not seem likely that college professors generally will adopt new roles suggested by the recently developed psychological theories.

Several promising developments, however, can be used to help the average college or university professor to become somewhat more proficient. The first of these developments is the increased emphasis on some efforts to evaluate teaching in the belief that those efforts will almost inevitably stimulate professors to think more about their classroom skills. In many respects, the one quasi-revolutionary development during the 1960s and 1970s was the widespread adoption of student course evaluation and the administrative use of those results. Suddenly faculty members, even in the major research universities, began to think about teaching and even occasionally to talk about it. This enhanced significance of the concept of pedagogy led many to experiment with such simple refinements as joint teaching of courses, duplication and advance distribution of lecture notes, more carefully coordinated bibliographies and course topics, and more carefully prepared examinations. Thus deans and presidents wishing to do something about college teaching might use their considerable influence to institutionalize the practice of student evaluation of teaching and then further to institutionalize other approaches to evaluation, including reports by the teachers themselves, their peers, and administrators.

A somewhat more difficult, but possible, development is the generation of an ethos in all kinds of institutions that professors should expect to spend a reasonable amount of time advising students and working with them in face-to-face consultation. We do not advocate that professors become psychological counselors or therapists, but we do suggest that if most students could experience a one-to-one relationship with one faculty member, the overall intellectual climate of an institution would probably improve.

In summary, we are saying that college teaching is an important, but limited, activity, capable of producing some distinguished outcomes but not intended to produce an infinite variety of outcomes. Some college teachers, as mature adults, can provide some nurturing to some students. However, this service should be viewed as the product of adulthood, rather than a part of the professional role of college professor. Basically, a college professor should introduce students to a subject, transmit information about that subject, help students to think about the subject, and encourage students to deepen their own comprehension and understanding. The subject taught should be selected in the belief that studying it will be useful for the intellectual growth and maturation of the student. For the average college professor, teaching is not a set of behaviors requiring assimilation of esoteric theories and technology; it is rather a type of human activity that can be improved in the same way that other basic human activities are improved — through efforts to enhance a limited number of skills.

If one adopts such a realistic view of teaching, the number of techniques to be mastered is reduced. As this chapter suggests, the future of college teaching is quite likely to resemble, in most detail, those practices that have prevailed for almost a century. In the final analysis, teaching excellence will continue to be primarily a product of the individual temperament, style, beliefs, and attitudes of the professor. Those elements are acquired over a lifetime, and collegiate administrators can do little except encourage their development and treasure the successes achieved.

EIGHT

Strengthening
Academic Leadership

The only entity that can actually restore and maintain academic quality in American higher education is the individual campus. Governmental policy formulation or the recommendations of national commissions will not enhance quality unless such recommendations are accepted and acted on by individuals and their institutions. Therefore, since leadership is critical to effective group action, an important step in improving academic quality is to restore to college and university presidents some necessary powers and prerogatives that have been diminished during the last three decades.

Historical Overview of the College Presidency

The traditional American university presidency, with its relative strength vis-à-vis other constituencies, resulted from the importation and marriage of two very different concepts regarding institutional governance. On the one hand, the unique roots for a lay board of trustees with absolute responsibility for conducting and maintaining an institution can be traced back at least to A.D. 1240 and the founding of the Brotherhood of Mercy in Florence, Italy. For seven centuries, a lay governing board

159

and an unpaid administrator have directed the voluntary members of this organization, usually referred to as the Misericordia, who agreed to contribute one hour per week to community service (see Houle, 1989, p. 3). Using similar arrangements to control educational institutions also seems to have originated in medieval Italy, where universities were initially created and run by students, until civil authorities assumed the responsibilities because student autocracy had become oppressive. City-state government, in turn, created essentially lay boards to oversee university affairs. The idea spread north through Switzerland and ultimately to Holland and Scotland, where lay control was consistent with ultimate lay control of Calvinistic Protestant churches. On the other hand, the idea of one individual as the sole spokesman for an entire institution seems to have originated in the office of rector of the University of Paris, who was responsible for watching the purse strings, convening the faculties, and certifying graduation and faculty appointment. Over time, the role was reinterpreted by the heads of colleges at Oxford and Cambridge and was then transplanted to the American colonies. In the colonies, the two elements came together, with a single or double board of trustees (or overseers) and a president to whom major responsibility was delegated. Once again, the combination seems to have gained strength from its consistency with the governance of the Calvinistic churches, whose boards of elders assigned considerable discretion to the pastor for the conduct of ecclesiastical affairs.

The emergence of the American college responsible for virtually all its own activities was, in large part, a product of frontier conditions characterized by poor transportation, limited communication channels, and a lack of available professional faculty members. Especially after the American Revolutionary War, as new colleges were created on the trans-Allegheny frontier, presidents acted at some distance from any scrutiny by members of boards of trustees, and they recruited as instructors quite young and inexperienced tutors who were no match for the professional qualifications of the president. Characterized by isolation and many responsibilities, the president's role quickly became a multifaceted one in which the president built the college building, cultivated college farms, solicited the college library, recruited and enrolled students, saw to their moral development, taught the major courses, conducted necessary examinations, and ultimately conferred the degrees. A good description of typical presidential duties is found in the chapter on the president in the Laws of the University of Nashville:

1. To the president is committed the general superintendence of the interests and reputation of the university, which he is bound to promote and maintain by every exertion in his power.
2. He is, ex officio, president of the board of trustees, and of the faculty, when present with them, and also the administrator of their decisions in cases of discipline.
3. He has the right to be present at the recitation of any class within the institution as often as he may see proper, and to conduct or hear recitation if he chooses.
4. He will take such branches of instruction into his own hands as he may judge that the number of other teachers and the exigencies of the institution shall render necessary and expedient.
5. All the religious exercises and studies of the university are committed to his direction: and the other members of the faculty are required to render him such assistance as may be deemed necessary to the punctual and faithful discharge of their duties.
6. He is to preside at examinations and commencements, and to confer all degrees [Schmidt, 1930, p. 54].

Presidents continued to do those things almost single-handedly throughout much of the nineteenth century, until enrollments began to expand and institutions became more complex. Then, presidents began to create subordinate offices, such as those held by deans, directors, and eventually vice-presidents.

From the office of dean flowed a variety of administrative sub-specialties (for example, dean of men, dean of admissions, dean of the faculty, dean of administration, registrar, and academic dean). However, the gradual appointments of these new assistants diminished neither the presidential responsibility for all activities nor the willingness of presidents to exercise those responsibilities.

That model of a dominating president would be emulated by the great entrepreneurial presidents of the late nineteenth century, through whose leadership the face and complexion of higher education would be changed for all time. In very similar ways, Andrew Dickson White (Cornell), James Burrill Angell (Michigan), and Daniel Coit Gilman (the University of California and Johns Hopkins University) all converted the university presidency, whose historic role was one of benevolent authoritarianism, into a position of great prestige and authority. Well-respected by other leaders in society, they put their imprint on the academic undertakings of their institutions. The personification of a strong educational officer was William Rainey Harper, who, with the financial backing of John D. Rockefeller, built the University of Chicago almost to his own design and in his own image. He decided on the design of buildings and the educational program; he established and maintained institutional priorities that stressed the primacy of research and ensured the financial vitality of the institution. He perceived the importance of an independent faculty to guide the curriculum, but he ensured that the curriculum always conformed to his own ideas. His concerns were universal: in a note he would propose a scholarly journal to a professor. He would review the thought of an educational scheme in a quarterly convocation statement. He would make a trip East to secure new members of the faculty. He alone was sure that the year-end deficit would somehow be taken care of (Frodlin, 1950, p. 26).

To the ideal of presidential omnipotence, exemplified by the entrepreneurial presidents of the nineteenth century, were wedded several other elements adding to the authoritarian centrality of the college or university president. Regardless of the type of institution, the model of the paternalistic and authoritarian public school superintendent became the model for normal schools turned into teacher's colleges and in time became the model for public junior colleges (whose presidents typically had been public school superintendents). In the church-related colleges (especially Catholic colleges), the considerable authority of heads of religious orders was simply adapted to college affairs as the head of the sponsoring order either became the head or designated the head of the sponsored college or university.

Another strand of potential influence on the role of college president is more difficult to document, although Thorstein Veblen came to believe it was predominant. This was the ideal of the corporate president wielding great power from the office itself, with that influence reinforced and intensified through a hierarchical bureaucracy. Certainly, twentieth-century presidents — a notable example is Chancellor Litchfield of the University of Pittsburgh — sought to model their administrations after the corporate ideal by appointing layer after layer of administrative officers who functioned in a highly bureaucratic manner.

By the end of World War I, the typical college or university president was influenced by several role models: religious leaders who felt paternalistically responsible for all their flock — faculty, students, or workers; the authoritarian small-college president; entrepreneurial presidents who, with adequate financial backing, created a new kind of institution; public school principals and superintendents who considered faculty members as quite interchangeable parts; and corporate executives accustomed to having their commands carried out by a well-organized bureaucracy. Nonetheless, since presidents increasingly came from the ranks of the professoriate, they understood the faculty point of view and recognized faculty contributions to academic values. Thus, in general, they did provide for consultation with faculties and did create organizations for the expression of faculty opinion. However, overall, college and university presidents viewed themselves as being individually responsible for their institutions and competent and able to decide on all issues — great and small. This self-image is illustrated by a cluster of twentieth-century presidents who single-handedly produced profound changes in their institution.

Arthur Morgan (Antioch College) and James Madison Woods (Stephens College) both became presidents when their institutions were in serious decline and facing bankruptcy and closure. Each had definite educational ideas and sublime confidence in his own wisdom and judgment. They quickly eliminated trustees who were unsympathetic with their visions for the futures of their institutions. They personally selected new board members and undertook faculty recruitment as an essential presidential prerogative. Thus, James Madison Woods sought interesting faculty members who shared his beliefs — regardless of their academic credentials. Both leaders felt free to create radical new programs and to staff them — even at the expense of, and over the opposition of, teaching faculties. Morgan single-handedly created the cooperative work-study program under which all students would alternate between academic work on-campus and supervised work experience off-campus. Woods saw admissions as the key to the role he had in mind for Stephens and created perhaps the first elaborate admissions office, with admissions counselors working all parts of the country and selling his educational program. Several decisions President Woods made without consultation illustrate the style of both these leaders. Woods felt free to appoint a consultant and instruct the consultant to design a full, new curriculum for Stephens College. He also would cancel all classes for a day if he believed campus morale was declining. He would tour the country searching for new faculty members and would make an appointment on the spot whenever he found someone who appealed to him, and he maintained with equanimity relatively high salaries for his immediate administrative associates and markedly low salaries for his aging faculty. By the 1970s, such conduct was unthinkable for a college president.

Coming into office a few years later than Woods and Morgan, Robert M. Hutchins demonstrated a similar pattern of behavior, but some details differed, because of the basic differences between their teaching institutions and his research university. From its creation, the University of Chicago had emphasized research and advanced graduate education and, for the most part, had merely tolerated undergraduate education;

indeed, some faculty hoped that the undergraduate curriculum would eventually be removed from the university. Of course, Chicago also engaged in big-time athletics and maintained a rather large extension program. The subject of reform of undergraduate education at Chicago had been discussed repeatedly under several different presidents to little avail. Hutchins, however, in his inaugural address in 1929, announced his intention to bring about reform. Throughout the succeeding ten years, although Hutchins worked through existing faculty and policy-discussion groups, he managed to transform the undergraduate program at Chicago and to present to the nation a significant educational experiment.

Hutchins clearly believed that he was the executive head of the university and had authority to exercise such supervision and direction as would promote the efficiency of every department. In that capacity, he recommended and quickly gained approval of a radical reorganization of the structure and administration of the university, as an initial step in generating significant curricular reform. His accomplishments included the creation of a lower-division college embracing the last two years of high school and the first two years of college, the creation of a prescribed program in general education as the chief escort of the college, a reorganization of the rest of the university into four divisions, the creation of a board of examiners to prepare external examinations on which the award of academic credit would be based, the creation of a new administrative office — dean of students, and, in time, the creation of a faculty for the college separate from the faculties of the academic departments and divisions. All these developments differed significantly from prevailing practice and from the attitudes and beliefs of many members of the Chicago faculty. Yet, Hutchins was able to reach decisions about all of them, decisions that later presidents would have judged to be beyond the prerogatives of the university presidency. Hutchins believed that he should generate reform, that his educational ideas were valid, and that he knew better than anyone else which individuals should be appointed to administrative and professional positions. Furthermore, he was willing to confront faculty opposition intellectually and to use

the influence of his office and his support from the board of
trustees to gain victory. After leaving the University of Chicago,
Hutchins remarked that he probably had moved too rapidly to
ensure that his reforms would last; nevertheless, at the time of
his presidency, he had acted clearly in the tradition of leadership exerted by the first president of the University of Chicago,
William Rainey Harper, and with the belief that the role he
assumed vis-à-vis faculty was a proper one. In summary, the
elements of the Hutchins presidency were an imposing physical
presence, an educationally informed mind, a powerful and pro-
lific pen when addressing educational ideas, a belief in his own
ability to select people, a willingness to use a full range of administrative sanctions to obtain approval for what he wanted,
and strong support from the board of trustees.

Another president who personified the zenith of presidential influence in American higher education was J. Wallace Sterling, who was president of Stanford University for nineteen years.
His major achievement was to move Stanford from a position
as a strong, regional institution to a position among the most
outstanding world-class research universities and to do so in a
relatively short time. Sterling brought with him to Stanford a
relatively straightforward set of beliefs. He saw private higher
education as an intellectual mainstay of the society, which could
best be sustained through intellectually stronger faculties, more
able students, and a steadily increasing variety of programs made
possible through constantly expanding resources. He had great
respect for faculties and stated that faculties were essential in
directing institutional affairs; nonetheless, he saw himself as being able to chart the direction the institution should take and
to make those decisions necessary to propel the institution in
that direction. His administrative style was relaxed and involved
a great deal of informal consultation with those in whom he had
confidence. While he did not object to formal faculty structures,
he believed he could accomplish more through the relatively
small group of associates with whom he surrounded himself.
He trusted his own judgment about people and appointed people who shared his vision for the institution. Thus, he appointed
Frederick Terman as provost and supported Terman's effort to

upgrade faculty qualifications radically. He also trusted his own perceptions of changing conditions, which led him to increase the selectivity of students, move a medical school from San Francisco to the Stanford campus, create an office in Washington to help exploit expanding federal programs for the benefit of Stanford, undertake a major restudy of undergraduate education, create a long-range plan by which his goals could be realized, and strengthen fund-raising activities that would place the institution among the two or three most successful institutions in the country. During Sterling's administration, Stanford moved from adequacy to superiority in quality of faculty, quality of students, receipt of federal contracts, yield from private benefaction, effectiveness of management, and research productivity. Behind each of these achievements lay the decisions and labor of a strong university president.

This same sort of strong presidential leadership was not restricted to the well-known institutions. During the 1950s, Leland Medsker created the Diablo Valley campus in the Contra Costa Junior College District and made it quite unique among California junior colleges in that it had a well-contrived program in general education, a vigorous advising system, and a climate in which academic matters were freely discussed. Benjamin Mays and Stephen J. Wright were but two of several strong black presidents who left lasting impressions on the institutions over which they presided and influenced in significant ways the national discourse about the purposes of higher education, especially as they pertain to black Americans. Presidents Rosemary Park, Mary Bunting, and Millicent McIntosh were all distinguished female leaders in American higher education, and the institutions over which they presided maintained coherent, demanding curricula comparable with those found in the academically elite male and coeducational institutions.

The point we want to make here is that strong campus presidents can make a significant difference in the intellectual quality of their institutions, provided they are granted the prerogatives necessary to govern. The principal danger of this reality is that those needed prerogatives also may be given to presidents who would use their powers to make consistent mistakes leading to serious campus problems and deterioration of academic quality. During the 1950s, Chancellor Litchfield of the University of Pittsburgh attempted to revolutionize that institution and move it to the front rank of American universities. Unfortunately, he tried to do too many things at once and allowed expenditures seriously to outstrip income so that by the time he left the chief executive office, the institution was so in debt that it had to appeal to the State of Pennsylvania for financial assistance and the status of a state-affiliated institution. The answer to this dilemma probably lies in allowing presidents a great deal of power but at the same time providing sufficient checks so that power is not used in ways destructive to the institution.

One can speculate that collegiate institutions in the United States operate with the same system of checks and balances that has allowed both state and federal governments to function with only a few true impasses in over 200 years. Within colleges and universities, faculties tend to be rather conservative with respect to educational change and innovation, while principal administrative officers tend to be somewhat liberal, constantly searching for new ways of improving their institutions. If an institution has a strong faculty with a variety of accumulated prerogatives and a relatively weak or ineffective president, the institution may stagnate because of the reluctance to change that characterizes many faculties. On the other hand, an institution with a weak and ineffectual faculty and a strong, driving president may attempt so many changes that institutional effectiveness is threatened; at worst, an unbridled, activist president can encourage such dilution of effort that the actual validity of the institution comes into question. In an ideal situation, strong faculties and strong presidents would be functioning in a condition of creative tension that allows reasonable progress but not too much change. Certainly, two opposing powers in one institution may produce impasse and confrontation, a danger that is mediated by the unique role of a board, which can eliminate the impasse by any of the large variety of actions allowed by the board's charter. We must place reliance on this system of checks and balances in order to prevent central administrative leadership from making grievous errors of judgment.

The Decline of the College Presidency

The strength and influence of the campus presidency began to decline almost simultaneously with the entry of American higher education into its most fruitful era. In many respects, a chief reason for that decline was the success of strong presidents who built institutions according to their own visions of academic excellence and inaugurated a variety of programs produced by able faculties using increased resources to teach increasingly able students. As faculty talent increased, faculty members wanted a greater role in institutional affairs and were less inclined to accept without question presidential decisions. President Sterling could appoint Provost Terman after brief consultation with a few senior faculty members; President Lyman was constrained to use an elaborate search mechanism, including faculty and students, to find an acceptable provost. Presidents Hannah and Hutchins could gain approval for radically new curricula by using the powers of personality and office to persuade deans, department heads, and senior professors; their successors were forced to watch university-wide curricular proposals disappear into the maelstrom of senatorial discussion. Presidents Woods, Morgan, and Hannah could personally recruit and appoint faculty members; for other presidents, that privilege was withheld whenever faculty members believed that their own insights into academic quality were better than those of the chief executive officer.

Other forces in the decline of the power of college or university president included the doubling or tripling of the size of institutions; presidents experienced difficulty in their attempts to use personal persuasion on a few individuals to achieve significant change. Before President Hannah of Michigan State University took leave to become Deputy Secretary of Defense, he saw no reason to have vice-presidents since he saw himself as able to handle all matters single-handedly. On his return from Washington, Michigan State University had grown so large that his personal style of leadership was no longer feasible, and Hannah created a tier of vice-presidents, although he continued to oversee the work of the deans of the various colleges. Increased size and complexity in the public sector produced multicampus institutions and statewide coordinating agencies and systems of control, all of which absorbed some of the powers and prerogatives previously reserved for the chief executive officer of a campus. Presidents of California state colleges before 1960 could appoint their personally selected deans and department heads, but, after the creation of a systems office, such appointments could not be made without review by the Chancellor's office.

Paralleling the growth of supracampus mechanisms of control came shifts in the size and nature of academic departments. In earlier times, with some notable exceptions, department heads were appointed and saw themselves as responsible through their deans to the campus president, and they were expected to agree with proposals of the president. As departments grew and their members saw themselves increasingly responsible to the department and to a discipline or field, the departmental leadership changed from being accountable to an administrative hierarchy to being chiefly accountable to departmental faculty members. Thus, in the 1960s, the powers of a campus president spread upward to system offices and downward to disciplinary departments.

The magnitude of those structural shifts was intensified by two other developments. The first development was the relatively sudden culmination of long-standing efforts by faculties at some institutions to gain full control over both their own membership and the full range of their own professional activities. Faculty members had long claimed such prerogatives, and skillful administrators had rhetorically conceded them. However, presidents actually did make or influence faculty appointments, establish teaching loads, and grant or withhold tenure according to their own criteria and judgment. By the 1960s, faculties in research universities and prestige colleges successfully insisted on the rights to recruit and recommend new appointments, determine their own use of time, and evaluate their own performance. In the 1940s and 1950s, faculty members usually requested permission to be gone from a campus for a few days. In the early 1960s, they simply informed their superiors of an anticipated absence. By the end of that decade, they announced an expected absence only when they would be gone

one week or more. This academic revolution did not extend to all types of institutions; faculty members in public community and state colleges remained supervised by the college administration, as did faculties in several private colleges and state regional universities. However, even in those institutions, the revolutionary goal of faculty autonomy was valued and frequently acquired through unionism and collective bargaining.

The other development was the student disruption and dissent of the 1960s and 1970s. Those events most certainly ended institutional and presidential power over the personal conduct of students. In 1958, the president of Stephens College could and did expel students for becoming pregnant. The central administration at Stanford could regulate residence hall hours for women, implement a student dress code, and prohibit the use of alcohol. Ten years later, such actions were not possible at many institutions; even more significant from the standpoint of the deterioration of presidential power was the creation of faculty senates as a device for coping with student unrest. Before the 1960s a few institutions (such as the University of California) had faculty senates, but most did not. Usually, a large and unwieldy total faculty existed to deliberate about such matters as graduation requirements and approval of new courses, but this group was too large to express a continuing voice concerning the full range of campus affairs. In institution after institution, the large total faculty proved to be unable to respond to student demands. This perception of impotency on the part of institutions, coupled with a long-smoldering faculty desire for a greater formal voice in setting institutional policy, resulted in the creation of senates that represented either only the teaching faculty or the various constituencies of a campus. The result was senatorial curtailment of presidential prerogatives in varying degrees among institutions and types of institutions. The most predominant provisions were senate committee approvals of appointment, retention, promotion and tenure; budget preparation; and changes in virtually all policies affecting the internal affairs of campuses.

These factors alone were sufficient to reduce considerably the power, prerogatives, and influence of campus presidents. In addition, that slippage was aggravated by the generally deteriorating regard for leadership during the 1960s and 1970s. Throughout the entire nation, military leadership came to be viewed as antagonistic to the national good, corporate leadership as destructive to the environment, and national political leadership as venal, corrupt, and self-serving. The leadership of higher education suffered less loss of public confidence than did the leadership of most other social institutions; nonetheless, the proportion of the public expressing confidence in the leaders of higher education slipped from 61 percent in 1966 to 33 percent in 1979 (Levine, 1980, p. 12). That loss of confidence beyond doubt reduced the discretion available to presidents and their associates.

　　　Theories and pronouncements about the nature of the college presidency may have helped bring about declining presidential power, but more likely they mirrored the change. Beginning in the late 1950s, a series of pronouncements alleged or advocated a decrease in presidential influence. Ruml and Morrison set the tone in 1959, arguing that the president had lost the power to influence education because of the increased complexity of presidential duties and that the faculty was unable to influence education because of its conservatism and fragmentation into departments. They argued that only the board of trustees could view educational needs dispassionately and with enough authority to produce needed changes. Clark Kerr (1977) observed that the role of the president of a comprehensive university had deteriorated to that of a mediator between the demands of the various quasi-autonomous units that comprised what he called the multiversity. John Kenneth Galbraith repeatedly contended that, rightfully, the faculty should control institutions and that administrators, including presidents, existed to conform to the will of the faculty. But perhaps the most influential idea was that expressed by Cohen and March (1974, p. 2) who observed: "The presidency is an illusion. Important aspects of the role seem to disappear on close examination. In particular, decision making in the university seems to result extensively from a process that decouples problems and choices and makes the president's role more commonly sporadic and symbolic than significant. Compared to the heroic expectations he and others might have, the president has modest control over the events of college life. The contributions he makes can easily be swamped by outside events or the diffused qualities of university decision making." Cohen and March (1974) proceeded to assert that such impotence derives from the essence of a collegiate institution as an organized anarchy unclear of its goals, possessing no technology for goal achievement, and lacking valid means for evaluating outcomes.

Current Conditions

Four major questions need to be asked and answered: What have been the significant consequences of the decline in presidential power? Have those consequences been mostly beneficial or harmful? If harmful, should the conditions of decline be reversed? If they should be reversed, are there plausible and realistic ways to reverse the decline?

In regard to the first question, possibly the greatest consequence (if one can be established) is the deterioration and fragmentation of the undergraduate curriculum. In the past, the great and lasting curricular innovations most frequently were introduced and established by presidents willing to expend a substantial portion of their good will to accomplish educational purposes. In fact, most campuses that offer high-quality programs are characterized by a high degree of presidential influence. Thus, President Charles W. Eliot, despite cautions from his board, proclaimed in his inaugural address his belief in the elective system that he established within six years. As noted previously, Arthur E. Morgan introduced cooperative work-study as an essential element of the Antioch College curriculum and was able to institutionalize it. Several decades later, President Asa Knowles established cooperative work-study at Northeastern University. The most visible and lasting formal programs of general education at the University of Chicago, the University of Minnesota, and Michigan State University were the products of presidential effort.

Since the early 1960s, no reformulations of undergraduate education have been implemented that were comparable in mag-

nitude to general education; the various reforms that have been
suggested have mostly proven to be transitory or acceptable only
to a few institutions. These attempted reforms include nontraditional programs and external degrees, competency-based education, experiential education, individual self-paced learning, and
interdisciplinary program-oriented seminars. Now and then, a
highly visible college or university president will speak out in
favor of some reformulation of undergraduate education, and
presidents of liberal arts colleges frequently publish speeches in
the magazine *Liberal Education* urging a return to some variation of arts and sciences. However, the principal arguments for
curricular reformulation come from such people as Paul L.
Dressel (1978), K. Patricia Cross (1972), Arthur Levine (1978),
Arthur Chickering (Chickering and Associates, 1981), Morris
Keeton (1976), or Mayhew and Ford (1974), none of whom have
the position and political power to effect any changes.

     The dynamics of this absence of significant curricular revi-
sion are quite easy to understand in large institutions with 5,000–
50,000 students. The various schools and departments have their
own interests, loyalties, and styles that they pursue with little
supervision by either central administration or the faculty senate.
These units usually have viewed themselves as agents of their
school or department rather than agents of the university, and
presidents either no longer have or are no longer willing to use
administrative sanctions to induce programmatic improvements.

     Increased demand on presidential time is a second con-
sequence of the upward movement of power and prerogative
from the president to supracampus boards and headquarters and
the downward movement of power to subordinate schools and
departments, senates and elaborate systems of faculty committees, and students. With each new element added to the institutional power formula, the amount of consultation and reporting increases to the point that presidents spend the bulk of their
time checking with various relevant constituencies before reaching a decision. With time scheduled so tightly and much of it
spent shifting from one potentially volatile conversation to another, the opportunities for reflection on educational matters
and for designing educational programs virtually disappear.

An occasional consequence in those institutions that adopted a senate and committee structure that excludes administrative participation has been the lack of input from a central administrative voice until the point of final decision. For example, before the 1960s, in all types of institutions, presidents and central administration played a major role — frequently too large a role — in the recruitment and appointment of faculties. Although an administration influence is still maintained in some institutions, sometimes administrative involvement is absent until the end of the process when, of necessity, it is either perfunctory or confrontational. At Stanislaus State College (in the California State University system), a recommendation for promotion is made by a department. The recommendation is then forwarded to an elected faculty committee on appointment, retention, promotion, and tenure. This committee, which has no administrative representation, reviews the recommendation; if the recommendation is approved, it is forwarded to the academic vice-president, who may approve or deny. However, by the time the recommendation reaches the vice-president's desk, the faculty already has considerable vested interest. Therefore, every denial becomes a potential spark for faculty-administration confrontation, and, indeed, in that institution, confrontation has been a major fact of institutional life for over a decade.

The net effect of the loss of presidential and central administrative authority appears to be an increase in the frequency and intensity of confrontation between faculty and administration, especially if the president seeks aggressively to regain administrative prerogative. Once eroded, presidential power is extremely difficult to retrieve. Some thoughtful individuals like Clark Kerr (1977) have suggested that capable, imaginative individuals may find the role of president so frustrating that it is undesirable. People seek to become presidents because of status and income, a desire to influence events, an opportunity to make a contribution, a feeling that they are better able than others to direct a complex organization, and a presumed interest in working with faculties and other interesting people. Fortunately, as of 1989, some evidence indicates that a positive shift in the quality of those becoming presidents has taken place.

Leadership and the Improvement
of Undergraduate Quality

The profound changes in American higher education have led some to question whether the prerogatives and influence can be restored to the leaders of individual campuses. Supracampus bureaucracies are a reality, and bureaucracies are not known for dismantling themselves. Faculty senates are another reality; many of these are neither particularly creative nor effective, but their existence is a constraint that will not go away. Unions, collective bargaining, and negotiated contracts that exist in over 700 institutions are further constraints, and that number may grow significantly in the public sector.

However, some steps can be suggested that might affect institutional leadership. First, presidents can contribute to quality through their own intellectual interests and proclivities. Clearly, a decline in central administrative discretion does not prevent a president from maintaining a strong and vigorous intellectual life. Cohen and March (1974, p. 149) have observed that presidents usually have heavy schedules and, therefore, little time for their own intellectual development. As legend has it, first they stop writing; then, they stop reading; and finally, they stop thinking. However, nonstop schedules are probably not all that necessary, and presidents might deny themselves some busy work for the sake of their own intellectual expansion. One good idea, for example, is that every campus president clear one full day each week to be devoted to study, reflection, and writing. Presidents should be encouraged not only to speak and write about academic and intellectual concerns on their own campuses, but also to contribute to national discourse and debate about academic and intellectual issues. Arden Smith found that the member institutions of the Council for the Advancement of Small Colleges — which had made significant progress toward getting accreditation, improving faculty salaries, increasing endowment, increasing enrollment, and expanding programs — were invariably presided over by individuals who identified with the higher education community, read widely, wrote and spoke frequently about educational matters, and seemed well aware of major educational and intellectual currents. Member colleges making little or no progress were invariably led by presidents with relatively more local and parochial interests and contacts (Smith, 1969). Several years later, Ford (1972) found the same phenomenon in dynamic and quiescent Jesuit colleges and universities. In February 1975, *Change* magazine published results of a poll of college and university presidents, foundation executives, journalists, and government officials, who were asked to nominate the most influential leaders of higher education in America ("Who's Who . . . ," 1975). Of 1,400 nominations, forty-four individuals were chosen on the basis of frequency of nomination. Less than one-half of the forty-four selected were or had been institutional presidents. Of the seventeen who had been presidents, eight gained their national reputation as influential for roles assumed after the conclusion of their presidencies. The present hope is that, if a similar poll is taken in 1995, a large majority of those selected will be sitting presidents.

Presidents who have continuously stressed academic quality in remarks to various constituencies and in writing can thereby personify high academic value and, over time, can lead an institution toward higher levels of quality. Father Theodore Hesburgh, for example, presided over a significant change at the University of Notre Dame, moving it to a highly prestigious position among Catholic universities. Father Hesburgh's leadership style argued eloquently for the compatibility of intellectual excellence and Catholicity. An institution of high academic quality has a culture of quality, that is, a generally shared value in the importance of quality. Cultivation of such a shared belief seems to be an appropriate one for a college president.

Also, presidents can become more active in national and international forums and assert academic values repeatedly. Too frequently, the most widely publicized writers on collegiate matters are professors of higher education, directors of institutional research, staff members in various professional organizations, and, occasionally, an economist or sociologist writing briefly about academic matters. More college and university presidents should take the time to reflect on the overall academic condition and then to write and speak about it. Not only could such actions contribute to a national debate on educational issues, but they could also lend force to a president's efforts to lead his or her institution.

Moreover, presidents, especially those of larger institutions, should try to develop traditions and even policies that would move promising individuals in the institution through various ranks — with the full expectation that the normal course of events could lead some of these individuals to a campus presidency. At the Massachusetts Institute of Technology (MIT), such a tradition is well established, with individuals moving from department head to dean to vice-president to chancellor and finally to president of the board of trustees. A similar tradition seems to be emerging at Stanford, where the two most recent presidents were promoted from the faculty ranks. In the past, many presidential search committees seemed to believe that an outsider would be more effective than an insider, if for no other reason than that the outsider would take office without many enemies and long-established blocks of opposition. However, many of the more widely known and successful twentieth-century presidents came from within their institutions, and they understood those institutions well before they assumed the presidency — for example, Clark Kerr (University of California), Theodore M. Hesburgh (Notre Dame), Edward H. Levi and Hannah Gray (University of Chicago), Paul C. Reinert (St. Louis University), and Derek Bok (Harvard).

Similarly, systems of institutions and organizations of institutions can begin systematic identification and cultivation of individuals for future positions of leadership. For example, each of the twenty-eight Jesuit collegiate institutions could identify a promising young assistant professor to be sent to a sister institution for a one-year internship in administration. For those who demonstrated administrative talents, further developmental activities could be provided, with the expectation that the next generation of Jesuit presidents probably would come from the ranks of these individuals. Some public systems already do this kind of cultivation informally; we suggest here a more formal endeavor, including establishing firm expectations of subsequent progress for successful individuals.

In addition to active presidential participation in dialogue regarding academic issues and a better system for grooming potential administrators, more leadership is needed from the president in some important internal institutional areas. The first, perhaps the most difficult but probably the most essential, is institutional self-denial, which is based on the belief that no institution can be completely comprehensive and, therefore, that many inherently good projects should not be undertaken. Not all universities need to maintain a medical school, and not all liberal arts colleges need to offer a music major. This principle appears to be equally valid for marginal institutions seeking sheer survival and for reasonably strong institutions seeking quality enhancement. Both types of institutions should examine what they are doing and what they would like to be doing, and they then should make decisions about what should be stressed and what should be de-emphasized or eliminated. The actual processes by which decisions are finally made to emphasize one program and to de-emphasize or eliminate another are laborious, emotional, and protracted, and they involve a great deal of discussion, consultation, and self-study. However, central administration must raise questions concerning programs, maintain the impetus for planning, and make the final budget decisions.

Another way for presidents of even large and complex universities to attend to academic quality is to expend some of their limited supply of presidential persuasiveness with faculties on reasserting some overall rationale for the undergraduate curriculum. Some of the strong presidents of the past were able to accomplish this feat, and perhaps others can do so in the future. Actual presidential discretion in decision making is limited; nonetheless, presidents are important, and others do listen to them. If a president of a reasonably secure institution decided that a major curriculum revision was the highest priority, that president probably could effect such a change gradually and achieve lasting results. Unfortunately, institutional leadership too often uses the rhetoric of curricular change ceremonially but does not follow up that rhetoric with institutional action.

Another — rather dangerous — suggestion for presidents and central administrative officers is the establishment of a system in which they receive recommendations for appointment, retention, and promotion of faculty and then make the final decisions. Both belief and tradition contend that judgment of professional quality can be made only by competent peers. Certainly, colleagues should have a voice in personnel decisions; however, central administration properly should create processes that ensure attention to standards of quality, and administrators should be prepared to overturn faculty recommendations if quality considerations have been overlooked or underemphasized. It is all too easy for members of a given department or school to allow biases, friendship, or disciplinary compatibility to sway judgments. Stanford's system seems to provide an appropriate balance. The recruitment process begins with a departmental or school request to the provost for a specific position, the dimensions of which are clearly indicated. The provost and staff review those requests critically and may grant them, reject them, or ask for modifications. After a search procedure, a dean or department head, on the recommendation of their faculties, presents a formal recommendation to the provost for review. The provost may approve, deny, defer, or ask for a still broader search. If the provost approves the candidate, the recommendation is reviewed by an elected advisory board to the president; with board approval, the recommendation goes to the president, who usually recommends it to the trustees. Thus, central administrative opinion is significantly involved in the decision at three points of the process. That same general procedure is also used for promotion and granting of tenure.

In order for the college or university president to influence faculty quality, program direction, and student quality, certain powers or prerogatives should be maintained (or restored if they have been allowed to lapse). The first of these powers is position control, by which every faculty position that becomes vacant automatically reverts to central administration, which can reassign the position wherever it is most needed or eliminate the position. Whatever administrative unit previously possessed the position should be required to argue a case for regaining it, and that argument should be viewed in the light of all other competing arguments for faculty appointment. The turnover of faculty did decrease during the 1970s and 1980s; nonetheless, within specific institutions or schools and departments within an institution, turnovers allow dramatic opportunities for institutional redirection, for example, if a particularly large group reaches retirement. The disposition or realignment of positions can radically affect a university; controlling these positions should be a presidential prerogative. The president and central administration require a clear voice and one that is widely understood and accepted in faculty personnel decisions, and that voice should be heard at every stage and not just at the last moment in the form of an acquiescence or a veto.

Despite the importance of this power for central administration, the faculty should be so organized that its judgment is expressed on all issues and decisions that come within its purview, namely, curriculum, faculty membership, admissions and graduation requirements, and the broad conditions of student life. Faculty advice should be available with respect to institutional purpose, financial and academic priorities, and any other matters involving the entire institution. Too many precarious institutions provide neither a clear faculty structure nor a clear understanding of faculty powers and prerogatives.

We offer here several specific suggestions as a context in which such renewed leadership can function. The first of these desirable arrangements is the unitary system of administrative responsibility that makes the president alone responsible and accountable to the board. In the last part of the nineteenth century, as business leaders and lawyers began to replace clergy on boards of trustees, some institutions adopted a dual structure, with the president and chief financial officer both responsible to the board. For example, in some liberal arts colleges the business manager is an ex officio member of the board of trustees and serves as treasurer of the institution. The business manager proposes the budget for board approval and defends it. The president may or may not know the intricacies of the financial condition of the institution. In a three-way split of responsibility, the business manager, the president, and the provost were responsible to the board of trustees for finances, external affairs, and internal affairs, respectively. But this type of bifurcated authority can impede the essential flow of information, place the board in a position of adjudicating differences between the president and other administrators, and actually divide the campus into antagonistic camps.

Consistent with the concept of unitary administration is the concept of a cabinet system of administrative coordination. The president normally has several principal administrative subordinates, perhaps officers in charge of academic affairs, financial affairs, student affairs, public relations, development, and admissions. These officers should be organized into a consultative, deliberative, and decision-making body that meets regularly, recognizes its collective responsibilities, and is recognized by all campus constituencies as one of the major policy-forming agencies of the institution.

The president also needs full authority to make major administrative appointments, such as the designation of vice-presidents and deans. The power of the president to appoint deans provides the president with the greatest opportunity to influence the academic destiny of the institution. Of course, widespread consultation and legitimate search procedures are needed, but presidents need to make abundantly clear the kinds of recommendations the search committee will make and the conditions under which he or she will accept these recommendations.

Academic quality requires adequate financing, and gaining the needed funds is clearly a presidential responsibility. Institutions receive funds from a variety of sources. Public institutions receive appropriations from the state, tuition, overhead charges on research contracts, and income from endowment and, (more recently) from fund raising. Private institutions tap the same sources, except usually they are not given direct appropriations from public sources. Presidents of both public and private institutions do, and should, devote a large amount of their official time to the cultivation of these financial sources.

It is also important that one individual oversee the major components of an overall institutional academic plan. Within the planning process, explicit attention should be given to faculty recruitment and policies; various academic programs, including indications of priorities, strategies, and development; physical plant plans, including land development; and the budget cycle and process (when appropriate). Whether this supervision is maintained by the president or by a provost closely attuned to presidential views depends on the institution's traditions and the general style of leadership, but some one individual should know in considerable detail all these plans and should be able to enforce consistency of goal and effort.

Above all, nothing should dilute the presidential power to propose the institution's budget. Ideally, budget preparation involves widespread consultation and negotiation, but the decisions are ultimately those that the chief executive officer makes before presenting recommendations to the board of trustees. Ultimate budgetary authority should not be the province of a senate or faculty budget committee.

We are advocating restored leadership — not the old-time authoritarian style that was the glory of a bygone era, but a system in which presidents have adequate operational authority commensurate with the final responsibility they bear for every important matter affecting the institution. In such an environment, responsibility for the various programs and activities are clearly assigned to subordinate officers and units who know what is expected and who are assigned sufficient power to perform. Exactly how to structure such an environment is the topic of the next chapter.

NINE

Rethinking
Decision-Making Roles
and Authority

Although it may be difficult to demonstrate, the ways that colleges and universities are organized, administered, and governed have some relationship to academic and intellectual quality. The purpose of organization and administration is essentially to obtain the requisite resources of money, people, and equipment needed to achieve fundamental educational purpose, as well as to orchestrate and focus those resources to ensure optimum achievement. A generally adopted pattern of organization, administration, and governance can be found in virtually all collegiate institutions in the United States. Its elements are well known: a board of trustees has responsibility for an entire institution, below which is a chief executive officer, exercising the will of the board through three principal subordinates, in charge of academic affairs, financial affairs, and student affairs, respectively. Depending on the size and type of institution, the chief executive officer is supported by a variety of service agencies, such as admissions, public relations, and fund-raising agencies. The subordinate officer most directly concerned with academic quality is obviously the one responsible for academic affairs.

184

Depending on the size of the institution, the typical form of organization provides schools, colleges, or divisions responsible to the chief academic officer and subdivided into academic departments and special institutes. In smaller institutions, departments themselves are responsible directly to the chief academic officer. In addition, a variety of support or service activities are lodged administratively in various places, including registrar's offices, placement services, various types of centers (for example, remedial centers), and, of course, the necessary arrangements to take care of finances, physical plant, and other miscellaneous services for students. The tenuous relationship of structure to quality is suggested by the fact that one institution carefully organized along those lines will be recognized as concerned with academic quality, while another is judged as seriously deficient. Another question arises when quite different organizational structures are developed by different institutions that, nonetheless, obtain similar levels of quality. For example, Stanford University operates without a formal undergraduate college, while Harvard, Columbia, and Chicago maintain one; yet the reputation and results of these universities are quite similar. In this chapter, an effort will be made to explore issues in organization, administration, and governance to determine whether some aspects of structure do have potential consequences for academic quality.

Criticisms of Collegiate Organization

Several endemic criticisms of collegiate organization and administration have been expressed. The first criticism is that the relatively straightforward organization of institutions into teaching departments represents an effective arrangement for a teaching mission but an inadequate mechanism to manage large-scale research or to provide significant services to local community, state, or federal government. Perkins (1973) elaborated this criticism in a monograph prepared for the Carnegie Commission for Higher Education. "These new structures [large-scale research enterprises] have, for the most part, escaped the direct control of the department and collegiate faculties. They deal directly with top university administration for space and personnel and with outside sources for funds and, when necessary, political backing. Clearly, the department could have only a minimal role in activities organized on such a scale. . . . There are two complications in the university's assumption of this function [public service]. First, public service requires institution-wide commitment, but such commitment is difficult to arrive at, given the decentralized structure of the university. Moreover, neither teaching nor scholarship operates happily or effectively when it must respond to a commitment made by the institution as a whole. The second serious problem is the contradiction between being of service to the public and maintaining the autonomy of the institution" (pp. 6–11).

While it is possible to find extreme pathological examples of competing missions, a more general condition is simply tension, which can be a by-product of intelligence. Thus, in a research university some tension may be generated as faculty members pursue research, direct graduate students, consult, and educate undergraduate students. However, results have generally been far from catastrophic.

A second major criticism is that academic administrators have not been prepared for administrative duties and, therefore, they may perform such duties with fumbling, bumbling amateurism. The criticism implies that administration requires esoteric knowledge and precise technical skills of a higher order that can be acquired only through formal training. In actual fact, people generally enter collegiate administrative roles quite well, having been prepared through long and expanding administrative experience. For example, an academic dean arrives at that position after years of serving on and chairing committees, performing a variety of administrative tasks, acting as an assistant to a dean or president, and serving as a department head. It was informally prepared administrators who expanded American higher education during its period of enormous growth, and it is likely that individuals with the same sort of preparation will need to, and will be able to, manage stability or even decline.

An emerging criticism of collegiate administration, which is related to the question of a lack of formal preparation, is that college administration has not taken adequate advantage of new theories of management and management information. The premise is that the scientific study of organizations and the evolving precepts in graduate schools of business have developed sophisticated approaches that, if embraced and adopted, could radically improve how collegiate institutions are organized, administered, and managed. The argument is that, if institutions develop better management-information systems and if they apply the latest theories about how organizations function, institutions will be better able to mount appropriate educational programs. This point of view has a reasonably long history. One theorist urged that strict imposition of bureaucratic principles would facilitate institutional functioning; another claimed that organizational theory could be used as a basis for improved administration; still another showed that at least one institution put its finances in equilibrium through sophisticated modeling (personal conversations with Herbert Stroup, J. Victor Baldridge, and William Massy). However, as March (1981) has observed, organizations succeed not by the use of macrotheories but by simple competence in dealing with the trivia of day-to-day relations with clients and day-to-day problems in maintaining and operating whatever technology has been adopted: "Accomplishing these trivia may involve considerable planning, complex coordination and central direction, but it is more commonly linked to the effectiveness of large numbers of people doing minor things competently" (p. 17).

A perennial criticism of collegiate administration, especially of the role of the chief executive officer, is that collegiate administrators are extraordinarily busy with the details of the office. One argument is that the responsibilities of presidents, deans, and vice-presidents are so demanding, yet so essential, that the work is never completely finished. The other argument is that presidents, deans, and vice-presidents are extremely busy because they want to be busy and see activity as evidence that they are performing their jobs satisfactorily. Regardless of the reasons, examples abound of collegiate administrators spending long hours at their jobs and assuming responsibility for virtually every detail under their purview. One dean felt obliged to reach his office at four o'clock every morning to handle the desk work so that the normal office hours of eight to five or six could be spent talking with people. Another dean reversed the matter, attending to miscellaneous paper work until six each evening and correspondence from six until ten or eleven each night. And one academic dean in a liberal arts college who served actively on twenty-one different committees also directly supervised sixteen departments, the library, the registrar's office, and the separate school of chiropractic medicine. This dean also insisted on teaching a course for undergraduate students. The alleged consequence of this hyperactivity is that administrators have no time to devote to their two principal obligations: exerting educational leadership and facilitating the development of the faculty. The implication, of course, is that educational quality suffers because of the overwhelming demands of managing even relatively small institutions.

Almost as frequently criticized as overly busy schedules of collegiate administrators is the organization of the academic department along disciplinary lines. Departments are judged appropriate to facilitate research, accomplish graduate education, and promote individual faculty well-being, but inappropriate to achieve institution-wide goals, including well-balanced undergraduate education. Departments are criticized for being too parochial and for stifling such educational innovation as interdisciplinary programs. Departments are also charged with placing their own interests ahead of institutional interests and are seen to have contributed to the loss of presidential power to govern. For example, a departmental development of a doctoral program may not be the best use of institutional resources, and departmental preoccupation with discipline-related, highly specialized courses denies faculty resources for institution-wide programs of general education. Harrington (1977, pp. 55–56) epitomized this type of criticism by remarking that, although they are

> useful in developing disciplines departments have
> championed specialization at the expense of gener-
> alizations, broad learning, and interdisciplinary and

multidisciplinary studies. They have been criticized, since their beginnings . . . for the break-up of knowledge into pieces and . . . for the maiming and mutilization of the mind that comes from over-absorption in one subject. . . . As the size of institutions increased, faculty members tended to live their lives inside their departments, to have less to do with members of other departments, and, after helping to build institutions, by their insistence on autonomy of departments have tended to pull these institutions apart, weakening the principle of college unity, the basic theory of the university. Strong departments have tended to build loyalty to the discipline, rather than to the institution. Raises, promotions, and chances for better jobs have depended more on recognition in one's special field than on contributions to faculty committees or one's reputation as a teacher.

Such criticism of departments was especially prevalent in the thinking of the egalitarian reformers and in some of the more widely publicized radical experiments of the 1960s and 1970s. For example, the planners for the University of Wisconsin, Green Bay, came to believe that the bulk of criticism of American higher education resulted from dysfunctions traceable to the traditional academic department: "it was based in a discipline; its professors normally had greater authority over programming, personnel, and budget decisions; and they had little incentive to relate their intellectual interests to those of other programs. In some ways, they existed in splendid isolation, turned inward on their own concerns, and the concerns of their discipline. At most, they paid minimal attention to the world outside the university or to the interface between subject matter and society" (Weidner, 1977, p. 64).

The 1985 AAC report, *Integrity in the College Curriculum,* also assigns considerable blame to departments that, in collusion with faculty curriculum committees, block needed reforms. "Every institution has a faculty committee charged with cur-

ricular responsibility. These committees have the power to author-
ize new courses and programs, but they are essentially helpless
to design and implement such courses and programs, which necessarily come to them from the departments. The committees
themselves are drawn from the departments, which must and do
protect their disciplinary turf. Curriculum committees are adept
at approving what departments want, skillful at cosmetic tinker-
ing that puts a new and fashionable face on old practices and
programs; but except in rare instances and under the prodding
of energetic academic leaders, they are seldom innovative" (p. 9).

Few of the new institutions that received publicity for having rejected a departmental organization have proven attractive
to students; moreover, few have attracted sufficient enrollment
for viability. Of course, other matters may have been involved,
such as location and time; however, too radical a departure from
orthodoxy apparently does affect institutional vitality.

A different kind of criticism is that the collegiate organization, with power residing in boards of trustees, presidents,
deans, directors, and department heads, is essentially undemo-
cratic, because it denies significant governance roles to the two
largest constituencies on campus: students and staff. These critics
argue that if students played a more significant role, the educational program probably would become more relevant to their
needs and hence higher in quality. A few institutions have tried
to accommodate that criticism through the creation of university senates in which all campus constituents, including students,
have legitimate representation.

An Alternative Perspective

A different point of view can contradict virtually all these
standard criticisms. Certainly, incompetent people sometimes
become collegiate administrators — just as incompetence can be
found in banking, business, or the military. However, the overall
record of collegiate administration, developed chiefly through
experience in an informal way, has been reasonably good. Institutions have grown, have acquired requisite resources, have responded to emerging needs of the society, have produced the

needed professional and technical manpower, and have produced graduates reasonably satisfied with their education and the lives they lead as adults. In fact, the serious criticisms leveled at higher education's performance, and on which demands for organizational reform are based, cannot, for the most part, be considered institutional failures. For example, the sixty-year-old attrition rate of 50 percent is probably more related to the unrealistic expectations of many entering freshmen than to institutional failure. Lack of interest in high culture of many Americans, even college graduates, is also probably more related to historic strands in American character than to failure of educational institutions. Similarly, changing social values, ethical standards, and possible loss of civility are developments that are much too profound to be attributed to any one social institution, especially to a social institution having one essentially important (but limited) purpose.

This system has produced thousands of presidents, deans, and department heads who, although perhaps little known outside their institutions and regions, have been involved with reasonably successful institutional development. In regard to the charge that the collegiate organization is inadequate to assimilate other than educational responsibilities, that charge, for the most part, is not demonstrable. Institutions have assimilated medical schools and teaching hospitals. They have accommodated research installations, such as the Stanford linear accelerator or the Lawrence Berkeley Laboratories, and, when necessary, they have accommodated a number of new organizations, such as centers and institutes. Occasionally, some institution is tempted to transcend its capabilities, as when a university attempts to administer a portion of a big-city school system. However, by and large, institutions have been careful to avoid entering into inappropriate activities and to withdraw as soon as some impropriety becomes apparent.

If we look at the success or failure of reforms attempted to correct alleged deficiencies, the overall record is not particularly impressive. The serious effort begun in the late 1950s to train future college administrators through programs in higher education produced mixed results. The number of university-based programs leading to master's and doctor's degrees in higher education administration increased from a relatively few in the mid-1950s to over 70 by 1981. The faculty memberships of these programs varied from one to fifteen full- and part-time members. Originally, such programs were created to provide such administrative leadership specialties as student-personnel officers and institutional research workers. Gradually, however, most of the programs assumed a somewhat more broad kind of responsibility to provide generalists who could fit into a variety of administrative roles. Graduates of these programs do enter or remain in such positions — in fact, most doctoral candidates in these programs already hold administrative positions. There is no good way of judging whether these formally prepared administrators possess skills and insights not possessed by those entering administrative work through the more traditional routes. Dressel and Mayhew (1974) were skeptical in their appraisal of programs in higher education:

> The scenario of graduate study which we believe to be all too typical is for students to matriculate in programs of higher education and to attend courses on a part-time basis until entitled to sabbatical leave from their institutions. During their sabbatical, they satisfy their residence requirements, pass preliminary or qualifying examinations, and begin the lonely quest for an appropriate thesis topic. Its discovery coincides with the end of the sabbatical, and they return home to develop their projects during evenings and weekends. From time to time, they may return to the university for brief consultations with their advisors, although these meetings more frequently than not consist of reporting on progress, rather than working together to solve difficult, substantive problems. Generally, because of the number of advisees, these part-time candidates pass through the system and graduate or disappear with minimum critique or assistance from their advisors [p. 119].

While programs in higher education have not succeeded as their founders might have wished, they have been somewhat productive. First, some programs provide graduate students with the technical and research skills needed in such growing activities as sophisticated budget modeling and planning, understanding of the political complexities that intrude on higher education, intricate institutional research and long-range planning, and newer theories and techniques of institutional development. Graduates of the Stanford program, for example, are very much in demand for these activities. Second, 1989 may be too soon to gauge the long-range significance of these programs; until the early 1950s, business schools were really not viewed as the primary source for corporate executives at the highest level. They tended to be simply schools of commerce that taught accounting and marketing, but they had not developed a general theory for the preparation of high-level administrators. Only since 1952 has the expansion occurred into the present exalted position that graduate schools of business possess as suppliers of chief executives. Possibly, in the next several decades, programs such as the one at Stanford, which stresses quantitative approaches to management and internship experience in high-level university offices, will achieve stature comparable to that of business graduate schools.

There have been a number of relatively brief workshops and in-service training programs for academic administrators, such as the workshops offered by the Council for the Advancement of Small Colleges or the Institute for Educational Management at Harvard. People who have attended these activities testify that the experience was valuable and contributed to enriched perception of the collegiate scene. Yet, it is difficult to find visible differences in administration in institutions as a result of administrator participation in those brief programs. One particularly valuable program for the preparation of administrators was developed by the Ellis Phillips Foundation and was continued for years by the American Council on Education. This program originally invited fifty nominations of junior faculty members for one-year administrative internships on some other campus. The purpose was to identify potential administrators and provide them with experiences that could help them decide whether they wish to enter administration and that might help them fulfill administrative roles more effectively. The program succeeded well and, over time, testimony of past participants in the program suggests that it was valuable. Again, this program did not seem to change administrative functioning in the way desired by the critics of the informal preparation of collegiate administrators, but it did prepare a whole generation of new presidents.

In response to the continuous criticism of academic departments, numerous efforts have been made to find a substitute. The creation of academic divisions and the creation of centers and institutes have been the most frequently used substitutes. However, except in relatively small institutions where a division of perhaps ten to fifteen faculty members makes more administrative sense than a department of one or two faculty members, divisions have not emerged as strong shapers of academic policy. Centers and institutes have, for the most part, proven to be transitory and have been supported mainly by external funding. When external funding disappeared (except in a few areas such as computer training, which evolved into a traditional department), centers and institutes tended to disappear. Departments have persisted and have generated the most lasting of curricular developments — sequences of disciplinary courses. In some institutions, departments have stimulated a flowering of usually adequate, and sometimes sublime, research. The persistence of departments and departmentalism despite the steady stream of criticism suggests that departments represent valid ways of organizing collegiate institutions and perhaps should be strengthened rather than continuously challenged.

Colleges and universities have not been significantly slower to adopt proven management technology and theory than have other social institutions. Quantitatively trained business administration graduates were a product of the late 1950s and 1960s. At first, most entered business, but they also began to enter small educational institutions by the early 1970s. Neither has the use of computers for administrators and management been notably slower in collegiate institutions than in other organizations.

The adoption of new and more sophisticated management information systems, the experimentation with new managerial roles, and the embracing of management and organization theory may eventually produce better results than improving preparation of administrators or devising substitutes for departmental organization. For example, after examining forty-two institutions that had received Exxon Education Foundation grants to develop management-information systems, Baldridge and Tierney (1979) detected that these systems led to somewhat improved administrative systems and processes, such as the examination of more alternatives to resolve a given problem. Wormley (1978) found that in a few privately supported liberal arts colleges, all of which had appointed younger chief financial officers who had been prepared in graduate schools of business, such appointments were associated with improved financial stability of the institutions. At Stanford University, the use of increasingly sophisticated simulation models was also associated with a steadily improving financial condition, as the institution evolved from a serious deficit-spending situation to one of budgetary equilibrium. However, in many smaller institutions, the results of installing a computer-based, management-information system seemed to be more cosmetic than substantive. In the larger institutions, computer-generated information was demanded by complex, suprainstitutional systems, but such information was used only infrequently by the operating academic units within the campus itself.

With respect to organization theory, collegiate institutions are eclectic, adopting at different times a bureaucratic model, an incremental model, a political model, a rational model, or the "garbage can" model suggested by Cohen, March, and Olsen (1972). Further, relatively few administrators or managers using these various models are consciously aware that they are actually using theoretical models. More studies of how collegiate organizations behave are probably needed. However, as of 1989, it is difficult to see that practice has indeed been modified, and it even could be argued that practice should not be modified. In *How We Talk and How We Act,* March (1981, p. 27) made these pertinent comments:

Theoretical rhetoric of change seems antithetical to routine, but I have argued that effective systems of routine behaviors are the primary bases of organizational adaptation to an environment. . . . the theoretical emphasis on problem solving of a classical sort, in which alternatives are assessed in terms of their consequences to prior goals that are stable, precise, and exogenous. I have argued that many situations in administration involve goals that are (and ought to be) ambiguous . . . I have argued that when an organizational system is working well, variations in outcomes will be due largely to variables unrelated to variations and attributes of top leaders. Where top leadership affects variation in outcomes, the system is probably not functioning well. The theoretical emphasis on administrative action as instrumental has been justified by the way it produces substantive consequences for important outcomes. I have argued that much of administration is symbolic, a way of interpreting organizational life in a way that allows individuals in organizations to fit their experience to their visions of human existence. Administrative processes are secret rituals at least as much as they are instrumental acts.

Over time, a number of administrative positions have been recommended as ways to improve administration and organization and academic quality. These include discrete offices of institutional research, offices of institutional planning, deans of undergraduate studies, directors of faculty development, and offices of evaluation services. While each of these new offices has, in some situations, seemed to achieve its goals fairly well, none of the roles have been widely adopted nor have any persisted for a significant amount of time. Perhaps 20 percent of collegiate institutions have created central offices of institutional research, and only a handful have created formal offices of evaluation services, faculty development, or centers for the improvement of instruction. Those institutions that have done so, have, for the most part, been relatively weak, little-known institutions; even in those institutions, evidence of significant impact is difficult to find. Commenting on faculty-development offices in several hundred institutions, Gaff (1975, p. 181) points out, "Presently little evidence about the effectiveness of campus programs is available, and what evidence exists tends to be either anecdotal or limited to elementary, descriptive information about the numbers and types of faculty members who participated in various activities."

Several administrative and organizational changes became relatively widespread and have presumably improved institutional quality. Most institutions now use some variation of a broadly constituted search committee to identify appropriate administrators. Standardized budgeting and financial reporting forms aid comparative examination of institutional financial conditions. Paralleling the increased educational levels of faculty members, higher educational achievement also characterizes current administrative officers. Techniques for obtaining student evaluation of teaching have been improved and widely used in making administrative decisions regarding pay, promotion, and tenure. Many institutions have developed reasonably complete administrative and faculty handbooks that codify organizational processes and procedures.

Some Approaches That Failed

Before proceeding with the advancement of some ideas as to how administration, organization, and governance might be modified positively to affect academic quality, we will review briefly some frequently encountered failures. The first is the inability of corporate faculties, academic councils, or academic senates to reach realistic agreement on institutional graduation requirements. A second concerns faculty and administrative appointment. Far too many uninteresting or marginally prepared people are appointed to faculties, and far too many people were casually advanced to tenure during the 1960s sellers' market for professorial services. The third malfunction is administrative failure to monitor central processes, such as admissions and expenditure of funds; this problem is often encountered in financially weaker institutions. Finally, many institutions allowed too many new programs to be developed during the period of expansion, and they either can no longer afford the programs or lack the requisite intellectual resources to implement the programs adequately.

Many errors or failures that affect quality are idiosyncratic to a particular president, dean, or department head. For example, one dean participated actively on so many committees that no time was left for essential administrative tasks. Another dean preoccupied himself with detailed collection of data and the publishing of routine reports. A new provost abruptly announced a major administrative policy of requiring complicated staff work by all administrative subordinates. An academic vice-president restricted himself to his office and to consultation primarily with the five division heads to such an extent that he lost any feel for the dynamics of the institution. His successor championed every faculty cause to such an extent that he polarized the institution between central administration and faculty and found himself alienated from central administration. Obviously, no guarantee exists to avoid such idiosyncratic errors. However, structural arrangements and organizational principles may exist that, if applied, can minimize the likelihood of these mistakes or, at least, minimize the damage they cause.

Conditions Conducive to Academic Quality

Organization and administration can influence at least five conditions essential for academic and intellectual quality. The first involves the recruitment and development of faculty. Equally important is the establishment of an environment in which the actual creative talents of faculty can be nurtured and enhanced. For best use of those creative talents, the organization should encourage a pervasive ethos of high regard for quality. This ethos seems to be highly important because the goals that a particular community values and discusses are often the goals that it achieves. The organization also should facilitate the essential processes of intellectual quality, as well as the processes of sustained discourse among students, between students and faculty, and among faculty. Further, the organization should inspire and aid efforts to understand and consider the needs of students; yet student needs should not become dictatorial. The organization should also limit the destructiveness of mistakes. Higher education is a conservative undertaking, and so is the process of improving quality. Perceived faculty reluctance to embrace innovations is worthy of attention. Although faculties can frustrate the efforts of administrators seeking change— especially the more extreme educational reforms, the very conservatism that produces the frustration probably contributes to the maintenance of academic quality.

Centralized-Decentralized Organization

Rather than searching for new organizational forms and administrative structures, individual campuses would do better to maintain most of their traditional elements, seeking only to improve them through clarification of responsibility. In Chapter Eight, the advantages of having a strong chief executive officer were stressed. Ultimately, that individual, subject to board support and ratification, should have the final decision with respect to every matter concerning the institution, including the budget, faculty appointments, and the admission of students. However, strong presidential authority can best be exercised in a decentralized system of organization and governance. With such a system, the chief executive officer and the rest of the central administration are ultimately responsible for academic planning, faculty recruitment and development, budget preparation, land and facilities planning and use, and (when appropriate) formal development activities. Eventually, the exercise of such power can allow subordinate units (schools, divisions, or departments) much latitude regarding matters essential to education. In their study of excellent corporations, Peters and Waterman (1982) concluded that this type of structure was one of the eight characteristics of innovative, dynamic organizations. They labeled it "simultaneous loose-tight properties. . . . It is in essence

the co-existence of firm central direction and maximum individual autonomy — what we have called 'having one's cake and
eating it too.' Organizations that live by the loose-tight principle are on the one hand rigidly controlled, yet at the same time
allow (indeed, insist on) autonomy, entrepreneurship, and innovation from the rank and file. They do this literally through
'faith' — through value systems . . . They do it also through pains-
taking attention to detail, to getting the 'itty-bitty, teeny-tiny
things' right" (p. 318).

This effective type of organization is illustrated well by
the following description of the organizational and administrative
arrangements at Stanford University. This example is used
because the authors are intimately familiar with the operation
of this university and because this institution accomplished a
qualitative revolution in quality within a short twenty-five years —
a revolution made possible in part by the institution's structure.

> The central administration at Stanford, although
> complex, is an informal structure comparable to
> central administration at similar institutions. How-
> ever, the actual functioning of the administration
> structure reveals at least two unique features. First,
> the office of the president is strong and influential,
> with final authority over all actions of the faculty,
> student organizations, and subordinate admini-
> strative units. The office is so organized that the
> president regularly expresses his opinions on mat-
> ters discussed throughout the university. By tra-
> dition, however, and because of the way constituent
> groups are organized, the president arrives at de-
> cisions through wide and varied consultation. In-
> deed, there has evolved a consultative style of ad-
> ministration that values and uses the views of all
> constituents. A second unique feature is the office
> of the vice-president and provost, who is the chief
> academic officer of the institution but who also, as
> a "first among equals," orchestrates the activities of
> the other vice-presidents. This arrangement as-

sumes and virtually mandates a strong team effort on the part of the president and provost, and the provost's activities are perceived as having essentially the import of the president's own.

Important to the consultative style of the administration are the relationships between the central administration and other components and constituencies of the university. The institution maintains a unitary system of administration, with the president responsible solely to the board of trustees. In practice, however, at the invitation of the president, other administrative officers routinely attend meetings of the board of trustees and participate in discussions, not only of their own concerns, but of board policy as well. The senate includes ex officio as non-voting members the president, provost, vice-provost, and dean of graduate studies and research, vice-provost and dean of undergraduate studies, and the deans of the seven schools. These administrative officers regularly attend meetings of the senate, periodically reporting on their stewardship and plans and seeking advice from the senate. The president and provost also meet regularly with the deans of the several schools to discuss all impending problems, issues and recommendations. And the provost meets periodically with faculties of the several schools to inform them of evolving policies and decisions and to seek advice. Thus, long before any decisions must be made that will affect them, the deans of the schools and their faculties have been informed as to what is likely to happen. The president and the president's chief associates meet regularly in both formal and informal sessions with students where wide-ranging and searching discussion is the rule.

While central administration is strong, the various schools' departments and special units enjoy considerable autonomy. In general, each school

is allowed to organize and conduct its programs as
the dean and the faculty see fit, and the schools do
present different administrative programs. The
schools are administered by deans recommended
to the president by the provost after an elaborate
search and are appointed by action of the board of
trustees. Some schools have strong, well-established
departments, headed by senior professors who generally hold administrative office for reasonably long
periods of time. Others are organized much more
flexibly, with committees for areas that deal with
specialized curricular or admissions matters. The
graduate and professional schools set their own admissions policies and, in fact, actually select their
students, although the graduate admissions office
makes the formal acceptances. With the exception
of university-wide graduation requirements for
undergraduates, the schools are also responsible for
their own curricula, with no approval needed from
the central administration. The schools determine
their own by-laws and, within broad guidelines,
determine appropriate work-loads for faculties. This
can, and does, produce different course-loads in
different schools. Schools and departments are encouraged to act responsibly through a budgetary
principle that once budgets have been appropriated,
the funds are the sole responsibility of the subordinate units, and they may keep in reserve funds
not expended each year [*Reaffirmation of Accreditation,* Stanford University, March, 1981, pp. 20, 21].

In a centralized-decentralized system, regardless of size
of institution, subordinate academic units should be delegated
complete responsibility for a curriculum, with the exception of
any institutionally mandated graduation requirement applicable
for all students. The separate schools, divisions, or departments
should decide which courses by which faculty members should
be offered at which times. For this kind of structure to work,

there should be no institution-wide curriculum committee reviewing what courses are to be offered as part of a particular program. Also, although one can anticipate cries of horror from many chief financial officers, subordinate units should have complete control over funds once they have been budgeted. Some may argue that many institutions retain central authority to recall all unexpended funds at the end of each year — funds that can then be used to balance the total institutional budget. Rather than support that system, institutions are better served ultimately to be more economical in budgetary appropriations, retaining needed discretionary funds before appropriations are made. Once funds have been granted, the subordinate units should be able to plan for their use over a longer period of time than a single budgetary year. This entire plan is based on the belief that men and women of good will will act responsibly when they are expected to do so and are held accountable for their actions. Further, this process assumes that the frequently encountered frenzied spending at the end of a fiscal year will not take place if subordinate units know that whatever they saved can be used in the future. States that mandate an automatic return of all unexpended funds from public institutions at year's end should re-examine the consequences and the effectiveness of such a policy.

For successful assignment of important responsibilities to subordinate academic units, the administrative leadership of these units must be expected to perform a variety of duties and be given the requisite resources to do them effectively and responsibly. Too frequently, deans, directors, and department heads either have not understood their administrative roles or have not been provided the necessary resources. In general, the head of any academic unit significant enough to receive a definite budget should be accountable for responsibilities including preparing and defending budgets and administering them once appropriated; advocating the interests of the unit to central administration and other constituencies; coordinating and orchestrating the efforts of members of the unit; evaluating faculty effort and facilitating professional development; making needed administrative arrangements; executing policies established by the unit;

adjudicating differences between members of the unit, including students; serving as the titular head of the unit; and, in some institutions, seeking needed external funds to accomplish the unit's purposes. As a general rule, the distribution of such responsibilities assumes that unit heads will serve a relatively long term and will be chosen from among the relatively senior professors. The practice of designating junior faculty members as department heads primarily to handle administrative detail should be discouraged. This rationale also assumes that administrative heads will be instructed about their responsibilities.

An important consequence of this doctrine is greater reliance on line officers rather than staff officers for a variety of services. If deans, directors, and department heads are responsible for the professional development of faculty, an institution-wide office for faculty development is probably not needed.

Curricular development, except for institution-wide general education requirements, should follow a similar process. The overall educational mission of a school or department should be decided through consultation among the faculty, its administrative leadership, and central administration. Central administrative decisions about the curriculum should be made through budgetary decisions and some role in faculty appointments. Thereafter, selection of courses to be offered should be the exclusive responsibility of the school or department, on the basis of the assumption that their faculties know best what should and can be offered and will, ultimately, be held accountable for the quality of their graduates. To deprive them of authority to decide on required courses for their majors releases them from responsibility for the results.

Similar decentralized responsibility for developing long-range academic plans and for budget preparation should be lodged in the subordinate units. However, those activities subsequently should be reviewed and consolidated for the entire institution. It can be argued that the discussions within those units of faculty need, curricular development, budget preparation, and long-range planning are the most potent devices to develop a sense of community within which a concern for quality is most likely to be expressed.

It should be cautioned that there are potential dangers in decentralizing these important matters. Departments may act frivolously with respect to funds, and as a unit they may abdicate curricular responsibility leaving decisions substantially up to individual faculty members. They may admit too many or too few students, and they may really divorce themselves from any institution-wide concerns. Protection against these dangers can be provided by ensuring that department heads and other subordinate administrative heads fully understand their responsibilities and how those relate to other activities within the institution.

In regard to adopting such a centralized-decentralized system for public institutions that are subordinate to statewide boards, committees, or agencies, certain prerogatives are denied institutions in some states — prerogatives such as maintaining budget surpluses at the end of a fiscal year. In other states, certain kinds of curricular requirements are imposed that limit how much authority can be granted to departments. However, as a general rule, nothing in the nature of public institutions seems to preclude considerable decentralization within the constraints of state legislative or executive limitations, and highly restrictive legislation is subject to change if administrators can demonstrate that such restrictions negatively affect academic quality. Proving such negative affects to responsible policy-makers and/or the electorate, may help eliminate or lessen the restrictions.

Other organizational matters relevant to the issue of quality include undergraduate admissions policy (which should probably be recommended by the senate, adopted by central administration and the board of trustees, and implemented by the director of admissions, directly responsible to the president of the institution or to the vice-president for academic affairs); overall grading policy (which should be established by the senate with approval of the president, but actually be implemented, within policy guidelines, by individual faculty members subject also to school or departmental criteria); and policies about which activities should be associated with academic credit (which should be decided institution-wide, although some latitude should be allowed schools and departments in interpreting those policies).

Critics of the point of view expressed here are likely to argue that virtually all suggestions will solidify traditional practices, relying on the informal system of converting academics into administrators. This opposing view suggests that conservative faculty opinions will likely be held by deans, vice-presidents, and presidents, but it would be preferable if those with different points of view were included. It will also be argued that reinforcing departments perpetuates each department's preoccupation with its discipline and with traditional values, and that only in breaking the control of departments can institutions become genuinely healthy. The response to this anticipated criticism is simply to plead guilty to the fact and to praise the outcome. Improvement of teaching, research, and service is essentially improvement within disciplines. Hence, strengthening organizations concerned with those disciplines is really the only valid way of stimulating improvement. Innovations, if they are to take hold, will likely be those innovations that grow out of disciplinary discussions of teaching, curriculum, budgeting, and planning.

Part Three

❖

Monitoring Quality

TEN

The Role of
Accreditation

American academics reflect a paradoxical view with respect to
maintaining quality. While some academics have beliefs about
political, social, and economic issues that are vastly different
from those of other academics, the political, social, and economic
beliefs of academics tend to be more liberal than the beliefs of
the general adult population. Accordingly, some academics have
little difficulty accepting the need for the federal government
to monitor drug preparation and distribution, airline safety, the
banking industry, automobile safety, and a host of other activities
that affect the general welfare. Likewise, many are not opposed
to state government assuming responsibility for hospital conditions, regulation of savings institutions, or the licensing of physicians and nurses to practice. Yet, almost universally, academics
of all political persuasions find repugnant the idea that government, especially state government, should monitor in any way
the substantive functioning of collegiate institutions. Rather,
they generally support the idea that higher education should be
self-monitoring, especially through the instrument of voluntary
accreditation. The right of self-regulation is, of course, the hall-
mark of advanced professional status. The academic community
widely believes it has achieved such status, and this chapter

will try to assess how self-monitoring has functioned in the educational community.

Voluntary Accreditation: Structures and Techniques

Some writers have eloquently praised the glories of self-monitoring. For example, Tucker and Mautz (1978, p. 314) remarked that "voluntary accreditation is one of the triumphs of higher education in the United States. For decades the accreditation process was a vehicle that helped pull higher education onto ascending plateaus of quality."

The American system of self-monitoring is unique among such systems in the developed nations, most of which use governmental agencies to monitor and control collegiate education. In America, regional voluntary accreditation evolved slowly, beginning in the late nineteenth century. The New England Association of Schools and Colleges was founded in 1885 to advance the cause of liberal education by promoting interests common to both colleges and preparatory schools. Two years later, the Middle States Association of Colleges and Schools was founded to strengthen relationships among institutions and to promote favorable educational legislation. By 1921, it had broadened its purposes to include the publication of a list of approved institutions. The North Central Association of Colleges and Schools was created in 1885, and, during its early years, it was concerned primarily with standardizing and evaluating high schools. This same preoccupation with monitoring secondary schools characterized the beginnings of the Southern Association of Colleges and Schools which was created in 1895. The Northwest Association of Schools and Colleges was established in 1917 to foster growth and cooperation between secondary schools and institutions of higher education in the northwestern United States. The youngest of the regional associations is the Western Association of Schools and Colleges, whose antecedent (the Western College Association) was established in 1924 for the purpose of discussing common problems. In 1948, this association assumed some monitoring responsibility for collegiate institutions in California.

Gradually, from the turn of the century to the end of World War II, these accrediting agencies took on more responsibilities, including the quality review of secondary schools, colleges, and universities; the publication of lists of accredited institutions; and the provision of some accreditation-related services for member institutions. This expansion of responsibility and activity is well illustrated by the pre–World War II history of the North Central Association of Colleges and Secondary Schools. Its first constitution proclaimed the objective of establishing closer relations between colleges and secondary schools of the north central states. Accordingly, during the nineteenth century, the association was mainly preoccupied with the preparation of high school students for higher education. During the early years, the annual meetings featured discussions of various controversial topics and preparation of related resolutions. This preoccupation persisted during the early years of the twentieth century, as evidenced by the creation of the Commission on Accredited Schools and its subcommittees on unit courses of study, high school inspection, and college credit for high school work. That commission was especially influential in establishing throughout the region the requirement that minimum high school graduation standards and college entrance standards must be expressed in Carnegie Units. (One unit of credit equals one class meeting five times a week for a full academic year.) By 1913, the Association had extended its influence to higher education and had published its first list of accredited colleges. The next step was to separate the commission on secondary schools from the commission on collegiate institutions; the commission on higher education then began to develop standards of acceptable institutional performance. Finally, just after the outbreak of World War II, the Association organized itself into three major commissions: one for secondary schools, one for collegiate institutions, and one designed to provide research and service.

After World War II, voluntary regional accreditation evolved and expanded in response to the profound changes taking place in higher education. As veteran enrollments flooded campuses, accreditation sought to ensure the maintenance of quality as institutions with small numbers of qualified faculty struggled to cope with large numbers of new students. On the other hand, as the demand for college teachers increased and institutions created new graduate programs to prepare them, accreditation also sought to ensure at least minimal quality in graduate programs. At the same time, the federal presence in higher education increased, so accreditation sought to provide judgments about institutions that could be accepted by federal agencies, thus preventing direct federal accreditation. Also, as big-time athletics emerged, with its intense competition, accreditation sought to ensure that academic ability was considered at least as important as athletic ability, a challenge that has continued to be elusive. During the late 1950s and the 1960s, as the number of new institutions increased, accreditation set up procedures to help them come into being and to ensure that they met at least minimal standards of quality. Unfortunately, as community colleges evolved from being simply junior colleges to becoming unique kinds of institutions, neither high school nor college regional accrediting bodies sought unique ways of dealing with their problems.

As a framework within which the performance of accreditation during the 1950s and 1960s can be judged, several issues facing higher education at that time must be discussed, along with the degrees to which accreditation actually helped resolve those issues. The first of the critical issues was the claim that higher education should become intrinsically more significant, especially with respect to such important matters as values, beliefs, and standards of personal conduct. The second issue involved the need for institutions to discover effective ways of self-renewal so that they could cope with the exponential increase in the amount of knowledge. The third issue was deciding who should go to college. A fourth, related issue was the matter of quality in education — what it was and how it might be achieved. The fifth of these transcendent issues was how to remove barriers to higher education (such as race, religion, geography, and finance) and at the same time maintain quality.

Organized accreditation also faced significant operational issues, the first of which was whether accreditation should restrict itself to minimum standard setting or seek a more expansive role. Deriving from that quandary was the issue of finding appropriate instruments, techniques, approaches, and theories for any new roles to be assumed and any new issues to be addressed by accrediting agencies. The older techniques (formal self-studies based on quantification of evidence, a brief site visit, and the review by the board and the total association membership) could identify gross weaknesses, but they seemed neither sufficiently refined nor even appropriate to help strong institutions to become stronger. A third operational issue involved finding and delineating appropriate areas of responsibility for regional accrediting agencies, professional accrediting agencies, coordinating agencies, and governmental agencies. Regardless of whether accreditation assumed a narrower or more expansive role, it faced the issue of identifying and training people who could do the actual work of evaluation and related activities. Finally, and centrally, were the issues of degree of power over higher education and who would wield it. Should power reside essentially in individual institutions, in accrediting agencies, in statewide coordinating or controlling boards, or in governmental bureaus and agencies?

Individual institutions also faced a number of issues, the resolution of which would affect accreditation. These issues ranged from quite simple problems (such as the cost of maintaining accredited status) to the conflicting demands on state institutions from the state government and regional and professional accrediting agencies. Additionally, the obviously strong and distinguished colleges and universities felt completely competent to decide their own standards, even when those standards ran counter to the standards suggested by an outside agency. Accreditation had come to be a fatiguing and costly activity, and strong institutions seriously questioned its worth. A related issue involved the time-consuming requirement for accreditation self-study: could self-studies done for accreditation purposes truly find institutional weaknesses or would the self-study report always be a self-serving, even cosmetic, effort? Another issue was whether institutions could gain any substantive help for institutional improvement from accreditation. Accrediting agencies made the claim that encouraging self-improvement was a legitimate activity for them, but many institutions remained unpersuaded. Starkly stated, very strong institutions had to decide whether accreditation could help them, particularly since the process was influenced by weak institutions that wanted approval more than they wanted help.

As it entered the 1980s, organized, voluntary accreditation consisted of a number of structures and made use of a limited number of techniques. Regional associations were incorporated by member institutions and organized into commissions for different levels of education, each maintaining a professional staff. The members of these commissions usually were appointed by the governing body of the total association and had responsibility for establishing policies and, ultimately, for making decisions about the accredited status of individual institutions. These regional associations, in cooperation with the special accrediting associations in nearly seventy specialized fields (such as nursing or medicine), created and then accepted coordination from the Council on Post-Secondary Accreditation (COPA), which had been established to ensure greater uniformity of accrediting policy, procedures, and practices. The professional staffs of these various organizations and the academic administrators and professors who actually performed the accreditation work formed a reasonably large group, although the actual professional staffs remained quite small.

The principal instruments of accreditation are the fulfilling of eligibility requirements for membership: the completion of an institutional self-study; a site visit by a team of academics, who presumably have specialized knowledge of the type of institution visited; a formal, written report of that team and, when desired, an institution's response to the report; and a review of the self-study and visiting team's report, first by the professional staff and then by the relevant commission, which makes the final determination of accreditation status. Finally, each accredited institution may be required to file an interim report at the end of a time stipulated by the accrediting agency — a report in which the institution makes an up-to-date commentary on its condition.

The institutional self-study is increasingly the keystone of the accreditation process. Presumably, by conducting a thorough examination of every important element of itself, an institution can detect deficiencies and make plans for improvement. This same self-study provides an accreditation visiting team with an overview of the institution and serves as a chart to guide on-site inquiries.

Generally, self-studies completed for accreditation can be classified into three types. The first (and most common) is the comprehensive self-study, an historical overview of recent developments in the institution's history and a gathering together of various data for a profile of the institution's situation with respect to mission, finances, enrollment, faculty, library holdings, curricula, and extracurricular activities. The goal for this kind of study is to provide an overall status report. The second variety (probably most suited for large, highly complex institutions) consists of a general, overall description of the institution accompanied by a much more detailed analysis of one or several important elements with which the institution is particularly concerned. The visiting team is expected to validate the overall description and to probe, in greater depth, the elements collected for such scrutiny. In 1981, for example, Stanford University opted for this restricted sort of self-analysis and presented an overall narrative together with detailed analyses of issues involved in undergraduate education, foreign language requirements, residential education, coterminal degree programs, and overseas campuses. A third, rarely used, type of self-study consists of a comprehensive study of all important elements of an institution; however, it is generated primarily for reasons unique to that particular institution at that particular point in its history. Whitman College used this approach in 1979. Located in Walla Walla, Washington, Whitman College possesses a reputation as a high-quality liberal arts college. Under the charisma of a relatively new, dynamic president, Whitman had engaged a wide variety of consultants with national reputations for a two-year period. The result of these extended consultations was a detailed blueprint for moving Whitman into the forefront of American liberal arts colleges. When the consultations had ended, the institution invited the Northwest Association to reaffirm its accreditation on the basis of this plan for future development. Much of the site visit was devoted to intense discussions among representatives of the institution, its consultants, and the site visitors.

Most accreditation self-studies, especially for small and middle-sized institutions, are of the first type. About two years before the expiration of its accredited status, an institution organizes a self-study, with a steering committee frequently chaired by the chief academic officer or a respected senior professor. The actual work of accumulating information may be done either by existing administrative units or by ad hoc committees whose responsibilities parallel the principal rubrics and guidelines developed by the regional association. Once information is accumulated, the actual draft of the self-study may be composed by a single individual (such as the chair of the self-study steering committee), or sections may be composed by individuals or committees responsible for major elements.

When the self-study report has been completed, the next stage of the accreditation process begins: an administrative review of the report by the professional staff of an accrediting agency to ensure that each of the stated criteria or guidelines has been discussed. Then, copies of the study are distributed to a site-visit team, whose members are expected to review the report before the site visit. This team varies in size from three members for small institutions to thirty members for large institutions. Members of site-visit teams are selected because of their presumed competence regarding some important element in the institution to be visited and because of considerable experience in making such visits.

The visiting team generally spends between one and one-half days to three days on-campus, and the visit follows a reasonably well-established routine. On the first evening, the team often has a dinner meeting to discuss overall strategy. On the following morning, the team meets with the chief administrative officers of the institution to inform them about the information that the team needs and the people team members wish to interview. After that meeting, team members fan out across the campus interviewing people and trying to form impressions. The second day is spent on similar activities, and, at the end of the day, the team meets to discuss preliminary findings. During the morning of the third day, team members may check on specific details and begin writing briefs of their individual reports. These reports are then reviewed by the team chair in preparation for an oral presentation at an early afternoon exit interview with the institution's chief administrative officer and his principal assistants. This interview usually lasts about one hour, during which the chair details institutional strengths and reveals the kind of criticisms that will appear in the final written report.

After leaving the campus, the team prepares a written report in one of two general styles. Either the team chair drafts the full report and sends it to team members for review, or individual members write much of the report, which is then edited by the team chair before he or she sends the draft to the institution for review. The final report is sent to the institution and to the association staff. The association distributes copies of the team report and any institutional responses to members of the accreditation commission. At its next meeting, the commission reviews all documents, hears all appropriate statements from institutional leadership, and reaches a decision on the accreditation status of the institution.

Several surveys have reported that administrative officers in institutions say the self-study effort is a worthwhile experience, and professionals active in the accreditation process claim that self-studies do motivate institutions to examine potential problems. In spite of this testimony, some problems do warrant attention. First, self-studies of especially weak and threatened institutions sometimes resemble a lawyer's brief, presenting all the favorable impressions. This kind of study enumerates obvious weaknesses and portrays glowing steps that have been taken to rectify deficiencies. Thus, an institution may point out the undeniable fact that the institution has experienced operating deficits for the preceding six years but conclude that a new management-control system will produce a deficit-free operation within just one year and the total elimination of deficits within a specified period of time. The evaluation team is in effect asked to bet on a future event when they make their recommendations on accreditation. In some other cases, the problems and deficiencies reported in a self-study have long been well known on-campus, and futile efforts have been made to solve them. The problems listed may include financial difficulties, certain obvious deterioration of the physical plant, the need for curricular change, the need to increase library holdings, the desirability of attracting more capable students, or the need to create some new student service. Self-studies have not often revealed major problems that were previously unsuspected. Moreover, the reporting of problems should not be the primary incentive for enhanced institutional performance. For example, an alert president should know that the number of applications for admission has been declining and should have been trying to improve the condition, regardless of the timing of the next self-study.

Some comprehensive self-studies are long on description and short on analysis and appraisal. According to a 1978 survey of 208 colleges and universities that had engaged in institutional self-studies in preparation for accreditation visits, only 33 percent had either generated or examined data on their students' learning and growth; only 23 percent had examined students' knowledge in their major fields; and only 11 percent had looked at their students' mental development (for example, analytic, synthesizing, and problem-solving capacities) (Kells and Kirkwood, 1979, pp. 25–45). Sometimes, the self-study report appears to be a stylized art form presenting a mosaic of information in ways most favorable to an institution. This same stylized quality is found in recommendations for improvement made in the self-study. Few institutions are satisfied with their advising system, attrition rate, grading system, financial resources, library holdings, proportion of faculty holding terminal degrees, emphasis placed on good teaching, donations from alumni, or administration of departments. Problems in these areas are endemic in all higher education, and sometimes require serious attention. Unfortunately, some self-studies appear to be more of a ritual than a serious effort to produce substantive change.

Self-studies, at least in the past, too often use a reasonably centralized hierarchical system of decision making through which the recommendations are to be accomplished. Thus, frequently made recommendations for changing the curriculum, improving advising, placing greater stress on teaching, or developing enriched extracurricular activities assume that central administration will be able to produce the suggested changes. As we have argued earlier, the effectual educational activities of an institution take place in the lowest academic administration units and are modified only when individuals in those units are motivated to change. Although a self-study report may exert some pressure on professors, counselors, admissions officers, and registrars, there are generally far more potent pressures that restrict change — until the individuals, usually for idiosyncratic reasons, decide on their own to modify practice.

The effectiveness of the site visit team is an important factor in an effective evaluation. The visiting team is often chaired by a president or a member of the commission. (Members are usually administrators and faculty members who possess presumed expertise.) An accrediting association seeks to ensure that the members of the team are at least somewhat competent in the major areas of concern and in the few areas indicated by the self-study report to be of specific concern. In general, on large teams, there is a financial officer, a librarian, a dean of students, a dean of academic affairs, and (possibly) a director of institutional research. Each team usually has one or two members making their first site-visit, but most will have made a number of similar visits. In the past, knowledge of the composition of a team and the institution from which the team members came could ensure a reasonably accurate prediction of the final recommendations. Thus, a dean of students would urge greater stress on counseling and advising, and a team member from a cluster-college would encourage greater innovation. During the visit to Stanford University mentioned above, a librarian from a centralized library system not unexpectedly urged greater centralization of the Stanford libraries; an internationally distinguished foreign language specialist urged restoration of a foreign language requirement; and a faculty member from Princeton urged that more full professors become intimately involved in actual undergraduate teaching.

The major instrument of inquiry used during a site-visit consists of personal interviews. Each team member interviews ten to twelve officials of the institution, and (especially since the late 1960s) some students are interviewed. These interviews are mostly unstructured, and, given the time limitations, sometimes the results are quite impressionistic. The information garnered through various interviews conducted over fourteen to fifteen hours becomes the basis for overall judgment of the institution and for quite specific recommendations regarding complicated matters. Obviously, the recommendations are as good or as bad as the reviewers who make them. A competent, skilled evaluator can elicit a remarkably accurate profile of an institution in a short time. On the other hand, sometimes only a caricature of institutional reality is produced by reviewers who are novices, dilettantes, individuals unaware of their own biases, or evaluators unable to distance themselves from the exigencies of their own campuses.

On the basis of these interviews and team discussion, a report is prepared that consists of a team recommendation regarding accreditation status, some discussion of principal institutional strengths and weaknesses, and several specific recommendations contributed by individual team members. On occasion, a certain ritualistic quality is detectable here, as well as in the self-study report. The team recommends reaccreditation for ten years and is pleased to note the improvement in library holdings, the elimination of accumulated deficit, the production of a faculty handbook, and the overall improvement in faculty salaries since the last visit. The team notes, however, the need for continuing effort to revise general education requirements, to place greater stress on improvement of instruction, to increase the emphasis placed on advising, and to increase the size of the endowment. Unfortunately, these observations are then sometimes followed by gratuitous suggestions made by individual team members that reflect idiosyncratic biases and interests. A typical list would include recommending that more women be recruited on the faculty, that a program for black studies be initiated, that the admissions office adopt a marketing strategy, that competency-based education be instituted, that the institution consider going from a quarter system to a semester system, that holdings in the music library be strengthened with eighteenth century materials, and that a language laboratory be created. The North Central Association has found a way to accommodate most such suggestions by including a category in the team's report labeled "Non-binding Suggestions from the Team."

Fortunately, the shortcomings of the site-visit and drafting of the report mentioned above do not occur in most cases. In fact, evidence indicates that they are occurring less frequently but that they do occur. Impetus for change has come from increased professionalization of the association staffs, from high-quality workshops to train new evaluators, and from a gradual abandonment of the practice of using the same small band of evaluators year after year.

The final step in this accreditation process is the review of the team report by the accrediting commission and the rendering of the judgment concerning accreditation status. As in the visiting teams, the commission is composed largely of middle-aged, white men from administration, the various academic disciplines, and professional education. However, some women and members of minority groups may be on commissions, and since the late 1970s, nonprofessional laypersons have represented the public interest on accrediting committees. Many commission members have had many years of successful experience doing accreditation work.

The commission usually meets twice a year for two days to two and one-half days and considers a large agenda including many action items regarding the accreditation status of individual institutions. Since self-studies average 120 pages each and each visiting team report averages 35 to 50 pages, it is impossible for all commission members to read all relevant documents. In the typical procedure, each commission member is asked to read all documents for one or two institutions and to suggest a recommendation for commission action. Consequently, a commission decision on the accreditation status of an institution is heavily influenced by the judgments of one or two commission members and merely ratified by the majority. The way commissions operate means that, for most institutions considered for accreditation, attention is occasionally superficial, especially if the overall reputation of an institution precludes any drastic

action. Unfortunately, sometimes the commission may spend
a few minutes discussing a 27,000-student university and two
hours considering a 500-student college.

Assessing Regional Accreditation

The salient issue here, of course, is how well or poorly
accreditation serves the purpose of ensuring and stimulating
educational quality. In order to address this issue, it is necessary
to confront the more transcendent, unresolved issue of the proper
role of voluntary, regional accreditation. Some advocates claim
that safeguarding the public interest by maintaining the comparability of academic credit is the major reason for accreditation's existence. Clearly, the definition of comparability requires
even greater attention to relative quality. Accordingly, if safeguarding the public interest is their primary reason for existence,
accrediting associations should clearly state that one institution
barely meets minimal standards, while another institution far
surpasses them. Yet, regional accreditation has thus far been
unwilling to make such fine discriminations.

Another role claimed for accreditation is to stimulate
educational innovation. However, the instruments used for accreditation must be judged, on balance, as inadequate for this
purpose. During the period of the ascendancy of accreditation
that has occurred since World War II, the form and substance
of undergraduate education has fluctuated wildly, seemingly in
response to such forces as the launching of the Russian satellite
Sputnik, the student protest movement in the late 1960s, and
the desire to draw previously unserved or underserved segments
of the population into postsecondary education. However, the
considerable experimentation that took place in collegiate institutions during that period seems more related to the innovations encouraged by availability of external funding than it does
to the stimulating influence of accreditation.

Some supporters of voluntary accreditation argue that accreditation should not be expected to affect national trends in
quality and that it has contributed to the improvement of quality
within campuses (because either the self-study process revealed

deficiencies, the insights of accreditation team members discovered the need for improvement, or the influence of the accreditation association lent its strength to improvement efforts
already under way). However, such claims are difficult to document with precision except in a few extreme situations. Self-
studies are reasonably rational reviews of institutional history
and status, but they are not necessarily techniques designed to
uncover hidden problems. Those on campus who prepare self-
studies are, for the most part, well aware of changes that should
be made and simply are awaiting more propitious times or more
acute need. An institution running deficits, experiencing enrollment declines, having a high attrition rate, or permitting a
decline in library holdings holds no surprises for leadership. Even
the steady improvement in the proportion of faculty holding the
doctorate probably correlates more with increases in the production of doctorates by the nation's graduate schools than with
any pressure asserted by accrediting bodies.

　　We agree that the primary, unequivocal, and overarching
purpose for accreditation should be the promotion and certification of quality higher education. In taking this position, we are
in substantial agreement with the finding of COPA's Self-Study
Panel (Council on Post-Secondary Accreditation, 1986), which
concluded that accreditation "falls short of providing the quality
assurance that our nation deserves . . . and that our civic and
political leaders increasingly, and correctly, demand." We also
support the panel's judgments that in most cases accreditation
is working better than it did in the 1970s. However, it is disturb-
ing that, during the period of accreditation's greatest ascendancy,
a steady decline occurred in student performance on ability and
achievement tests, such as the GRE (average scores dropped
in eleven of fifteen categories).

　　Accreditation presumably influences quality by withhold-
ing accredited status from institutions until they achieve at least
minimal levels of quality. The record of this happening is somewhat mixed, at best; relatively few institutions have been denied
some form of accredited status as long as their financial base
appears reasonably secure. Furthermore, examples abound
throughout the nation of the inability of the regional accrediting

associations to force institutions to cease questionable activities. The North Central Association took ten years to act conclusively with respect to Parsons College in Iowa, when accreditation was removed. In both California and Florida, accreditation commissions have devoted fifteen years or more to reviewing institutions offering doctoral degrees based on as few as seven weeks of formal instruction; yet, the associations have been unable to completely deny these institutions accredited status. The Western College Association spent more than twelve years attempting to control an institution that offered a variety of underfinanced, off-campus programs around the world, only to find that, in 1981, the institution was continuing its questionable practices of colonization without adequate resources. The North Central Association also struggled for about twelve years to control another colonizing institution, which had been forced, through financial exigencies, gradually to eliminate about half of the centers and programs it maintained throughout the nation. In 1981, a visiting team failed by one vote to recommend removal of accreditation, although the report did point out glaring deficiencies. The somewhat critical report was significantly softened by the review mechanism, in effect allowing the institution to continue its questionable practices. The general problems faced by accrediting associations are illustrated by the story of Tarkio College in Tarkio, Missouri.

Tarkio College received substantial coverage in the national media because of gross abuses relating to off-campus course offerings. By 1988, 647 courses were being offered in twenty-eight counties throughout Missouri, some as far as 547 miles from the home campus. In February 1988 (after serious allegations in the *St. Louis Post-Dispatch*), the FBI, Internal Revenue Service, U.S. Postal Service, and U.S. Department of Education raided the college's Brentwood branch office in St. Louis and seized boxes of records and financial information. Welfare agencies (such as the Salvation Army, the Harbor Light Mission, and the Missouri Division of Family Services) accused the college of sending recruiters who worked on commission to enroll street people, the homeless, parolees, and even the mentally ill in Tarkio courses. The affidavit accompanying the search warrant said "so-called 'street people' were induced to enroll in Tarkio-related programs by offers to pay them cash rebates from student loans" (Poor, 1988, p. A-1). A social worker, describing the type of students who were being recruited, indicated one student who had signed up to study computers "thinks he's from another planet." Another, studying to be a security guard, "always wears camouflage clothing, carries a large knife and has delusions of battle" (Mannies, 1988, pp. A-1, 4). Recruits were assisted in filing for guaranteed student loans for as much as $2,600. Most of them subsequently defaulted, leaving the college with the default rate of 78 percent — the highest in the nation.

Teams from the North Central Association (NCA) made three focused visits to the St. Louis branch of Tarkio College. Apparently, team members were informed neither about all the programs being offered nor about all the recruiting methods. In 1989, the Missouri Department of Elementary and Secondary Education decertified the school's education programs. Since the college is scheduled for a ten-year review in 1990 and since the accrediting process centers on peer judgments arrived at through self-studies and site visits, NCA staff members expressed reluctance to go outside that process to enforce conformance, although the Director and Deputy Director of the Commission on Institutions of Higher Education did visit the campus and warned of possible sanctions following the conclusion of the federal investigations. Finally, after considerable pressure from other institutions, the school was placed on probation in November 1989. By that time, some state officials had already expressed the opinion that regional accreditation is useless in terms of ensuring quality.

Since the end of World War II, the present authors know of only one publicly supported accredited institution that has lost its accreditation. Additionally, most newly created institutions have received accredited status. In the private sector, no institution established for ten years or more and having a reasonably secure financial base has lost its accreditation. Increasingly, an institution in difficulty either is embarrassed by being granted a shorter period of accreditation than the normal ten years or is required to prepare and submit interim reports and financial statements. However, for the most part, the submission of interim reports has virtually no effect on the actual accredited status of the institution. At best, reports that flag serious difficulties can accelerate the next scheduled comprehensive self-study and full-team review. We can predict safely that, under current procedures, if an institution has a reasonable longevity, a definite campus, and reasonably recognizable programs and it is not in danger of imminent bankruptcy, it will continue to receive accredited status regardless of how its graduates perform.

In addition to the issue of sanctions, voluntary accreditation must resolve the issue of which criteria will be used to judge quality. During the 1960s and 1970s, regional accreditation adopted the policy of trying to judge institutional achievement by whatever purposes the college had set for itself. This approach is quite different from earlier rather rigid demands that all institutions be measured by the same, typically quantitative, standards. The shift away from precise standards took place for a number of reasons. Rigid standards, it was claimed, discouraged experimentation and innovation. Rigid standards also seemed to some to be incompatible with the increased variety of institutions seeking to achieve many different kinds of outcomes. This approach is understandable and appealing since it also avoids such problems as academic freedom in church-related schools or the appropriateness of awarding credit for vocational or remedial courses. However, in operational terms, this approach leaves site-visit teams totally adrift when they are confronted with obvious deficiencies. As has been repeatedly stressed in this book, there are norms for the fundamental purposes of a collegiate institution and for the strategies most likely to achieve them. Those norms should be clearly stated and should govern the judgments of accrediting associations; if an institution wishes to set other goals, it certainly may do so, but programs set up to achieve other goals do not entitle it to accredited status. It is entirely appropriate for some institutions to teach refugees basic English, to teach women basic automobile maintenance, or even to teach income-tax avoidance—but not for a collegiate institution granted accreditation. The revised eligibility standards of the Northwest Association of Schools and Colleges

(1988) demonstrate that clear progress in defining eligibility requirements is possible.

As of 1989, accreditation is still struggling to cope effectively with the hundreds of nontraditional programs that began to emerge all over the country in about 1970. As these programs began, some regional associations, quite sensitive to complaints that they were overly rigid and tended to stifle innovation, adopted exceedingly lenient attitudes toward new programs. For example, one institution that was granted candidacy status had developed a baccalaureate program essentially requiring one year of academic work; a master's program requiring another year of one class a week; and, through a cooperative arrangement with another nontraditional institution, a doctoral program. As public criticism grew regarding this kind of institution, the associations tried to tighten their requirements and did develop qualitative criteria that new programs were expected to meet. However, associations were reluctant to apply those criteria. Redd (1980), using the criteria developed by the Western College Association for doctoral programs, found that doctoral programs in educational administration offered in the nontraditional mode by accredited institutions usually did not conform to those criteria and were judged deficient; yet these institutions remained accredited. In 1978, Dressel, after reviewing many accredited, nontraditional doctoral programs, raised several issues that accrediting agencies have not confronted, such as the possible exploitation of off-campus programs to prop up the finances of the home campus, the extensive use of faculty from local institutions to teach part-time (and the potential negative impact this practice has on the primary employer of such individuals), and the awarding of traditional degrees for programs that are different in fundamental ways from programs implied by the degree awarded (pp. 157–159).

A fourth challenge involves the ability of accreditation, using historic instruments, to provide obvious benefits to strong, high-quality, prestige institutions. As described above, when Stanford University was reviewed for reaccreditation in 1981, a visiting team composed of ten distinguished members made a series of comments and recommendations that addressed what had long been obvious to the institution's leadership (that is, issues that had been under study by the institution). Stanford participated in the reaccreditation process because its officers recognized that some form of institutional certification probably should be accomplished and that it was better to support voluntary accreditation than have accreditation handled by state and federal agencies. Apart from such symbolic value, one can wonder what good to the institution came from an expenditure of over $25,000 and the commitment of considerable amounts of administrative time.

Another major issue contributing to ambiguity in the process of evaluation and judgment by accrediting associations is the relationship between accreditation and institutional eligibility to participate in the many federal support programs. Congress has written into much of its higher education legislation that funds may go only to accredited institutions or institutions that have established a quasi-accredited status, such as candidacy for accreditation or the recognition of their academic credit by three accredited institutions. Since most of the institutions over which accreditation might have real power are absolutely dependent on federal programs for continued existence, acquiring and retaining accredited status is a life-and-death matter. Institutions may even threaten litigation if accreditation is not granted. This particular issue is extraordinarily complicated, involving — among other matters — a constitutional question as to whether the federal use of accreditation to establish eligibility is an illegal delegation of the congressional power to make law. The fundamental quality concern is the federal assumption that accreditation establishes that a given institution is providing educational programs of acceptable quality. As we have noted, there is no clear evidence to support that contention.

It appears that, for most institutions, financial stability is the primary factor on which accredited status rests and that the typical sanction for obvious deficiencies is awarding accredited status for less than the maximum period allowed. One reason for the seeming inability of accreditation boards to act on matters of educational quality may be fear: fear of being sued, fear of being regarded as reactionary, fear of offending friends and colleagues, or fear of destroying honored and respected institutions that are going through difficult times. Such fear is understandable, and it shows itself in an unwillingness to make judgments primarily on the basis of inputs — for example, faculty preparation, library holdings, or quality of students or on measures of output — such as student test performance. The argument may be stated like this: It is true that only part-time instructors or marginal qualifications are used, that the students do not spend much time in class, that the financial basis is shaky and relies entirely on tuition, and that academic credit is given for nonacademic life experience; nonetheless, there is no way of determining that students in such a program receive any better or worse education than do students in traditional programs. In the absence of such evidence, we should tolerate such programs on the ground that they might be doing some good.

In order to break this cycle and develop and enforce more precise standards by which quality can be judged, accrediting agencies must focus attention on the composition and preparation of site-visit teams. Clearly, the experience, quality, and judgment of visiting team members is one of the most significant components in the entire process. The National Commission on Higher Education Issues (1982, p. 6) suggested that "the accreditation system, especially the policy-making bodies and evaluating teams, should include more administrators and faculty members from institutions known and respected for their high quality. Such persons should consider it part of their professional responsibility to participate in the accreditation process."

While the associations have not been able to resolve all these issues definitively, there is a sense that progress is being made. Well-attended workshops are now being held for those who will serve on site-visit teams. Also, regional accrediting associations are placing more emphasis on the on-going nature of self-studies, and there is increasing insistence that self-study processes involve a broad campus constituency. Accreditation standards are beginning to consider as important the measurement of the outcomes of the educational enterprise. Highly informative workshops on the self-study process are now offered annually in several regions, and effective guides have been de-

veloped (see Kells, 1988). If the various associations continue
to improve the quality of their site-visit teams and the institutional self-studies, significant progress toward enhancing the
quality of the American educational enterprise will be made.
Ordinary faculty members, student personnel workers, and
librarians may yet come to see self-studies as opportunities for
continuing self-improvement through reflection rather than as
externally generated intrusions on their time.

Attempts to improve the process will not be effective unless
accrediting associations heed the advice of the COPA Self-Study
Panel (Council on Post-Secondary Accreditation), that the accrediting mechanism should be used to enhance educational
quality rather than simply ratify the existence of minimal standards. To accomplish this task, the associations need to certify
levels of institutional achievement. Such an effort will require
expanded professional staff and sufficient resources of all kinds.

Alternatively, if regional accreditation is unwilling or
unable to fulfill such an expanded role, it would do well to
retrench from its present position and to focus narrowly and
sharply on the single matter of ensuring that colleges and universities meet minimal standards to warrant accreditation as a
higher educational institution. This will also require specifically
and operationally defining that the North Central Association
(*Handbook of Accreditation,* 1990, p. 15) calls purposes "appropriate
to a post-secondary institution."

If regional accrediting agencies opt for the more circum-
scribed and limited role, their relationships with state and federal
government would be simplified. Accreditation would then say,
"Here is what a collegiate institution is, and here are its characteristics. We will certify institutions that demonstrate those
characteristics, and the federal government may, if it wishes,
use that certification as a basis for eligibility to participate in
various federal programs. Accreditation will not modify its concept of what is a collegiate institution so that a variety of noncollegiate activities may become qualified for federal funds. If
the federal government wishes to provide financial aid for area
vocational schools, for remedial institutions, or for institutions
offering basically short vocational courses, then Congress should
enact appropriate legislation."

On the other hand, some signs are troublesome. For example, fearing legal exposure arising from a general lack of precision regarding the attributes of quality, North Central Association asked its member institutions in July 1989 to vote on proposed revisions to the Association's constitution that would move responsibility for monitoring quality to the separate commissions and at the same time soften the language dealing with the Association's obligations regarding quality. Specifically, under "Article II — Purposes," the wording is changed from: "The development and maintenance of high standards of educational excellence" to "The encouragement of educational excellence" and "The development and perfection of accreditation processes which assure quality" to "The development, through its commissions, of accreditation processes which foster quality." Under "Article VIII — Commissions," two additions were made to the powers and duties of each commission: "To develop accreditation processes which encourage quality and educational excellence" and "To stimulate improvement of educational programs and effectiveness of instruction, with concern for freedom to teach and learn" (Gose, 1989). Clearly, "encouraging" and "fostering" quality are not as strong as the "maintenance of high standards" that "assure quality."

The influence voluntary accreditation has in the future will depend in great measure on the view accrediting commissions ultimately adopt about their responsibilities for defining and assuring quality. If they abandon maintaining and enhancing quality as their primary reasons for existence, then the federal government or the states can be expected to move into this arena. We have served as members of three regional accreditation commissions and have much experience with the accrediting process. We believe that voluntary accreditation is still the best mechanism for certifying undergraduate quality, and we strongly urge that the accrediting associations take this challenge seriously.

ELEVEN

Governing Boards and Coordinating Agencies

Although the trend toward centralization of authority above individual campuses in publicly controlled higher education cannot and perhaps should not be reversed, coordinating boards,
boards controlling a number of separate campuses, and statewide
regulatory agencies with jurisdiction over individual campuses
have had limited positive effect on academic quality. The principal effects may even be negative. Indeed, in view of the elaborate rationale that has been used to justify these suprainstitutional mechanisms, perhaps these boards resemble the emperor's
new clothes, in that everyone assumes they perform an important function despite contradictory evidence.

The American system of higher education has established
some remarkable achievements in quality. Indeed, the Study
Group on the Conditions of Excellence in American Higher
Education (1984, p. 1) concluded that the American system of
higher education "is by far the largest, most complex, and most
advanced in the world." After having met the unexpected demands of veterans at the end of World War II, the system produced the high-quality faculty needed for the expanded enrollments of the 1960s; the needed doctors and other health workers
to cope with rising health expectations on the part of a growing

population; established a research apparatus that, for a time, established the United States as the world leader of scholarship and technological advances; and, for an even shorter time, achieved some agreement concerning the purposes of undergraduate education and the best ways to achieve them. However, these achievements are the accomplishments of an earlier era and not the results of the era of coordination and supracampus control.

Before exploring such matters, a restatement of the definition or criteria of quality is in order. American society maintains three functions for higher education: teaching, research or the production of knowledge, and certain kinds of service to society. Arguments presented earlier suggested that the educational mission of college and universities is to use words, numbers, and abstract concepts in order to prepare learners to understand, cope with, and ultimately control their environments. Moreover, these institutions exist to prepare people for a limited number of professions or vocations that rest on a broad theoretical or conceptual base. Collegiate scholarship, research, or the production of knowledge also can be sharply defined. Three general types of research and scholarship are appropriate to colleges and universities. First, research and scholarship are expected of professors as they prepare the courses they teach; this is, theoretically at least, an enormously time-consuming activity. Professors claim they spend around fifty-five hours a week in professional work, of which only six to twelve hours are spent in classes; much of the remainder of their time is spent researching material for those classes. Second, research is conducted by graduate students under professorial supervision, which is designed both to uncover new knowledge and to teach the student the processes of research and scholarship. Third, efforts to discover new knowledge, either for its own sake or to contribute to solutions of complex practical problems, may be supported by the institutions in faculty salaries or by outside agencies.

These three modes of research permit a wide variety of activity but still not an unlimited variety. One touchstone for appropriateness of research is the disciplinary divisions of a particular college or university. Appropriate collegiate research consists of efforts to understand those disciplines and to add knowledge to them. The second touchstone is the judgment of individuals who have engaged in research and scholarship in a systematic way. This criterion is illustrated by the peer-review system by which research grants are awarded. In the United States, support has rested on the identification of worthwhile, creative, original, and significant research proposed by individuals. Support for research in the United States is thus based on the talent and merit of the individual researcher.

Similarly, service is derivative of the disciplinary efforts in the teaching and research of college professors. The collegiate institution is not an all-purpose, service-rendering enterprise that will offer whatever kind of service individuals want, as long as they are willing to pay. Rather, the institution provides service directly related to professorial enterprise in a discipline that characterizes a particular college or university. The clearest examples of appropriate service are agricultural short courses and agricultural advice given to farmers by professors from schools of agriculture, whose courses and expertise grow from their ongoing agricultural research. An example of a service that would be valuable but inappropriate in a collegiate setting is the operation of a child-care center in institutions without academic programs in child growth and development. Institutions that try to offer whatever kind of services the surrounding community desires but do not have a critical mass of scholarship and professional expertise to undergird that service may contribute to deterioration of quality education.

In this chapter, we will explore the actual and potential relationships between supracampus agencies and quality performance in teaching, research, and university service to the community.

The Background and Functioning of Supracampus Agencies

The surge in state creation of supracampus agencies actually began about 1958, as state governments realized that they would need to create many new collegiate institutions to accommodate the growing number of college-age residents with educational aspirations. As states began to act on the emerging premise that there should be a higher educational institution within commuting distance for most students in a state, leaders realized that required expansion could not occur by simply doubling the size of existing campuses but would necessitate the establishing of additional separate campuses. Although legislative higher-education and budget committees could deal with a single state university, five or six state colleges, and even a handful of state-related community colleges, the task of holding budget hearings for fifteen or more institutions was seen realistically as impossible. So, in order to keep within manageable limits the number of educational organizations appealing directly to the legislature for support, the search began for some way of combining institutions.

The other reasons for consolidation also grew from conditions of growth and expansion. An agency concerned with statewide educational policy was needed to recommend or decide where new institutions should be located. Without some such analysis, expansion would very likely take place in politically powerful regions of the state—even if the greatest need was elsewhere. Also, an agency was needed to ensure that expensive and unnecessary program duplication was either prevented or kept to a minimum. Legislative bodies reasoned that individual campuses might well be tempted to create prestigious but expensive programs such as colleges of medicine or dentistry, regardless of need or the state's ability to support them.

Wise planning required reliable information that reflected the actual educational situation of the entire state. Such information should be compatible with other sources of information. Since, historically, each campus had created its own—frequently rudimentary—information system, an agency was needed to develop a uniform information system. A related need was an agency to undertake detailed and sustained planning based on accurate and compatible information, so that state concerns would be accommodated and the expansion of higher education would be in harmony with other statewide programs.

Thus, as states began to create coordinating agencies, they were assigned a typical set of responsibilities: collect compatible information from institutions, develop long-range state plans for higher education, recommend and/or approve locations for new campuses, recommend and/or approve educational programs, and either review budget requests from individual institutions to make recommendations or consolidate requests into a single higher education budget.

Although each state created structures on the basis of its own traditions and situation (and some states changed structures over time as conditions changed), four general organization types were used. The first was a consolidated governing board responsible for all publicly supported institutions in the state (used, for example, in Georgia, Idaho, Montana, and, eventually, Wisconsin). The second type consisted of a consolidated board for all four-year public institutions and some other separate agency responsible for two-year community colleges (used, for example, in Arizona, North Carolina, and Florida). The third form consisted of coordinating boards, with authority either to approve programs or only to review programs and make recommendations. Illinois, Ohio, and Maryland created coordinating boards that actually consolidate budgets; Missouri, Colorado, Texas, and Virginia created boards that only review and recommend budgets. The Missouri Coordinating Board for Higher Education must also approve all new programs, but it can only recommend that existing programs be closed. Of other states with boards that have program review and recommendation authority only, Alabama's board consolidates budgets; California's board reviews and recommends budgets; Nebraska's board has no statutory budgetary role; and, in Delaware, Vermont, and Wyoming, the coordinating board was created by the governor and is used primarily for advice to the chief executive on higher educational matters (in 1988, the governor of Maryland convinced the legislature to convert that state's coordinating board into this last type).

During the 1960s, a typical development pattern began with state initiation of studies of higher educational needs within the state. These studies were often followed by the creation of some form of a coordinating board, which, after developing a staff, created the first master plan for the state's higher-education development. State master plans were followed by demands that institutions also develop master plans. Usually, some division of the statewide plan was followed by some structural or organizational changes, such as either creating systems of institutions (or multicampus institutions) or changing from a coordinating board to some variant of the consolidated governing board. These various steps are so interrelated that, for evaluation purposes, we will consider them all together.

Supracampus Management: Successes and Failures

By 1970, the successes and failures of early attempts at supracampus management revealed some reasonable conclusions. On the plus side, educational statistics and other information were considerably improved over the information available before. Also, the processes of long-range planning had been improved so that the 1970 plans were considerably clearer and more realistic than plans developed a decade earlier. Moreover, because of the efforts of staffs from these suprainstitutional organizations, legislators seemed to be better informed and more sophisticated about educational problems and issues. Finally, in some states, the creation of a statewide system of two-year community colleges was directly the result of coordinating council efforts.

Balancing these successes were a number of failures or consequences for which there is no persuasive evidence of success. The record of states creating new campuses in appropriate numbers and in effective places was not particularly good. For example, California created two university campuses and three college campuses that either were not needed or were so located as to deter student enrollments at planned levels. Wisconsin created two branches of the university that the state could not afford and were not, in the long run, critically needed. Florida mislocated the placement of Florida Atlantic University in Boca Raton and created a specialized campus in Orlando that proved not to be particularly needed.

Moreover, the record of the 1960s in preventing unnecessary duplication of expensive programs was not particularly good. Flagship university campuses had more political power than coordinating boards and so could influence legislation. Other political forces could gain support for institutions or programs in a certain region whether or not they served statewide needs. California, Michigan, and Alabama each ended up with one medical school too many, and Colorado was saddled with an unnecessary dental school. Virginia and Illinois ended up with a variety of new doctoral programs in various disciplines of the humanities that duplicated the efforts of other institutions in those states. In general, it seemed that a persistent individual institution could, through perseverance, overcome the resistance of the statewide agency to whatever new program the institution desired. Such persistence might take the form of bootlegging a new medical school into existence through gradually creating most of the courses needed for a medical school and then making the argument that a medical school could be created with virtually no increased cost to the state. Or persistence could be reflected in the marshalling of local political power to overcome the efforts of the coordinating board.

Although statewide agencies were instructed to accommodate the private institutions in order to ensure their vitality, statewide boards mostly concerned themselves only with public institutions; for example, they might locate two institutions near a successful private institution. Also, even though a major reason for creating statewide agencies was to contain costs, by 1970, no data indicated that a coordinated or controlled statewide system could offer educational services any more economically than could systems in somewhat less controlled states.

The preceding paragraphs describe the situation as the creation of supracampus organizations reached its peak in 1970. Five years later, after continued expansion of statewide coordination and control, no new information had been gathered concerning the success of these organizations. Berdahl (1975, pp. 1–13) indicated that, although some particular state agencies had been evaluated informally, actually there was little more than subjective judgments (all of which reflected the underlying biases of individuals making them). The authors whom Berdahl recruited for his report, all of whom had had experience with suprainstitutional agencies, agreed that higher education had problems and that some form of statewide organization was a possible way of solving them, but they could adduce no persuasive evidence to validate this assertion. Indeed, the authors present a perplexing set of propositions or affirmations. One argued that state boards lead to planning, and planning is especially necessary in times of debility; therefore, state boards are probably essential. Another seemed to say that statewide boards are good, but they have not been evaluated properly; perhaps if higher education used a modified business model, it might learn something. Still another, then a member of the Florida House of Representatives, simply argued that state boards have existed long enough that they now needed to be evaluated. Other authors argued in similarly abstract ways. Not one of these essays concerned with evaluating statewide boards dealt with the concept of educational quality and how boards might affect it.

A similar sense of the inevitability of increased statewide centralization — and the lack of information about its results — is found in the remarks of the board of the Carnegie Foundation for the Advancement of Teaching (1977, pp. 11–12), which observed that centralization seemed to have had no measurable, direct impact on policies or practices and disagreed with the tendency toward centralization of authority from the campus to multicampus systems and from governing boards to state mechanisms. This Carnegie board asserted that such movement reduced the influence of students, faculty members, and campus administrators who knew the most about the institution and who were most directly involved. Furthermore, while recognizing that institutions of higher education could not proceed without restraints, this board claimed the best restraints were competition between campuses and the limitations imposed by the state budget.

The board of trustees of the foundation, however, weakened its case somewhat by insisting on the urgency of long-range planning and implying that this activity should be done at the state level. The most desirable possibility seemed to be considerable authority given to campuses plus some statewide mechanism with limited power to conduct planning and to coordinate campus activities. A less desirable, but still tolerable, arrangement would be a consolidated board for higher education that would perceive itself as part of higher education and not outside it. The board mirrored the council's advice by suggesting that it might be better public policy for states to create several competitive institutions or segments, which would allow the dynamics of the marketplace to operate to some degree. The worst possible scenario would be the creation of state regulatory agencies, because, as the board pointed out, the staffs of these agencies often come from outside higher education.

The popularly labeled Second Newman Report (Newman, 1973) similarly revealed a state of disenchanted inevitability as it pointed out the increased number of multicampus institutions and the tendency for statewide boards to assume more and more prerogatives. Although Newman deplored these developments, he accepted the conventional rationale that "given the growth in numbers of students, the number of institutions, and the size of budgets, some system of organization and management of institutions is required. It is manifestly impossible for a legislature to supervise the operation of 10 or 50 or 100 campuses. The use of the multi-campus system concept is thus the logical outcome of growth" (p. 55). That report, too, failed to address the issues of quality.

The Sloan Commission on Government and Higher Education (1980) seemed uneasy with the growth of statewide higher education boards; nonetheless, it argued that the boards might help enhance quality somewhat by initiating reviews of programs in the public and private institutions. However, the commission presented no evidence to support its expectation that program review might affect quality and, essentially, used a negative argument to support its contention: "Candid evaluations of program quality, made by competent and disinterested reviewers, would be particularly valuable during a period of retrenchment. They can both provide warnings to administrators in a particular institution and help institutions as a group resist the temptation to compete for students by lowering academic standards. Further, independent judgments of program quality should be an important consideration when a state agency redefines the mission of an institution and changes its role or even recommends closing it" (pp. 16–17).

This argument (that program review requires disinterested effort by agencies above the campus level) can be disputed. The more removed a reviewer is from the locale of the educational effort, the less valid and productive review exercises are likely to be. Their argument also implies that participants on-campus have vested interests so deep that they would preclude recommending hard decisions; yet, an examination of several institutions reveals a great deal of responsible objectivity when institutional needs are being pondered. A different point of view suggests that (1) program review is a process in which those most intimately involved ponder what they are doing and might do in the future and (2) from such discussions will gradually emerge consensus. So, perhaps, program review can best take place in departments and divisions (or in separate schools in complex institutions). The best motivation for change in higher education is usually internal motivation. Too frequently, program review engaged in for externally motivated reasons results merely in a defense of the status quo.

Overall, the critical professional writing about suprainstitutional organizations has a timid quality — as though the creation of these agencies were so inevitable that their performance should not be assailed because then even more highly centralized agencies would be created. Not only is there a reluctance to criticize, there is typically acceptance of some need for supracampus organizations to mandate long-range planning, to accomplish ways of ensuring accountability, and to bring about rational allocation of scarce resources in a time of stability or even decline.

Actually, statewide coordinating boards, consolidated boards of trustees, and multicampus institutions are vulnerable to additional criticisms, especially concerning the achievement or maintenance of quality with respect to the three major purposes of teaching, research, and service. An overly simplified example can make an important point: The University of California, Berkeley, is part of a highly concentrated system that, in turn, is coordinated by a long-established coordinating agency, whereas the University of Michigan operates quite independently of a rather weak coordinating agency and, for the longer portion of the growth years of 1950 to 1970, operated with no coordination at all. No persuasive evidence has shown that there are major, essential differences in quality of education between Berkeley and the University of Michigan.

The expectation may be inappropriate that suprainstitutional agencies could affect quality with respect to the three major purposes of higher education because these are products of several internal factors. The campus president, in even the larger institutions, keeps overall track of the educational program, the research thrust, and the services offered and the relationships between them. Within the campus departments, curriculum is actually fashioned and standards are set and maintained. The individual department, in cooperation with campus central administration, succeeds or fails in recruiting a qualified faculty. Of course, the individual faculty member either does or does not do high-quality research and teaching.

Some argue that essential statewide concerns can be ensured only through agencies above the campus level. Lee and Bowen (1975, p. 146) analyze nine multicampus systems.

> With a few exceptions, the increase in statewide activity has been meritorious. Academic planning and program review are more comprehensive and of higher quality, budgeting is technically more sophisticated and more sensitive to academic criteria, multi-campus programs are increasing, faculty personnel planning is being initiated, and student mobility is being facilitated. To be sure, few of these activities are limited to multi-campus systems; indeed, the experiences of individual campuses, public and private, offer many lessons for statewide administrators. But the record is sound. Multi-campus systems have made a difference for students, for faculty, and for the educational enterprise of their states. The difference has been positive—more so, we believe than would have been the case had the

policies and decisions described in earlier chapters
been the responsibility of single campuses, whether
dealing with each other as autonomous institutions
or dealing directly with state executive and legislative officials and with coordinating agencies.

However, throughout their comprehensive review of nine systems, there are statements that raise questions about whether
the systems are achieving their purposes effectively. The authors
describe in detail the various plans that have been developed
by the system headquarters of multicampus institutions, but
detail is lacking about actual accomplishments, except for either
negative ones or positive ones that actually were the result of
accident or a particular individual (for example, the six campuses of the University of Texas were created not as a result
of comprehensive planning but of ad hoc decisions over time).
Political pressures in New York can force the conversion of a
community college into a four-year campus at almost any time.
Program review, which in theory should be concerned with
quality, is described essentially as an economic device that can
generate a moratorium on development of new programs or at
least slow down the process of creating new programs. Again,
the impression is that, except for certain gross decisions (such
as denying doctoral-level work in the California State University and College system), a persevering campus can maintain
existing, albeit unproductive, programs and create new ones.
In one of the two examples of comprehensive system-based
review of existing academic programs, the system administration was pleased with the results at the University of Missouri,
but no results are mentioned. In the other example, the University of Wisconsin, the major accomplishment was phasing out
fifty-one marginal programs, resulting only in minimal cost
savings.

　　　With respect to innovative development of new programs
in the system, Lee and Bowen (1975, p. 77) point out what
theoretically could be done, observing that "the multi-campus
system would seem to enjoy several advantages in the search
for new approaches; it can be a source of financial and technical

support for campuses, but limit risk to one campus; it can be an objective judge of experimental success or failure; it has interior lines of communication to transfer successful programs to wider, perhaps captive, audiences." Again, what is lacking is the dramatic example to show that those potentialities have been actually realized. They mentioned the Empire State College of the State University of New York as an important innovation, but, as of this writing, it has served only a tiny minority of people receiving bachelor's degrees from New York public institutions. They also cite some of the efforts to establish nontraditional external degree programs in California. However, actual programs seem to have flowered only on campuses at which the chief executive had a long-time personal commitment to external degree activities (for example, the campus of Dominguez Hills).

To understand why suprainstitutional agencies such as multicampus systems cannot be shown to have positively influenced the quality of teaching, research, or public service, the claimed elements of an exemplary model should be examined. Lee and Bowen (1975, p. 149) proposed a model that stressed several elements: (1) Most decisions are better made at a campus level rather than a central level, (2) some decisions must, however, still be made centrally, (3) both campus and central decisions require all available information, and (4) both campus and central administrators require great flexibility with respect to resources, and a spirit of high cooperation should be maintained at all levels.

This model assumes that significant academic decision making is a rational act and, by implication, that there are persuasive examples that demonstrate rationality. Both of these assumptions can be disputed. Decision making in colleges and universities can be incremental, bureaucratic, political, capricious, accidental, or rational. A review of several presumably significant academic decisions throughout the country suggests a variety of modes. Thus, the decision of Fordham University to create Ben Salem College in 1967 was reached almost capriciously, in connection with a lunchtime conversation of the president of the institution and a faculty member who was also a poet. Similarly, the decision of the University of California to create the Santa Cruz campus in the form of many small colleges seems to have been an inspiration of the president, Clark Kerr, conditioned by his own undergraduate experience at Swarthmore. The decision of the University of Wisconsin to create the Green Bay campus as a distinctively innovative institution was first of all political — the demand of that region for the presence of a state university — and the instinct of the president of the University of Wisconsin that, in view of the times, the university should have an innovative campus of some sort. The far-reaching decision of Dartmouth to become coeducational illustrates political effort of a most sensitive variety, since the needs of alumni, faculty, administration, students, and a concerned wider community had to be satisfied. On the day of the vote, even the president did not know how it would come out.

Supracampus agencies have a rather poor record of using information in a sophisticated way to reach rational, effective decisions. During the late 1960s, virtually no institution anticipated or made plans for an eventual stabilization of demand, although relevant information was available in census data and birth and fertility rates. In 1972, the Federal Higher Education Amendments provided a presumably rational system of commissions in each state to facilitate the planning for and use of funds from federal subsidies. Essentially, the goal proved to be unattainable, as the various states adopted other means of anticipating and providing for the future. West Virginia, for a variety of reasons, embraced the idea of vigorous statewide coordination, and a system was put into effect under experienced and presumably capable leadership. The result was a hodgepodge of educational activity.

Perhaps the biggest single reason for skepticism about the efficacy of suprainstitutional influence on the actual practice of higher education is that education's successes have resulted more from reacting to unexpected events than from grand statewide master plans. Of course, sometimes higher education's reaction to events has been detrimental. Nonetheless, of the major developments in the quality of American higher education since the beginning of World War II, only one appears to have resulted from academics examining their enterprise, finding it wanting, and attempting to do something about it. That was the general education movement.

The cooperative venture of the federal government and universities in developing a sophisticated research effort and apparatus stemmed directly from the unexpectedly fruitful cooperative effort with war-related research. Although some academics certainly sensed the contours of the future and attempted to prepare for it, the flowering of research in the major research universities was not a long-range, planned activity. Similarly, the expansion of high-quality graduate programs stemmed in part from the growing need for people to staff the new research apparatus. Additionally, that expansion was driven by the collective decision of the post–World War II "baby boomers" to attend college. Those students would need teachers, and the graduate schools represented the only agencies that could produce the needed educators rather quickly. The same pressure of numbers stimulated the move toward selectivity by those institutions which were relatively well known and which did not choose to expand indiscriminately. The increased concern with academic rigor that characterized the 1960s was not the result of a thoughtful analysis and a rational decision to impose more stringent standards; rather, it was an almost knee-jerk reaction to the public outcry over the launching of the first Russian satellite. Likewise, current concerns with quality stem from the slide in the nation's competitiveness, rather than from the tomes of state master plans. Perhaps the nation's needs are served better by diverse individual institutions that are sensitive to local and national needs within their purview and plan accordingly.

If no persuasive evidence shows that supracampus agencies facilitate accomplishment of the fundamental purposes of higher education and if their demonstrable gains (such as more elaborate data and precise budgeting formulas) are of marginal value, then why have these agencies been sustained and why do they continue to grow in size, complexity, and influence? There is no clear answer to these questions. However, reasonable speculation sees the logical elegance of the rhetoric used to defend these agencies. The syllogism runs thus: "As higher education moves into a period of stability and restricted resources, those resources must be managed well and there must be no costly duplication of educational services. Therefore, coordinating boards (or consolidated boards of control of systems or campuses) are essential to manage those resources." Expressions of that syllogism are embellished with value claims, such as the protection of academic freedom, preservation of diversity, stimulation of innovation, and best service of the common welfare.

That logic and the accompanying value claims become plausible when one recognizes that in most states there are too many separate campuses to allow them all to deal directly with the executive and legislative branches of government. Some fewer number of direct links is essential to avoid legislative chaos. However, that particular purpose could be achieved by relatively small staffs collating campus budget requests and forwarding them to the governor and legislature with explanatory comment. Centralized agencies seek to do much more, including the preparation of consolidated budgets, substantive review of program plans, and deliberate allocation of resources to the several campuses. In the case of multicampus institutions, chief executives of the system assume a major role in the appointment of campus executives, substantive review of indigenous campus problems, and actual control over the professorial positions available on every campus. However, no evidence suggests that a system president select more capable campus executives than local campus search committees do. Nor is there evidence that system officers are better judges of program quality than the interacting elements of faculties and administrators on a local campus.

One reason that these agencies are sustained is that they exist and have developed influential bureaucracies. Efforts to eliminate these agencies when they have demonstrably failed, as in Colorado and in Florida, have not been successful. These bureaucracies gain strength from the occasional support of a campus that believes the bureaucracy might help in its competition with other campuses. For example, as Virginia Polytechnic Institute (VPI) began to grow, its leadership supported statewide coordination with the belief that VPI would gain with coordination and that the University of Virginia might very well lose. Fear also plays an important part in generating campus support for a system of coordinating-board arrangement; campus officials hope that these agencies might prevent an even more onerous centralized system of controls, such as a consolidated board that has a large staff to regulate collegiate institutions in the state. The specter is constantly raised that if a state did not have a coordinating board, other state agencies and bureaus would undoubtedly begin to exercise tighter control but without sensitivity to essential educational values. Consider, for example, the remark, that "boards which fail to come to grips with state internal priorities will find those decisions made for them by governors and legislatures" (Berdahl, 1975, p. 18).

The bureaucracies also gain strength as bureaucrats gain sophistication with such things as esoteric budget and planning systems. The expansion of quantitative systems such as those developed by the National Center for Higher Education Management Systems (NCHEMS) also seemed to have accomplished an expansion and an entrenching of suprainstitutional bureaucracies.

Despite the lack of evidence that supracampus organizations positively affect educational and academic quality and their checkered performance record with respect to other missions, these agencies probably will persist and, given their bureaucratic nature, seek to expand their power and influence. We believe that there is a limited, beneficial role for statewide coordinating bodies, but we believe also that a variety of measures need to be taken to minimize expansionist tendencies and to restore a considerable amount of responsibility to individual campuses — where all quality issues ultimately must be resolved.

Coordination to Improve Quality

The statements of major policy-recommending groups should be pondered carefully and injected more frequently into the public debate regarding the structure of higher education. Even thoughtful apologists for multicampus systems argue that most decisions, most of the time, are better made on campuses than at central governing boards. Their overall point of view is that there should be a creative use of unique organizational structures combining coordination and governance. "Coordination implies a continuing high level of campus autonomy — the prerogative of the campuses to promote their own institutional stamp and style. Governance, on the other hand, implies that central administration had direct operational responsibility and is accountable to the state for the sum of activity across campuses. The tension between campus and central responsibility cannot be resolved by abandoning either" (Lee and Bowen, 1975, p. 148).

The current system operating in the state of Missouri seems to reflect this ideal. The state supports four regional universities; one regional university that is currently changing its mission to become a liberal arts institution; one land-grant, historically black university; three state colleges; and the land-grant University of Missouri system with four campuses. Additionally, the state provides 47 percent of the budget for eleven community college districts. Each unit is governed by a board with constitutional authority to enter into contracts, set salaries, close programs, develop budgets, make purchases, and otherwise operate the institution. Three of the boards can be drawn from anywhere in the state: the University of Missouri; Lincoln University — the land-grant, historically black institution; and Northeast Missouri State University — the recently designated liberal arts institution. Members for the boards of the other institutions must all come from designated regions (or counties in the case of the state colleges and community colleges). Members are appointed by the governor and confirmed by the senate for six-year, staggered terms. Fifty percent of the members must come from each major political party.

Also appointed by the governor and confirmed by the senate is an eight-member Coordinating Board for Higher Education. This body reviews budgets prepared by the several institutions and makes recommendations to the governor and general assembly. A rather small staff, including a commissioner for higher education, is appointed by the board and serves at its pleasure. The staff gathers data from the institutions, issues comparative reports, and lobbies the legislature for funding.

While the board must approve new programs, it can only recommend to local boards the closure of existing ones. The board does have authority to conduct program reviews, a process that is ongoing. In 1984, the board issued its second master plan and has since received master plans from the various four-year institutions.

The dynamics of this system are instructive. Each spring, the commissioner meets with the presidents to agree on general categories to be designated for special emphasis and funding for the ensuing fiscal year. Examples include locally developed assessment programs, the improvement of undergraduate quality, and retention of minorities — all categories broad enough to encompass a wide range of initiative. The presidents convert this information to plans and appear several times each year before the board and its subcommittees to argue on behalf of their institutions. The presidents also present their cases before the legislative subcommittees and frequently to the governor and his staff. Institutions compete vigorously for the attention and favor of the board and the legislature. Those presidents who can sell a particularly innovative program to the commissioner, the coordinating board, the governor, and the legislature are rewarded with significant funding. Recent examples include Northeast's Value-Added assessment program and Northwest's Electronic Campus. An innovation started on one campus quickly spawns competing strategies on other campuses. For example, even though Northwest's restoring of a month to the school year was not popular among other institutions, the plan was quickly mimicked when it received vocal support from the governor. Also, all the institutions began developing assessment plans after Northeast received a substantial increase in its base appropriation in recognition of its efforts. Such competition also acts as a constraint on certain institutional initiatives (for example, the attempt of Southwest Missouri State University to change its status relative to the other regional universities in the state). Program reviews have also frequently been efficacious, particularly when they have been used to call attention to statewide needs, such as additional computing resources or laboratory equipment. Whether this approach will endure in Missouri is a subject of conjecture. The former commissioner and a few influential legislators have lobbied persistently for a single board to govern the regional universities. Also, the coordinating board has been trying to expand its authority vis-à-vis the local boards.

Beginning in 1984, then commissioner Shaila Aery developed substantial influence with the board, the legislature, and (to a lesser degree) the governor and his staff. During two subsequent years, her recommendations regarding funding for the various institutions were accepted without modification by the legislature and governor. She was able to exercise such influence because of her personal political skills, her facility with information regarding the state and its institutions, and the support of the various presidents. When some of the presidents began to withdraw their support in the fall of 1988, her influence began to wane. This is not surprising since the presidents regularly communicate with their local legislators and with the governor and his staff.

In considering such systems, we should remember one of the basic premises on which this society was founded: competition between ideas, individuals, parties, entities, goods, and services. Competition is not only the best form of price control, it is also the best form of quality control. This is true in education as it is in other areas of activity. Accordingly, state coordinating agencies ought to see as one of their primary tasks the establishment and nurturing of an environment within which the various institutions in the state can compete. Such an environment, properly structured, can be remarkably effective and efficient.

We are convinced that suprainstitutional organizations, like individual campuses, would be more effective in terms of improving quality if they too would adopt a more realistic view of their task. Ellen Chaffee (1989) has proposed a more limited and focused list of responsibilities for an effective coordinating board. In her model, an effective system

- Has conscious, explicit identity, purposes, beliefs, priorities, and expectations of its institutions
- Knows what the state needs and wants with respect to higher education
- Recognizes and corrects when the system does not meet appropriate state needs

- Acts to acquire or reallocate resources necessary to meet state needs
- Communicates effectively with key internal and external constituencies
- Ensures that institutions know what is expected of them
- Decentralizes authority to the institution except with regard to systemwide concerns
- Draws conflicting interests together in a way that ensures credibility and support for the system
- Promotes interinstitutional cooperation, rather than competition [we believe that competition and cooperation are both needed, in some system of checks and balances]
- Corrects deficiencies in a manner that is consistent with its own authority and the norms of the academic community

If such a limited agenda were adopted, discussion could center on answering the following types of questions: How can we clarify and define the nature and purposes of higher education sufficiently to enable institutions, government, and the public to recognize what is and is not appropriate collegiate activity? How can the nature of academic credit be sufficiently defined so that quality can be partially achieved through control of the granting of academic credit? Can institutions be persuaded rather than forced to limit what they will undertake in the face of limited finances? How can the two goals of quality and equality be reconciled and brought into relative balance?

In summary, coordinating boards should limit their functions to information gathering and dissemination; developing broadly conceived state plans for higher education and encouraging sharply focused local planning; reviewing budgets and formulating funding recommendations for presentation to state government; identifying possible areas of unnecessary program duplication and jawboning recalcitrant institutions; and informing legislators regarding problems and issues in higher education. Their base of power should reside in the fact that they make informed recommendations regarding funding to the governor and legislature. The potential negative consequences of not taking the board seriously are generally too great for any president to ignore their recommendations.

Presidents and other institutional representatives can play an important role in stemming the demand for more centralized control. In many respects, the case for supracampus agencies has been strengthened by examples of campus overaggressiveness and even campus greed. When a campus manipulates accounting procedures in order to gain increased funding through a formula that grants higher appropriations to certain categories of expenditure, the case for monitoring campuses is strengthened. When a campus uses the political power of the community in which it is located to gain approval for a new professional school when there is already an oversupply of those professionals in the region, the case for strengthening the powers of supracampus agencies is enhanced. Overall, it may be likely that the best defense against growing centralization is for individual campuses to perform more responsibly with respect to claims and aspirations and to be accountable for the validity of its programs.

In this connection, a most healthy point of view would be for appropriate campuses to accept declines in traditional enrollments and demand for programs and to tailor requests for appropriations accordingly. Too frequently, the argument is advanced that, although enrollments seem about to decline, for the sake of quality, expenditures should continue to advance. As the 1970s began and institutional leadership realized that within a decade there would be a decline in the number of college-age students, intensive efforts were made to find new markets. Off-campus programs proliferated and on-campus new programs were developed that would attract many different kinds of enrollees. Further, institutions sought approval for upgrading programs to graduate levels, especially the doctoral level, because the state-funding formula created financial advantages for campuses offering doctoral level work. Some of these efforts were probably warranted. However, the impression persists that campus efforts to prevent decline and even to increase enrollment through new programs created a powerful reason for the creation of some agency that could contain these aggressive tendencies. Were campuses less expensive, outside accountability, program review, coordination, and control probably would be demanded less often. A regional state institution in western Illinois of 15,000 full-time equivalent students might, in the long

run, be stronger by accepting a reduction to 10,000 students
on campus than by maintaining an enrollment of 15,000 through
certain off-campus centers located in bordering states.

One important way in which public campuses could blunt
the demand for accountability and control might be to follow the
self-restraining practices of those private institutions which have
remained vital and in strong intellectual and financial health.
These private institutions, recognizing the financial limitations
of tuition, endowments, and gift income, have been unwilling
to attempt new programs and expansion beyond their capabilities. They have recognized that the maintenance of quality requires concentration on those things the institution has been able
to do best. If public campuses exercised similar restraint, perhaps
supracampus control would be less necessary. Spokesmen for
public institutions would obviously argue that as publicly mandated and supported activities, they must be responsive to public
needs and demands, and, to a certain extent, this is true. However, presumed public demands have been used as a justification for entry into activities that are really and primarily for
purposes of institutional growth and aggrandizement.

Here a variety of rhetorical questions can be raised. For
example, to what extent did the insatiable expansionism of
California public two-year community colleges (supported primarily by property taxes) contribute to the disenchantment that
led to the overwhelming passage of Proposition 13, which limited
property taxes? Self-restraint on the part of those institutions
might have produced a different outcome. Similarly, what was
the relationship between the creation and planned-for expansion of two University of Wisconsin campuses and the statewide
decision to create a single board to control growth and program
development throughout the state? In another case, during the
1960s, the Board of Curators of the University of Missouri took
over the previously private University of Kansas City and expanded the two-year St. Louis branch to the status of a comprehensive university. The original plan was that the four campuses would be loosely coordinated, so that they might better
respond to the needs of the communities served. However, both
the University of Missouri, Kansas City, and the University

of Missouri, St. Louis, embarked on aggressive expansion that included stressing graduate work and research. The very aggressiveness of the campuses led the second president of the multicampus system to increase control over campuses so as to ensure that institutional growth did not exceed the state's resources. If these two campuses had been more economical in their plans, would tight central control have been prevented?

In summary, we believe the most effective approach is for states to assume that campuses under the control of local boards can, if properly motivated and rewarded by a restrained coordinating board, discipline themselves and generate the innovations needed to improve quality with only minimal intrusion from agencies above the campus level.

TWELVE

Strengthening Undergraduate Education: A National Imperative

Before attempting a synthesis of the points made in this book, we need to make several prefatory remarks to establish a context for our beliefs. First, the thesis around which our arguments have been developed is our belief that the history of American higher education is a chronicle of persistently confronting and successfully responding to challenges coming from the larger society. Since World War II, the challenges have been demographic, financial, egalitarian, and now qualitative. Since the egalitarian movement provided the immediate context within which quality must now be addressed, we have tried to explain carefully its assertions and consequences. The egalitarian movement was not started by academics; it had its roots in the broader society, in Harry Truman's integration of the armed forces, Martin Luther King, Jr., and the civil rights marches, the student protest movement, and even Vatican II. It reached the nation's campuses at a time when administrators were beginning to worry about enrollment declines because of dropping birth rates and the dire financial exigencies predicted for the 1970s. Thus, egalitarianism was played out on campuses through a series of innovations that were designed to shore up higher education's fortunes in general and at the same time to draw the underserved into the net. Many of these innovations had merit in certain restricted environments (for example, individualized self-paced instruction and competency-based curricula). On the other hand, other attempted reforms seemed deleterious wherever practiced; pass-fail grading systems, credit for experience, and changed temporal arrangements belong in this category. However, such generalizations notwithstanding, the fundamental problem was not attempts to improve higher education through innovation; rather, it was the loss of focus about the essential task of higher education and a lack of appreciation for the limitations endemic to the academy. These lapses allowed reformers to expand the domain of higher education's responsibility to include virtually any kind of social activity. The net result was that, although higher education had been able to respond to previous challenges without compromising academic standards, the innovations growing out of the egalitarian movement, in the aggregate, had a negative impact on quality.

During the 1960s and 1970s, an important societal battle was won: College campuses were opened to increasing numbers of ethnic minorities, women, older adults, and members of the lower socioeconomic classes. However, the war was almost lost as far as quality was concerned. This sacrifice of academic quality in the interest of egalitarian gains was extremely unfortunate because it came at a time of increased global competitiveness. The extent of the problem began to emerge in 1980 when it became clear that America was rapidly losing ground to seemingly better educated competitors. For example, U.S. trade in manufactured goods slid from a surplus of $15.5 billion in 1981 to a deficit of $119.1 billion in 1988. This change was reflected in the U.S. share of world trade in manufactured goods, which went from 15 percent in 1970 to 13 percent in 1980 and to little more than 10 percent in 1989. The export of services, which was supposed to make up the difference, has not been the expected panacea, as evidenced by the fact that the nation's debt increased 40 percent in 1988 alone (Truell, 1989, p. 1).

Although higher education is only one element in the equation, most observers agree that any long-term solution to the problem will require a well-trained workforce. Thus, the task confronting higher education now is to respond effectively to this new challenge without sacrificing all the gains in access that were made during the 1970s. Our highly competitive global economy requires us to move in the direction of higher quality; otherwise, our society will have nothing to offer to anyone. The problems of attempting pure equality are reflected in the current disintegration of communism around the world. Although communism may be more effective than capitalism at eliminating poverty, communism has not been able to generate wealth. Even many communists are beginning to realize the flaws of such a system. An overriding emphasis on giving everyone an equal share may attenuate the mechanisms and the incentive for outstanding performance. As far as higher education is concerned, the crucial question then becomes whether an institution can provide access and yet maintain rigor. We believe that it can, but not easily. This observation suggests a corollary to our thesis: An inevitable and necessary tension—reminiscent of Aristotle's Golden Mean—must be managed between access and rigor, egalitarianism and meritocracy, and the needs of non-traditional and traditional students.

There are grounds for optimism as American higher education struggles to reconcile these tensions. One of the unique differences between higher education in the United States and the systems found in most of the other developed, industrial democracies is America's rather broad conception of higher education. Over time, the American system could subsume undergraduate education in the liberal arts and sciences, graduate education, and (as need arose) a wide variety of professional education, which added to the older professions of theology, medicine, and law the emerging professions of engineering, business, education, home economics, agriculture, forestry, social work, journalism, and public policy. Just by linking all these fields of study under a central rubric, the American system became highly flexible, allowing students to shift without appreciable loss of time from the study of one profession to another. This flexibility and interchangeability of educational preparation was made possible in large measure by the self-discipline of the various professional programs in maintaining a balance between theoretical and applied work and reasonable adherence to canons of scholarship and rigor. To the extent that such nimbleness and discipline still exist in American higher education, the current challenge to improve quality can be successfully confronted. America's wide range of institutional types has the potential to provide broad access, within limits. However, at the access end of the continuum, some lines clearly need to be drawn if an institution is going to award credit for something called "higher education." On the other hand, at the rigor end of the continuum, there probably should be no compromises. The finest institutions must continue to confront not only the boundaries of knowledge but also the intellect and creative capacities of America's brightest youth.

However, as stressed throughout this book, higher education is only one player in the drama. Other forces beyond the control of higher education can combine to shape its destiny. One such force is secondary education. Although we have deliberately limited our concern to higher education, college quality is, in many ways, dependent on the quality of secondary education. Few will question the premise that the quality of secondary education declined during the 1960s and 1970s. Evidence includes the well-documented decline in academic aptitude test scores, the increasingly vocal testimony as to the overall decline in the literacy of high school graduates, and the documented decline in the percentage of high school students who take intellectually demanding academic courses. During the 1960s, serious attempts were made to revise the secondary curricula in mathematics, physical science, biological science, and English in the direction of facilitating greater student understanding of those fields. However, for the most part, those reforms did not succeed for several reasons: they attempted an extreme reformulation of the subjects; teachers were unprepared to use a new nomenclature; and, like so many of the subsequent collegiate reform efforts, they were characterized by unrealistic expectations that teachers could and would learn quickly the complex new skills required. The overall effect seems to have been significant drops in enrollments in the reformulated subjects.

Coupled with curricular failure has been a decline in the quality of secondary school teaching. Atkin (1981) observed that "those who sought teaching positions in the 1930s and 1940s included significant numbers of academically able people . . . things are different now. In the first place, today's entering freshman is less likely to aim toward a career in teaching than college freshmen at any time during the last thirty years. Furthermore, the intellectual ability of those who do intend to teach, as measured by standardized tests, is markedly lower than for college majors in every other field except ethnic studies." The decline in the quality of those choosing the teaching profession was produced by several factors, including (1) the opening up to women of careers other than teaching, nursing, and librarianship and (2) the shift of qualified secondary school teachers into college teaching positions, especially during the 1960s. Also, prospective teachers may have been discouraged by the lack of economic incentives for elementary and secondary school teaching, the perceived lack of intellectual stimulation in schools, and the low public esteem for teachers.

A possible explanation for the slide in quality in secondary school performance parallels the phenomenon that began to appear in higher education during the 1970s: expansion into new activities unrelated to the historic mission of preparing students for college. As a result, academic efforts were simply overcome by the draining of resources to newer sorts of activities. Hofstadter and Smith (1961, pp. 354–355) eloquently described that situation that had begun in the 1950s:

> to fit the views of the new education, the curriculum of many junior and senior high schools has been enriched with new courses in band, chorus, driver education, human relations, home and family living, homemaking, and consumer education. It has been possible for an American child to reach his majority in some communities without having had an opportunity to understand that the curricula available in his public high school are not everywhere regarded as an education, and may be wholly

unsuited to his own aspirations. . . . Traditional
education had been founded upon a primary conviction about the value of the various subject matter disciplines and on the assumption that the child,
through some degree of mastery of academic subjects, would enlarge his mind for the general ends
of life and establish the preparation for the professions of business or other desirable occupations (it
was assumed that vocational education could serve
those who could not or would not enter into such
competition). Contrary to the allegations of the new
educators, traditional education was not altogether
unmindful of the child but it assumed, on the whole,
that he would find some pleasure in mental activity
which was offered him in an academically disci-
plined education and that he would gain satisfaction from his sense of accomplishment as he moved
from stage to stage. Insofar as the learning process
was irksome to him, it assumed that self-discipline
came from overcoming irksomeness and it would
be at least a net gain . . . politically the older education was conservative, in that it accepted the existing order of society and called upon the child to
assert himself within its framework — which was
largely that of nineteenth century individualism.
But it was also democratic in that it did not commonly assume, much less rejoice in the idea, that
large numbers, from any class of society, were
necessarily incapable by native endowment of entering with some degree of hope into the world of
academic competition, mastery of subject matter,
and discipline of mind and character.

What Hofstadter and Smith imply is that the secondary school
would be much more effective if it would return to a more limited
conception of its mission. Perhaps secondary education can be
improved significantly, not by eliminating such things as band,
chorus, debate, and intramural athletics, but by treating them

as what they are: extracurricular amenities to brighten the lives of pupils who wish to participate, but by no means part of the principal academic mission for which academic credit is awarded.

Yet a pious plea to return to the basics, alone, will not bring about the needed renaissance in secondary education because of the nature of the clientele that the enterprise presently attempts to serve. American high schoolers in 1990 are, in many ways, more socially handicapped than any of their predecessors. Such diverse realities as the near instant availability of some form of mood-altering drugs (even in the elementary schools), the economic pressures that seem to drive both parents into full-time employment, and the single-parent families that often result from a record-high divorce rate combine to generate in contemporary youth an intense preoccupation with their own physical and psychological survival, which seriously compromises the peace of mind and lack of distraction that learning requires. It is not surprising that students upset with the psychological problems generated by a lack of a durable identity will not be overly concerned with the niceties of Shakespeare, Thucydides, or quadratic equations.

While exhortation to secondary education will probably not produce any significant change, colleges and universities do possess a power that might serve to help bring it about: the power to set admissions requirements for entry into collegiate programs. The Southern Regional Education Board (1985, p. 2) recognized the impact such an approach could have on secondary schools: "Collegiate standards send clear signals to the public schools about the expected level of achievement; high standards challenge secondary school students to higher levels of preparation. It is equally important to remember that the quality of public school teachers depends greatly on the quality of undergraduate education."

Prior to the 1930s, college admissions requirements were probably overly rigorous and frequently somewhat irrelevant (for example, the requirement in the late 1920s of knowledge of Greek and Latin for entry into some institutions). However, the virtually complete laissez-faire approach of the 1970s, which allowed high school graduates to present a completely self-selected array of high school credits went too far in the other direction and contributed to the overall deterioration of collegiate quality. Although individual institutions properly should be allowed some latitude, all institutions should impose some standard requirements, including four years of English (with clear guidelines that only certain English courses would be considered as meeting entrance requirements), at least two years of mathematics (again, some high school mathematics courses would not be acceptable), one full year of American history (not social studies), a one-year course stressing technological knowledge, and a one-year laboratory course in biology or physical science. We realize that such prescriptions can be assailed by both academic purists and by those favoring a life-adjustment emphasis to secondary education, but they are presented here as a minimum set of standards on which to build a college experience.

The Principle of Parsimony

Our argument throughout the book has been that the first and most important agenda item for improving the quality of education at any level and in any type of institution is a limited view of what the institution can and should be about. This principle applies equally to the high school, the community college, the technical institute, the university, and the liberal arts college. A limited, realistic approach view is requisite to sharpening the focus of an institution, to establishing a clear identity and appropriate place in the educational system for the institution, and to generating loyalty and commitment on the part of its participants, be they faculty, students, or the broader society. Charles Hughes (1965, pp. 8–9) made this observation: "We can know what we are as individuals or as a group only after we have first considered what it is we are trying to become. We can know whether what we are doing is absurd only after we have identified the goals we are trying to achieve. We can know the meaning of our individual jobs only after we have recognized the reason for our coming together as an organization. We are nothing more than what we do, and we can become nothing more than what we see ourselves achieving in terms of goals."

If this limited view were adopted nationally, there could be sharper focus for the allocation of resources, and institutions could better decide what to emphasize at the local level. Granted, since the nature of the enterprise itself precludes successfully addressing every perceived need, and since no institution can be truly comprehensive, this view would necessitate exercising self-denial, as various types of institutions focused on what they do best. The result on the individual institutional level would be a reduction in the number of courses and programs offered, coupled with the acceptance that the full range of desirable human traits or skills cannot possibly be the responsibility of any one type of institution. Institutions would restrict their activities to those programs or services for which they possess the requisite knowledge, personnel, and sophistication to perform honestly and effectively.

From this perspective would come a clear differentiation between the curricular and the extracurricular, between that for which academic credit is offered and that for which some other kind of recognition is given, and between that which is appropriate for transfer and that which is not. Those activities supported with public funds should, of necessity, be curtailed in the expectation that many desirable activities should be supported by participants. Any other approach is economically, socially, and educationally unsound.

The focus of this book has been on undergraduate higher education, and institutions purporting to be in that business should center their activities around the definitions advanced earlier for quality undergraduate education, appropriate research, and appropriate service:

> Quality undergraduate education consists of using words, numbers, and abstract concepts to prepare learners to understand, cope with, and positively influence their environments.

> Appropriate collegiate research consists of an individual faculty member's efforts to understand and add to the knowledge of his or her discipline.

Appropriate collegiate service is a derivative of an individual faculty member's disciplinary efforts in teaching and/or research.

Ideas and Abstractions

A natural extension of the above definitions and a second essential perspective for improving the quality of undergraduate education is the notion that the primary focus of the curriculum should be on ideas and abstractions. Pondering and expanding intellectual traditions through rational processes (that is, critical and analytical thinking) have been the central missions and purpose of collegiate education since the establishment of medieval universities. Success in this endeavor is measured by how well participants are able to analyze, synthesize, and evaluate in verbal, written, and numeric form. Achievement of such goals generally requires extensive exposure to reading, writing, and numerical calculation in an environment of sustained, intensive interaction among and between students and faculty. Added to the equation is independent effort closely supervised by informed faculty, an environment that values ideas in and of themselves, a culture in which uncertainty is accepted as part of the natural order, and a community that celebrates all forms of intellectual and creative effort. Over time, the culture and structure of academic institutions have evolved in a manner generally supportive of such interaction.

This concept obviously concentrates on postadolescent youth and the intellect. However, it does not ignore the needs of the so-called nontraditional adult learners; rather, it assumes that many adult learners can also benefit from this same formulation. Those learners of any age or station in life who have other self-improvement goals, such as learning basic English or acquiring the technical skills needed for a wide variety of vocations, should seek fulfillment in other settings and should not expect to receive academic credit for their efforts. We do not deny that such needs may deserve attention in institutional ways; yet we insist that to include them as essential components of undergraduate education is to confuse educational purpose and dissipate the educational effort. We believe that it is unrealistic to ask the same faculty that supervises traditional undergraduate education to supervise avocational training, prison-based programs focused on preparing inmates for release, or programs for the aged. Furthermore, institutions that do insist on such criteria for collegiate level work may still participate in Elderhostel programs or the offering of occasional short courses, seminars, conferences, and colloquia, providing the institutions possess the appropriate expertise and do not attempt to equate such activities with the central mission.

In regard to community colleges, we believe that they should continue to offer technical-vocational training and a limited number of avocational and recreational courses as long as they can finance them, as long as there is student demand, and as long as they do not generate credits for academic degrees. One possible improvement would be to create within community colleges a separate unit, possibly labeled "the college," which would offer only collegiate level parallel courses. This unit would concentrate on programs developed around the above definition of quality undergraduate education and would have its own faculty for whom there would be different expectations, such as terminal degrees and publishable scholarly or creative activity.

Respect for Tradition

A third view that has been urged in this book can best be described as a cautious suspicion of those who would casually discard traditional values and approaches that have weathered the test of time. Although education—like any other endeavor—should constantly be evaluating itself while searching for new and more effective technologies, the shortcomings of long-respected traditional approaches should be clearly demonstrated before the approaches are dismissed as inadequate. The most frequently voiced criticisms of higher education, especially undergraduate education, should be reviewed to determine whether there is a general, widespread basis in fact for such charges. Some of these common criticisms have been discussed earlier; six are briefly reviewed and answered below:

1. The Ph.D. is a research degree and as such does not prepare people for college teaching. This criticism has validity only if collegiate education is essentially concerned with something other than knowledge, understanding of knowledge, and ability to apply and communicate knowledge. The Ph.D. has evolved over one hundred years as an effective way of gaining knowledge, understanding knowledge, and expanding knowledge.

2. When lecture is the predominant mode of instruction, development of a range of other student traits and aptitudes is not allowed. Certainly, lecturing can be frequently dull, disorganized, and desultory; yet, in its ideal form, it appears to be essential. Ideally, new knowledge appears first in primary research reports, then in summaries of research reports, and finally in textbooks. In the ideal setting, students search out and master the knowledge presented in original sources, and the lecture is used for introducing expanding knowledge and for organizing that knowledge to facilitate its acquisition.

3. Dividing the undergraduate curriculum into a major, a minor, and a few graduation requirements encourages students to concentrate and specialize and does not allow time or encouragement for broader learning. This critique may be evaluated in several ways. One might see students as divided roughly into two classes—devotees and dabblers. The devotee gains satisfaction from intense specialization, whereas the dabbler gains satisfaction from sampling different topics. Proving that one approach is "better" than the other is extraordinarily difficult. A more reasonable approach is providing the opportunity for students to move in whichever direction they wish without prejudice (except in a few professional subjects such as engineering or nursing). There has always been sufficient flexibility for the dilettante to explore widely and for the fanatic to concentrate.

4. Because of the credit hour and letter grade system, educational progress has been reduced to numerical accounting that cannot reveal the nuances of various kinds of student educational achievements. It is difficult to understand the vehemence with which numerical accounting is attacked. Some individuals who would feel happy with digital readouts regarding their blood pressure, heart rate, red and white blood cells, cholesterol level,

and other indexes of health nonetheless reject the possibility that numerical indexes also can measure educational health. Of course, letter grades are sometimes given capriciously and, of course, the accumulation of credit hours for a miscellany of experience might present a distorted view of educational competence. The significance lies not in the fact that three semester hours credit of A is shown on a student's transcript, but in the fact that three semester hours credit of A is given for one subject that is related to other subjects and to an overall bank of knowledge.

5. The traditional academic calendar of quarters or semesters and the traditional academic scheduling of classes meeting a specified number of hours per week in a symmetrical pattern produces a lockstep that prevents the spontaneity of learning possible in a more flexible arrangement. Without arguing that spontaneity is valueless and should not be encouraged, we observe that routine scheduling and allocation of activities to particular times and days is a fairly common human phenomenon. The best predictor of an individual's activities next Sunday is that individual's activities on the last three or four Sundays. All organizations develop metabolic rates based on their essential functions, whether they are hospitals, military organizations, or engineering construction firms. The symmetry and regularity of college classes is probably related to the fact that education is incremental and, for the most part, takes place over time rather than in some moment of intense poignancy.

6. Faculty members are excessively academically conservative and unwilling to experiment and innovate, and this intransigence leads to rigid and routine education practice. Beyond doubt, a case can be made that faculty members are conservative, since most of the subjects they value represent conservation of certain kinds of knowledge. Some professors rarely change and repeat each year the lectures and jokes of the previous year, just as some generals plan to fight the next war exactly as they fought the previous one. A guess is that professors typically will experiment with those things they believe to be important. They will examine new textbooks; they will attempt different ways of presenting information; they will, from time to time, create

new courses that rearrange their subjects; and they will experiment with different ways of testing for student achievement. The charge of unwillingness to experiment may very well be based on professors' unwillingness to undertake inappropriate projects. For example, a professor of French may be reluctant to organize a class as a T-group; try role-playing situations; attempt nondirective group therapy; or use films, television, tape recordings, and other embellishments to simulate the flavor of the civilization whose language he or she teaches.

Careful analysis of commonly criticized matters may reveal faulty practice or evidence that a practice has outlived its usefulness. Thus, the availability of textbooks probably facilitated elimination of recitation as a primary mode of instruction. Such analysis, however, may also indicate that there are substantial reasons for common practices and that only refinement is actually necessary. The general point of view of faculties and administrations is that, before traditional practices are rejected in favor of something new, there should be massive and persuasive evidence against those traditions (such as academic majors; graduation requirements; formal classes taught by full-time faculty; formal tests and letter grades; clear distinctions between the curricular and the extracurricular; expectations that there be two hours of study for each hour of class; and the acceptance of lectures, discussions, laboratory work, libraries, and necessary field trips as the major instructional elements.

Rather than seeking to discard traditional practice, institutions might very well opt for urging greater individual competence with respect to the established aims and techniques of education in order to enhance quality. Rather than searching for some new grand design, institutions, small or large, should encourage clear lecturing, more careful textbook selection, increasing use of original sources, more reliable grading, more regular office hours for advisement, more intensive preparation for class, clearer and more detailed criticism of student writing, and clear bibliographies of material actually in the library. Heroic measures rarely produce the achievements promised and may very well siphon off time, energy, and attention from those elements that need change. Quality enhancement in most activities is simply improved competence with respect to routine activities, whether the activities are preparation of legal briefs, open heart surgery, a theatrical performance, or university teaching.

In the companion volume to this one, which deals with institutional survival through the potentially troublesome 1980s and 1990s, we make a strong argument that institutions should, for the most part, remain faithful to their traditions rather than departing in new and uncharted directions (see Mayhew, 1979). That same advice seems highly appropriate with respect to the matter of quality. Quality does seem related to well-understood missions, long experience with specific kinds of routines that are well established in the collective memory of individuals in the institution, and recognition, over time, of the appropriate activities of the institution. Institutions should look at their past successes and simply seek to perform as well or better in the future.

Institutions might also seriously consider, as a matter of institutional policy, embracing high selectivity in the hiring of faculty members; decentralization of important substantive educational matters; and a feeling of trust that competent faculty members given responsibility will behave responsibly. Many recent developments of centralization of campus authority, creation of suprainstitutional agencies, creation of specialists to deal with faculty development, the curriculum or evaluation, and even increases in presumed prerogatives of accreditation appear based on the doctrine of distrust. A plausible doctrine for collegiate institutional practice is the belief that competent faculty members will achieve good results, with the understanding that they cannot be expected to produce miracles — or historic changes and achievements.

Realistic Expectations

This evaluation of tradition leads to the fourth perspective that we have urged for administrators, professors, critics, reformers, legislators, and, indeed, the entire society: the adoption of the realistic view that human beings and institutions are fundamentally resistant to radical change and that the greatest enemy of the good is often the perfect. Lecturing went on constantly in medieval universities, and lecturing goes on constantly in American higher education in the waning years of the twentieth century. Medieval education was essentially verbal, and so is American higher education. In the second century A.D., Marcus Aurelius discussed the intractability of the human condition, as well as the obligation of individuals to attempt to modify it, remaining tranquil during the effort and accepting the improbability of immediate, dramatic results (Aurelius, [second century] 1961). This ideal suggests that the conscientious professional administrator or professor probably should seek to improve advising, instructional techniques, the curriculum, and every other aspect of education, while recognizing that such effort will at best produce slow change. A wise president or dean will encourage and even goad, at times, serious faculty discussion, but will refrain from predicting heroic reforms.

As a concluding thought for this book, some response should be made to the anticipated criticism that the entire book reflects a worship of the status quo and does not encourage experiment, innovation, and change. To the contrary, nothing has been argued that would preclude such activities so long as expectation for heroic change is not encouraged and so long as experiment and innovation do not attempt to ask formal education to do something for which it is simply not prepared. In medicine, the great post–World War II developments (such as increased group practice, health insurance, biomedical laboratory tests, body scans, techniques of surgery, and genetic analysis and counseling) were all refinements of the traditional activities of medical doctors (that is, diagnosis of and intervention in illness). Recommended changes in medical practice did not suggest that medical doctors become theologians or social workers, although the work of theologians and social workers has increasing implications for sickness and health. Similarly, changes in legal practice have not altered the essential traditional activities of interviewing clients, doing diligent legal research, preparing documents, and appearing and performing in the courtroom. There have been changes in the legal practice, including greater specialization and more efficient ways of locating relevant legal precedents. Even though legal services have been extended to groups previously not well served, the significant change lies in the financing of that service and not in the essential nature of the service provided. All too frequently, the experimentation, innovation, and change suggested for higher education have really called for significant departure from traditional practice (for example, urging professors to concentrate on improving students' interpersonal relationships or asking professors to undertake sophisticated, psychological therapeutic interventions).

Throughout this book, as we have struggled to identify ways for improving undergraduate education, we have stressed notions and attitudes such as acceptance of limitations, persistence, leadership, courage, a sense of proportion, and realistic expectations. It occurs to us that the list is not complete. In fact, we think that a rather good case can be made that the traits most needed for professional workers in institutionalized higher education are a stoic sense of duty, a ribald sense of humor, and a sympathy for the absurd. Stoicism is essential in order to manage an organized anarchy (see Cohen and March, 1974). A sense of humor is needed to tolerate the pomposity and self-aggrandizement exhibited by so many academics, and a sympathy for the absurd allows toleration for endless academic debate on matters of little consequence.

References

AAUP/AAC Commission on Academic Tenure. *Faculty Tenure: A Report and Recommendation.* San Francisco: Jossey-Bass, 1973.

Abbott, L. *Quality in Competition.* New York: Columbia University Press, 1955.

Alkin, I. M. "Who Will Teach High School?" *Daedalus,* 1981, *110* (3), 91–104.

American Council on Education. *Cooperation in General Education.* Washington, D.C.: American Council on Education, 1947.

American Council on Education. *Campus Trends.* Washington, D.C.: American Council on Education, 1989.

Arrowsmith, W. "Future of Teaching." In A. C. Eurich (ed.), *Campus 1980.* New York: Delacorte Press, 1968.

Ashcroft, J., and others. "Task Force on College Quality. *Time for Results: The Governors' 1991 Report on Education.* Washington, D.C.: National Governors' Association, 1986.

Association of American Colleges. *Integrity in the College Curriculum: A Report to the Academic Community.* Washington, D.C.: Association of American Colleges, 1985.

Astin, A. W. *Four Critical Years: Effects of College on Beliefs, Attitudes, and Knowledge.* San Francisco: Jossey-Bass, 1977.

273

Astin, A. W. *Achieving Educational Excellence: A Critical Assessment of Priorities and Practices in Higher Education.* San Francisco: Jossey-Bass, 1985.

Atkin, J. M. "Who Will Teach in High School?" Paper presented at Stanford University, 1981.

Aurelius, M. "To Himself." In M. Madas (ed.), *Essential Works of Stoicism.* New York: Bantam Books, 1961.

Baldridge, J. V., and Tierney, M. L. *New Approaches to Objectives.* San Francisco: Jossey-Bass, 1979.

Barzun, J. "The Wasteland of American Education." *The New York Review of Books.* Nov. 5, 1981, *28* (17).

Bennett, W. J. *To Reclaim a Legacy.* Washington, D.C.: National Endowment for the Humanities, 1984.

Berdahl, R. O. *Evaluating State-Wide Boards.* New Directions for Institutional Research, no. 5. San Francisco: Jossey-Bass, 1975.

Bloom, B. S. *A Taxonomy of Educational Objectives: The Cognitive Domain.* New York: Longmans, Green, 1950.

Bok, D. *Higher Learning.* Cambridge, Mass.: Harvard University Press, 1986.

Bowen, H. R. *The Costs of Higher Education: How Much Do Colleges and Universities Spend Per Student and How Much Should They Spend?* San Francisco: Jossey-Bass, 1980.

Boyer, E. L. "Breaking Up the Youth Ghetto." In D. W. Vermilye (ed.), *Lifelong Learners: A New Clientele for Education.* San Francisco: Jossey-Bass, 1974.

Boyer, E. L. *College: The Undergraduate Experience in America.* New York: Harper & Row, 1987.

Breneman, D., and Nelson, S. *Financing Community Colleges: An Economic Perspective.* Washington, D.C.: The Brookings Institution, 1981.

Broh, R. A. *Managing Quality for Higher Profits.* New York: McGraw-Hill, 1982.

Carnegie Commission for Higher Education. *Quality and Equality: Levels of Federal Responsibility for Higher Education.* New York: McGraw-Hill, 1968.

Carnegie Council on Policy Studies in Higher Education. *Three Thousand Futures: The Next Twenty Years for Higher Education.* San Francisco: Jossey-Bass, 1980.

The Carnegie Foundation for the Advancement of Teaching. *Missions of the College Curriculum: A Contemporary Review with Suggestions.* San Francisco: Jossey-Bass, 1977.

Cartter, A. M. *The Ph.D. and the Man-Power Needs.* New York: McGraw-Hill, 1974.

Cartter, A. M. *Ph.D.s and the Academic Labor Market.* New York: McGraw-Hill, 1976.

Chaffee, E. E. "Strategy and Effectiveness in Systems of Higher Education." In J. C. Smart (ed.), *Higher Education: Handbook of Theory and Research.* Vol. 5. New York: Agathon Press, 1989.

Cheit, E. J. *The New Depression in Higher Education.* New York: McGraw-Hill, 1971.

Cheney, L. V. *50 Hours: A Core Curriculum for College Students.* Washington, D.C.: National Endowment for the Humanities, 1989.

Chickering, A. W., and Associates. *The Modern American College: Responding to the New Realities of Diverse Students and a Changing Society.* San Francisco: Jossey-Bass, 1981.

Clark, B. *The Open Door College.* New York: McGraw-Hill, 1960.

Cohen, A. M., and Brawer, F. B. *The American College.* San Francisco: Jossey-Bass, 1982 (2nd ed. 1989).

Cohen, M. D., and March, J. G. *Leadership and Ambiguity: The American College President.* New York: McGraw-Hill, 1974.

Cohen, M. D., March, J. G., and Olsen, J. P. "A Garbage Can Model of Organizational Choice." *Administrative Science Quarterly,* Mar. 1972, *17,* 1.

Commission on Nontraditional Study. *Diversity by Design.* San Francisco: Jossey-Bass, 1973.

Cooper, R. M. "Improving College Teaching and Administration." In S. Baskin (ed.), *Higher Education: Some New Developments.* New York: McGraw-Hill, 1965.

Copperman, P. *The Literacy Hoax.* New York: William Morrow, 1978.

Council on Post-Secondary Accreditation. *COPA Self-Study Panel Findings and Recommendations.* Washington, D.C.: Council on Post-Secondary Accreditation, 1986.

Crosby, P. B. *Quality Is Free.* New York: New American Library, 1979.

Cross, K. P. "Problems in Access." In S. B. Gould and K. P. Cross (eds.), *Expectations in Traditional Study.* San Francisco: Jossey-Bass, 1972.

Current Issues in Higher Education. Washington, D.C.: American Association for Higher Education, 1974.

Dearing, B. "Pressures Jeopardizing Qualities of Undergraduate Teaching." In G. K. Smith (ed.), *Current Issues in Higher Education.* Washington, D.C.: American Association for Higher Education, 1965.

Delworth, U., and Associates. *Student Services: A Handbook for the Profession.* San Francisco: Jossey-Bass, 1980.

Deming, W. E. *Out of the Crisis.* Cambridge, Mass.: MIT Press, 1986.

Dressel, P. L. "A Review of Non-Traditional Graduate Degrees with Particular Emphasis on the Problems of Accreditation." In G. K. Smith and others (eds.), *Research Reports.* Vol. 2. Washington, D.C.: Council on Post-Secondary Accreditation, 1978.

Dressel, P. L., and Mayhew, L. B. *General Education: Explorations in Evaluation.* Washington, D.C.: American Council on Education, 1954a.

Dressel, P. L., and Mayhew, L. B. *Science Reasoning and Understanding.* Dubuque, Ia.: Brown, 1954b.

Dressel, P. L., and Mayhew, L. B. *Higher Education as a Field of Study.* San Francisco: Jossey-Bass, 1974.

Eble, K. E. *Professors as Teachers.* San Francisco: Jossey-Bass, 1972.

Eble, K. E. *The Craft of Teaching.* San Francisco: Jossey-Bass, 1976.

English, W. F. "Efforts to Improve College Teaching." In G. K. Smith (ed.), *Current Issues in Higher Education.* Washington, D.C.: National Education Association, 1955.

Ford, P. J. "Factors Contributing to Academic Vitality at Jesuit Liberal Arts Colleges." Unpublished doctoral dissertation, Department of Education, Stanford University, 1972.

Frodlin, R. (ed). "The Very Simple But Thorough Going." *The Ideas and Ideal of General Education.* Chicago: Chicago University Press, 1950.

Gaff, J. G. *Toward Faculty Renewal.* San Francisco: Jossey-Bass, 1975.

Gardner, J. W. *Excellence: Can We Be Equal and Excellent Too?* New York: Harper & Row, 1961.

Garvin, D. A. *Managing Quality: The Strategic and Competitive Edge.* New York: Free Press, 1988.

General Education in a Free Society. Cambridge, Mass.: Harvard University Press, 1947.

Gollattscheck, J., and others. *College Leadership for Community Renewal.* San Francisco: Jossey-Bass, 1976.

Gose, K. F. "Proposed Changes in the NCA Constitution and Rules of Procedure." Letter sent to member institutions of the North Central Association (NCA), July 5, 1989.

Grant, G., and others. *On Competence: A Critical Analysis of Competence-Based Reforms in Higher Education.* San Francisco: Jossey-Bass, 1979.

Grant, G., and Riesman, D. *The Perpetual Dream.* Chicago: Chicago University Press, 1978.

Hall, L., and others. *New Colleges for New Students.* San Francisco: Jossey-Bass, 1974.

Handbook of Accreditation, 1990–92. Chicago: North Central Association of Colleges and Schools, Commission on Institutions of Higher Education, 1990.

Harrington, F. H. "Shortcomings of Conventional Departments." In D. E. McHenry and Associates (eds.), *Academic Departments: Problems, Variations, and Alternatives.* San Francisco: Jossey-Bass, 1977.

Harvard University. *General Education in a Free Society.* Cambridge: Harvard University, 1947.

Henry, D. D. *Challenges Past, Challenges Present: An Analysis of American Higher Education Since 1930.* San Francisco: Jossey-Bass, 1975.

Hofstadter, R., and Smith, W. (eds.). *American Higher Education, A Documentary History.* Chicago: Chicago University Press, 1961.

Houle, C. O. *Governing Boards: Their Nature and Nurture.* San Francisco: Jossey-Bass, 1989.

Hughes, C. L. *Goal Setting: Key to Individual and Organizational*

Effectiveness. New York: American Management Association, 1965.

Hutchins, R. M. *The Higher Learning in America.* New Haven, Conn.: Yale University Press, 1936.

Higher Education and American Democracy. Vol. 1: *Establishing the Goals.* New York: Harper & Row, 1947.

Jacob, P. *Changing Values in Colleges: An Exploratory Study of Impact of College Teaching.* New York: Harper & Row, 1957.

Jencks, C., and Riesman, D. *The Academic Revolution.* Garden City, N.Y.: Doubleday, 1968.

Jencks, C., and Riesman, D. "The Art of Teaching." In C. Anderson and D. Murray (eds.), *The Professors.* Cambridge, Mass.: Schenkman, 1971.

Juran, J. W. (ed.). *Quality Control Handbook.* (3rd ed.) New York: McGraw-Hill, 1974.

Katz, J. "Personality and Interpersonal Relations in the College Classroom." In N. Sanford (ed.), *The American College.* New York: Wiley, 1962.

Katz, J., and Associates. *No Time for Youth: Growth and Constraint in College Students.* San Francisco: Jossey-Bass, 1968.

Keeton, M. T. "Networks and Quality." In D. W. Vermilye (ed.), *Lifelong Learners—A New Clientele for Higher Education: Current Issues in Higher Education 1974.* San Francisco: Jossey-Bass, 1974.

Keeton, M. T. "Beyond the Cloister." *The Third Century.* New Rochelle, N.Y.: Change Magazine Press, 1977.

Keeton, M. T., and Associates. *Experiential Learning: Rationale, Characteristics, and Assessment.* San Francisco: Jossey-Bass, 1976.

Kells, H. R. *Self-Study Process: A Guide for Postsecondary Institutions.* Washington, D.C.: The American Council on Education, 1988.

Kells, H. R., and Kirkwood, R. "Institutional Self-Evaluation Process." *Educational Record,* Winter 1979, pp. 25–45.

Kerr, C. "En Attendant 2000." *The Third Century.* New Rochelle, N.Y.: Change Magazine Press, 1977.

Kirk, R. *The Intemperate Professor.* Baton Rouge: Louisiana State University Press, 1965.

Knapp, R. H., and Greenbaum, J. J. *The Younger American*

Scholar. Chicago: University of Chicago Press and Wesleyan University Press, 1953.

Ladd, E. C., and Lipset, S. M. *The Divided Academy.* New York: McGraw-Hill, 1975.

Lee, E. C., and Bowen, F. M., *Managing Multi-Campus Systems: Effective Administration in an Unsteady State.* San Francisco: Jossey-Bass, 1975.

Levine, A. *Handbook on Undergraduate Curriculum.* San Francisco: Jossey-Bass, 1978.

Levine, A. *When Dreams and Heroes Died: A Portrait of Today's College Student.* San Francisco: Jossey-Bass, 1980.

McKeachie, W. J. "Research on Teachers at the College and University Level." In N. L. Gage (ed.), *Handbook of Research on Teaching.* Skokie, Ill.: Rand McNally, 1963.

McKeachie, W. J. *Teaching Tips: A Guidebook for the Beginning College Teacher.* Lexington, Mass.: Heath, 1978.

Mannies, J. "Vocational Schools Recruiting Homeless." *St. Louis Post-Dispatch,* Feb. 10, 1988, pp. A-1, 4.

March, J. G. "Commitment and Competence in Educational Administration." In L. B. Mayhew (ed.), *Educational Leadership and Declining Enrollments.* Berkeley, Calif.: McCutchan, 1974.

March, J. G. *How We Talk and How We Act.* Urbana, Ill.: University of Illinois Press, 1981.

Mayhew, L. B. *General Education: An Account and an Appraisal.* New York: Harper & Row, 1959.

Mayhew, L. B. *The Smaller Liberal Arts College.* Garden City, N.Y.: Prentice-Hall, 1962.

Mayhew, L. B. *Arrogance on Campus.* San Francisco: Jossey-Bass, 1970.

Mayhew, L. B. *Legacy of the Seventies.* San Francisco: Jossey-Bass, 1977.

Mayhew, L. B. *Surviving the Eighties: Strategies and Procedures for Solving Fiscal and Enrollment Problems.* San Francisco: Jossey-Bass, 1979.

Mayhew, L. B., and Ford, P. J. *Reform in Graduate and Professional Education.* San Francisco: Jossey-Bass, 1974.

Medsker, L. *Junior College Progress and Prospect.* New York: Harper & Row, 1960.

Meeth, L. R. *Quality Education for Less Money: A Sourcebook for Improving Cost Effectiveness.* San Francisco: Jossey-Bass, 1974.

Millett, J. D. *Financing Higher Education in the United States.* New York: Columbia University Press, 1952.

Morison, S. E. *The Developing of Harvard University.* Cambridge, Mass.: Harvard University Press, 1930.

Morrill, R. L. *Teaching Values in College: Facilitating Development of Ethical, Moral, and Value Awareness in Students.* San Francisco: Jossey-Bass, 1980.

National Commission on Excellence in Education. *A Nation at Risk: The Imperative for Educational Reform.* Washington, D.C.: U.S. Government Printing Office, 1983.

National Commission on Higher Education Issues. *To Strengthen Quality in Higher Education.* Washington, D.C.: American Council on Education, 1982.

National Commission on the Role and Future of State Colleges and Universities. *To Secure the Blessings of Liberty.* Washington, D.C.: American Association of State Colleges and Universities, 1986.

Newman, F. *The Second Newman Report: National Policy and Higher Education.* Cambridge, Mass.: MIT University Press, 1973.

Northwest Association of Schools and Colleges. *Accreditation Handbook.* Seattle, Wash.: Northwest Association of Schools and Colleges, 1988.

Pace, C. R. *Measuring Outcomes of College: Fifty Years of Findings and Recommendations for the Future.* San Francisco: Jossey-Bass, 1979.

Pace, C. R. *Measuring the Quality of College Student Experiences.* Los Angeles: Graduate School of Education, University of California, 1984.

Perkins, J. A. *The University as an Organization.* New York: McGraw-Hill, 1973.

Peters, T. J., and Waterman, R. H., Jr. *In Search of Excellence: Lessons from America's Best-Run Companies.* New York: Harper & Row, 1982.

Poor, T. "Data Seized at Tarkio's Office Here." *St. Louis Post-Dispatch,* Feb. 13, 1988, p. A-1.

Rashdal, H. *The Universities of Europe in the Middle Ages.* New York: Oxford University Press, 1936.

Reaffirmation of Accreditation. Stanford, Calif.: Stanford University Press, 1981.

Redd, J. F. "Non-Traditional and Traditional Doctoral Programs in Educational Administration: A Comparative Analysis." Unpublished doctoral dissertation, Department of Education, Stanford University, 1980.

Report of the President Truman Commission on Higher Education, Vol. 6. Washington, D.C.: U.S. Government Printing Office, 1947.

Riesman, D., and others. *Academic Values and Mass Education.* New York: Doubleday, 1970.

Rosecrance, F. C. *The American College and Its Teachers.* New York: Macmillan, 1962.

Ruml, B., and Morrison, D. H., *Memo to a College Trustee.* New York: McGraw-Hill, 1959.

Schmidt, G. B. *The Old Time College President.* New York: Columbia University Press, 1930.

Schumacher, E. F. "Good Work." In D. W. Vermilye (ed.), *Relating Work and Education: Current Issues in Higher Education 1977.* San Francisco: Jossey-Bass, 1977.

Sloan Commission on Government and Higher Education. *A Program for Renewed Partnership.* Cambridge, Mass.: Bassinger, 1980.

Smith, A. K. "Factors Related to Survival and Progress in the Small Liberal Arts College." Unpublished doctoral dissertation, Department of Education, Stanford University, 1969.

Southern Regional Education Board. *Access to Quality Undergraduate Education.* Atlanta, Ga.: Southern Regional Education Board, 1985.

Study Group on the Conditions of Excellence in American Higher Education. *Involvement in Learning: Realizing the Promise of American Higher Education.* Washington, D.C.: National Institute of Education, 1984.

Taylor, H. "The Teacher at His Best." In R. M. Cooper (ed.), *Two Ends of the Log.* Minneapolis: Minnesota University Press, 1958.

Thompson, R. *The Impending Tidal Wave of Students.* Washington, D.C.: The American Council on Education, 1954.

Truell, P. "All Exports Aren't Created Equal." *The Wall Street Journal,* July 3, 1989, p. 1.

Tuchman, B. W. "Decline of Quality." *New York Times Magazine,* Nov. 2, 1980, p. 38.

Tucker, A., and Mautz, R. "Involvement of Statewide Governing Boards in Accreditation." *Educational Record,* 1978, *59,* 4.

Tyler, R. W. *Basic Principles of Curriculum Construction.* Columbus: Ohio State University Press, 1932.

University of California, Santa Cruz. *General Catalog 1970–71,* July 1970, *8* (1), p. 41.

Warnath, C. F. *New Directions for College Counselors: A Handbook for Redesigning Professional Roles.* San Francisco: Jossey-Bass, 1973.

Weidner, E. W. "Problem Based Departments." In D. E. McHenry and Associates (eds.), *Academic Departments: Problems, Variations, and Alternatives.* San Francisco: Jossey-Bass, 1977.

Whitehead, A. N. *The Aims of Education.* New York: Mentor Books, 1951.

"Who's Who in Higher Education." *Change,* 1975, *7* (1), 24–31.

Wormley, W. M. "Factors Related to the Ability of Certain Small Private Liberal Arts Colleges to Cope with the New Depression in Higher Education." Unpublished doctoral dissertation, Department of Education, Stanford University, 1978.

Index